Sociological Theory and the Problem of Values

Sociological Theory and the Problem of Values

Don A. Martindale
University of Minnesota

CHARLES E. MERRILL PUBLISHING COMPANY
A Bell & Howell Company
Columbus, Ohio

Published by
Charles E. Merrill Publishing Company
A Bell & Howell Company
Columbus, Ohio 43216

ISBN: 0-675-08841-0

Library of Congress Catalog Card Number: 73-89962

1 2 3 4 5 6 7 — 79 78 77 76 75 74

Printed in the United States of America

For
Hans and Nobi Gerth

Preface

Since World War I the interests and concerns of sociologists in the Western world have had a roughly "decade" rhythm. This periodicity seems to have been brought about in part by the character of historical experience and in part by the tendency of contemporary nations to collect statistics at ten-year intervals. World War I left the Western world changed: the social and cultural readjustments of the 1920s gave the decade an image that led to its characterization as the Jazz Age; the 1930s were dominated by the Great Depression; the 1940s were dominated by World War II and its immediate aftermath; the 1950s were a decade of worldwide readjustment somewhat comparable to the 1920s, a period of cold war and the Affluent Society; and the 1960s were dominated by the IndoChina War and the protest of minorities (Blacks, Chicanos, youth, and women). Meanwhile the practice by modern states of gathering demographic and other statistics primarily at the turn of the decade has been accompanied by the tendency of social scientists to reformulate their hypotheses on the same cycle.

In the period since World War II this decade periodization has been manifest in distinctive preoccupations. Already in retrospect the 1950s appear as the first period in American sociology when theory ceased to be a European import and became a home-manufactured product. These years also marked the first period when a collectivistic theory (in this case structure-functionalism) rose to a position of unquestioned dominance in America. The major events of American sociology in the 1960s centered on the shattering of the theoretical monopoly of functionalism and an intensified concern with sociology's epistemological foundations, manifested in the preoccupation with theory construction.

One cannot say what may typify American sociology in the 1970s, but it seems likely that the problem of values will be among its foremost influences. Two major developments in the late 1960s point this way: an increased inclination by representatives of one point of view to undertake unmasking operations against others, and the rise of what is variously described as a "radical sociology" or a "sociology of involvement." These developments which thrust the problem of values forward are on a collision course with other developments which attempt to reconceptualize theory formation in terms of the findings of various trends in analytical philosophy and the philosophy of science.

At the same time that the place of values in sociological theory is being moved to central concern in the councils of sociological theory, the empirical study of various categories of value has been quietly growing. It is high time for sociologists to recognize that the various empirical studies of value constitute a family of disciplines which could well be described as branches of the sociology of culture. Along with a renewed concern with the problem of values, the sociology of the 1970s might be characterized by the attempt to bring coherence to the sociology of culture.

As sociology drifts toward the point where a more adequate conceptualization of the distinction between fact and value is attained, the fundamental substantive problems of sociology become capable of reconceptualization. The substantive problems of sociology are three in number: social persons, social structure, and social change. They are reviewed in this book to determine major areas of ambiguity and areas in need of further theoretical interpretation and research.

Finally, it may be observed that the findings of recent attempts at theory construction on the one hand and at clarifying the problems of the sociology of values on the other indicate lines along which the reconceptualization of the types of sociological theory may be desirable.

Contents

Contents

PART I

Sociology
and the
Problem of Values

It has been suggested that the sociologists' attempt to achieve an ethically neutral scientific stance is evidence of senility, and an interest in the value problem is an indication of a guilt complex from a prodigal youth. As Alvin Gouldner said,

> Perhaps their quest [of those seeking ethical neutrality] is the first sign of professional senility; perhaps it is the last sign of youthful yearnings and perhaps a concern with the value problem is just a way of trying to take back something that was, in youthful enthusiasm, given too hastily.[1]

Inasmuch as Gouldner's address itself was concerned with the problem of values, one cannot help wondering in which category he would place himself.

Actually, the same general processes responsible for sociology's general epistemological problems also played a role in its concern over values and their consequences for the science. The nineteenth-century drive toward a system of knowledge which swept aside so many hard-won distinctions also wiped away those that had been drawn between fact and value.

When one deals with human social behavior one is unavoidably concerned with the pursuit of values, or ends, or things people experience as desirable and the various principles or norms—moral, ethical, aesthetic, and legal—by which they adjudge behavior in pursuit of values as right. The impulse that established sociology tended to assimilate values to facts and moral, ethical, aesthetic, and legal rules to the natural science laws. The epistemological and methodological problems of sociology were complicated by the tension between some scholars who felt it necessary to resist this identification and others who have sought to perpetuate it.

A division appears between those who insist that the task is to establish a value-free sociology and those who insist that it is in principle impossible to do so and remain concerned with social behavior. Meanwhile a number of spheres of sociocultural life structured by their normative orders have been established as objects of empirical study. These include the sociology of knowledge, the sociology of play, and the sociology of art.

NOTES

1. Alvin W. Gouldner, "Anti-Minotaur: The Myth of a Value-Free Sociology." A presidential address delivered at the annual meeting of the Society for the Study of Social Problems, August 28, 1961. Appearing in *Social Problems*, 9, no. 3 (Winter 1962):199-213. Reprinted in *Sociology on Trial*, ed. Maurice Stein and Arthur Vidich (Englewood Cliffs, N. J.: Prentice-Hall, 1963), p. 35.

CHAPTER 1

The Place of Values
in Sociological Theory

Three major attempts have been made in the West to unify normative with other types of knowledge. In the classical Greek view brought to a high stage of development by Plato, the good, the true, and the beautiful belong to an ideal realm directly accessible to reason. However, since these ideals are directly given to reason, the problem is to explain why, in fact, there should be endless dispute about them. Plato's answer was that the imperfect world of the body and of the senses casts up endless imperfections which obscure the operations of pure reason.

With some modifications this Platonic view was taken over by the medieval Christian theologians. The mind of God was substituted for pure reason. For the rest the attitude toward the world of the body, of the senses and passions, was similar to that of Plato. The world of the flesh was the source of sin and error.

By elevating the world of matter to a plane of equality with the world of mind and spirit, Descartes posed anew the problem of the unity of knowledge. While he retained the program of the rationalists and scholastics, his problems were complicated by the fact that the world of the flesh no longer represented a convenient device for accounting for normative conflicts. The rationalists (particularly Spinoza) made heroic attempts to formulate ethical principles into an axiomatic system. However, the program to fuse empirical, logical, and ethical knowledge into a single system once again proved to be intractable, leading to Kant's expedients which gave these spheres a kind of formal similarity while making them *in principle* separate.

The great systems of the nineteenth century, including positivistic sociology, resumed the task of demonstrating the unity of thought, and undertook the derivation of man's ethical principles from his collective life (in contrast to the rationalistic derivation of them from the structure of the rational mind and the theological derivation of them from the arrangements of God).

Society as Religious and Moral Agent: Comte to Durkheim

In the fourth volume of his *Positive Polity* Comte undertook the construction of a positivist religion which he argues is the final step in the elaboration of a positivistic sociology. In it Comte assigned morals to a primacy over all the sciences.

> Morals will take their place at the head of the encyclopaedic hierarchy as a direct consequence of the normal convergence of all positive theories toward the regulation of the conduct of nations and individuals.[1]

The position irreversibly assigned to morals results, Comte maintains, in the subjection of man's life at long last to a complete discipline in harmony with his true wants.[2] Moreover, positive religion and positive ethics are one and the same thing. Positive religion and ethics constitute applied sociology. When later generations need more detailed rules, they will "draw them from moral science by the aid of an advance in sociological science."[3]

The central element in the positive religion is the theory of the Great Being. This is the discovery that the only object worthy of worship is society, which has been raised to the positive stage.

> The Family and the Country, these are the two collective beings which in due succession were to lead by a natural process to the

4

> conception and the feeling of Humanity, which may be looked on
> as the common country or the universal family.[4]

Humanity or the Great Being is the whole constituted by the beings past, future, and present which cooperate in the perfection of the world.[5] "Every being must be composed of parts similar to itself, so Humanity is divisible primarily into States, then into Families, never into individuals."[6]

In the positive society, in Comte's opinion, a clear distinction will be drawn between public and private morality. He believes men are superior to women in intellect; women are superior in feeling. Public morality will be in the hands of sociologist-priests whose primary functions will consist in the direction of education and the continuous censorship of public morality. The proper place of women is in the home, where they will be supreme. Practical affairs will be in the hands of a business patriciate who will be protected from greed by the fact that they will own everything.[7]

The priests for the religion of humanity will be limited to the number required for maximum effectiveness. Each positive school will be served by seven priests and three vicars. Each professor will be bound to two lectures a week during the ten months of the positivist year. Every school will be annexed to the temple of the district. On this basis, Comte argued, the spiritual wants of the West can be met by a corporation of twenty thousand philosophers. France would require one-fourth that number.[8] The high priest of humanity, for which post Comte's services were available, was to have his headquarters in Paris. To aid him in his office he was to be able to draw on the assistance of seven national superiors, each with a salary half of that of the high priest over and above necessary expenses. Four were to be allotted to Italy, Spain, Great Britain, and Germany, respectively, and three others for colonial settlements of the West. However, it was anticipated that as the positive religion expanded, so too would its needs for eminent priests until the number eventually would reach forty-nine.[9]

The system of worship contemplated by Comte divides into public and private. A special feature of private worship is its primary emphasis on the adoration of Woman.

> The immediate basis of Sociolatry, personal worship, is characterized above all by the heartfelt adoration of the affective sex, on the ground of the inherent capacity of every true woman to be a

representative of Humanity. As composite, the highest form of existence can hardly be appreciated unless personified. . . . As sympathy is the greatest source of unity, and sympathy is strongest in woman, woman must be the best personification of a being, the foundation of whose existence, as a whole, is love.[10]

Comte sought to develop down to the smallest detail the various aspects of the doctrine, life, and organization of the religion of humanity. He developed a positive calendar divided into thirteen months, in each of which some major element of the positive religion was celebrated. He visualized a series of eighty-one annual festivals of the worship of humanity under all its aspects. New Year's day, for example, opens with the Synthetical Festival of the Great Being, and the first month of the positive year is devoted to humanity with special festivals of the social union, religious, historical, national, and municipal. The Complementary Day of the positive year is devoted to the Festival of all the Dead and the additional day in leap year to a General Festival of Holy Women. The tenth month of the positive year is primarily centered on the worship of women in their various roles as mother, wife, daughter, and sister. The eleventh month featuring the positive priesthood celebrates the Festival of Art, the Festival of Science, and the Festival of Old Men.[11]

Further details are quite unnecessary for our purposes. It is clear that Comte was not troubled by a distinction between empirical, moral, and religious knowledge. Ethics and religion were for him merely applied sociology; such applications could only be entrusted to the hands of sociologist-priests.

The critique of positivistic sociology from a traditional Christian point of view was carried out with acumen by Tolstoy. He observed that moral philosophy has, from time to time, justified every sort of cruelty and harshness, but with positive sociology this is now supposed to be a finding of science. "And it is on this new doctrine that the justification for men's idleness and cruelty is now founded."[12] The essence of Comte's positivistic theory, Tolstoy correctly observed, consists in conceiving all mankind as an undying organism with men as particles of the organism, each with his special task in the service of the others with respect to the organism as a whole.[13] Since everything that happens in the organism serves the whole, persons who have freed themselves from labor, Tolstoy observes, must not be judged from the standpoint of common sense and justice, but from the standpoint of organic laws such as differentiation, integration, and the like.

6

Slavery, for example, may seem regrettable, but in terms of the development of the social organism it was justified, performing important functions at its particular time and place.

> The whole significance of scientific sciences lies in this alone. It has now become a distributor of diplomas for idleness: for it alone, in its sanctuaries, selects and determines what is parasitical, and what is organic activity, in the social organism. Just as though every man could not find this out for himself much more accurately and more speedily, by taking counsel of his reason and his conscience. It seems to men of scientific science that there can be no doubt of this, and their activity is also indubitably organic; they, the scientific and artistic workers, are the brain cells, and the most precious cells in the whole organism.[14]

In the course of his comments on the reception of Comte, Tolstoy observes that in general the learned world had only adopted the first part of Comte's argument "that part which justified, on new premises, the existent evil of human society; but the second part, treating of the moral obligations of altruism, arising from the recognition of mankind as an organism, was regarded as not only of no importance, but as trivial and unscientific."[15]

While Comte's derivation of a system of society and religion from his sociology was largely ignored by his scientific-minded colleagues, there was a widespread acceptance of his sociology. However, Comte's sociology already rested on the assumption that ultimate scientific, moral, and religious ideas form a single consistent system. Comte's *Positive Polity* was a reasonable set of deductions from his sociology, once it was accepted. There is a direct relation between this sociology and Durkheim's attempt to derive not only all religious, but all logical and scientific notions from the collective.

In *The Elementary Forms of the Religious Life*, Durkheim proposed to seek the origin of religious conceptions and to examine their bearing on the theory of knowledge. The most primitive religious system, he believed, will be one in a society of utmost simplicity and one in which no element is borrowed from a previous religion.[16] Durkheim was convinced that he found such a simple society and elementary religion in the Australian Aborigines and Totemism. This society proved, he thought, that the most fundamental of all religious notions was that of sacredness (of a realm set off in opposition to the profane), that it could not be derived from either man or nature but must have originated in the

7

primitive clan with its atmosphere of an extra-individual sanctity and compulsion.[17] All other religious ideas and concepts were, in Durkheim's view, differentiations from the sacred character of the group itself.

However, Durkheim was not content to halt his analysis with the derivation of all religious notions from the collective but proposed to derive all key notions of logic and science as well from the socioreligious complex.

> At the roots of all our judgment there are a certain number of essential ideas which dominate all our intellectual life; they are what philosophers since Aristotle have called the categories of the understanding: ideas of time, space, class, number, cause, substance, personality, etc. They correspond to the most universal properties of things; they are like the social frame which encloses all thought. . . . Now when primitive religious beliefs are systematically analyzed, the principle categories are naturally found. They are born in religion and of religion; they are a product of religious thought.[18]

The idea of time, Durkheim argues, could not be derived from the subjective experience of duration,[19] for it has an objective and super-individual character as a process by which we divide, measure, and express in objective signs the course of events in years, months, weeks, days, and hours. This notion of an objective time could only originally have had reference to the periodical occurrences of rites, feasts, and public ceremonies. "A calendar expresses the rhythm of the collective activities, while at the same time its function is to assure their regularity."[20] Similarly, Durkheim believes that the notion of space is of collective and religious origin, deriving the structure of the primitive camp with regions distinguished in terms of the number and comparative location of the clans of the tribe. "The social organization has been the model for the spatial organization and a reproduction of it."[21] Even the distinction between right and left, he speculates, is probably of religious and collective origin. Similar reflections are urged to hold for such things as the principle of identity, the rules of logic, and the basic notions of science.

> Up to the present there have been only two doctrines in the field. For some, the categories cannot be derived from experience: they are logically prior to it and condition it. They are represented as so many simple and irreducible data, imminent in the human mind by virtue of its inborn constitution. For this reason they are

said to be *a priori*. Others, however, hold that they are constructed and made up of pieces and bits, and that the individual is artisan of this construction.[22]

Rationalism and empiricism, in short, are seen as the two contrasting ways of accounting for various forms of knowledge. Durkheim proposes his form of collectivism as a method for overcoming the fatal shortcomings of each. In contrast to both the rationalists and empiricists, he maintains, the basic forms of thought are derived neither from the rational constitution of the mind nor from miscellaneous bits of experience. These categories "are, essentially, collective representations."[23]

Society "is a reality *sui generis;* it has its own peculiar characteristics which are not met with again in the same form in all the rest of the universe."[24] The categories of thought are derived from the collective which simultaneously endows them with both an a priori character (this same social character leads to an understanding of the origin of the necessity of the categories) and an empirical character.

> From the fact that the ideas of time, space, class, cause, or personality are constructed out of social elements, it is not necessary to conclude that they are devoid of all objective value. On the contrary, the social origin rather leads to the belief that they are not without foundation in the nature of things.
>
> Thus renovated, the theory of knowledge seems destined to unite the opposing advantages of the two rival theories, without incurring their inconveniences. It keeps all the essential principles of the a priorists; but at the same time it is inspired by that positive spirit which the empiricists have striven to satisfy.[25]

Both Comte and Durkheim, thus, assimilate the various classes of knowledge (religious, moral, logical) to one another. In terms of the basic model from which these problems were approached in the first place, the temptation is continually present to carry out a sweeping reductionistic program: reducing judgments of value to judgment of fact, ethical and moral principles to laws, and social phenomena to physical phenomena. This keeps the door open to movements such as physicalism and some types of logical positivism; the view that every legitimate sentence in sociology or psychology may be translated into a sentence in physics.[26] The incorporation of physicalism into the program of logical empiricism was rigorously promoted by Neurath.[27] The position was followed for a time by Carnap and Hempel. It led to the view that value judgments can either be disposed of as distorted statements of fact or as mere ejaculations, expressions of feelings, with no empirical content.

On the other hand, the assimilation of the various classes of knowledge to one another and the derivation of them from the collective itself also keeps open the possibility to the individual sociologist of launching upon elaborate programs of sermonizing in the name of "letting the facts speak for themselves."

The Problem of Relativity
of Social Science Knowledge

Positivistic sociology was only one major form of nineteenth-century monism. From positivism sociology inherited one major form of its value problem. However, sociology also inherited a form of the value problem in the program of value reductionism from the other major monistic system, objective idealism, which brought the problem of the relativity of social science knowledge.

Objective idealism had many similarities to positivistic sociology. It, too, considered man's total sociocultural (historical) development to be a single unit. However, at any time, only a small phase of the whole is revealed. The process of understanding consists in the proper location of the aspect in the whole. The key to understanding of man's sociocultural development is not provided by natural science procedure, but in paradigms of moral or ethical experience. "Throughout history a living, active, creative, and responsive soul is present at all times and places."[28]

> The connections in the mind-affected world arise in the human subject and it is the effort of the mind to determine the systematic meaning of the world which links the individual logical processes involved to each other. . . . Understanding is the rediscovery of the I in the Thou; the mind rediscovers itself at ever higher levels of connectedness; this sameness of the mind in the I and the Thou and in every subject of a community, in every system of culture, and finally, in the totality of mind and universal history, make the working together of the different process in the human studies possible. Only in the world of the mind which, active, responsible, and self-determined, moves with us and, in it alone, has life its value, its goal and its meaning. What we must grasp in experience and understanding is life as the context which embraces mankind. . . . We must construct the whole form, its parts, and yet, the whole must contain the reason for the meaning given to the part and the place assigned to it.[29]

In Mandelbaum's compact summary, for Dilthey the historical process "is an ultimate, every-changing one, imminent in all of its objectifications." To understand reality is to understand it as a whole and "no understanding which falls short of this goal is ultimate."[30] For such understanding any given individual is disadvantaged: his experience is only a tiny fragment of that of his age; the experience of his age, moreover, is only one phase of the whole.

Every experience, Dilthey maintains, presents life under a special aspect. When experiences repeat, they coalesce to form attitudes. Among the more comprehensive attitudes toward life are optimism and pessimism with their manifold nuances.[31] The coalescence of similar attitudes among people establishes a common orientation or world view constituted by peculiar values which assign importance and meaning to the various items of social experience.[32] World views develop in great multiplicity in response to the conditions of climate, race, nationality, history, political organization, and epoch. The source of their diffusion lies in the uniformity stamped upon the specific structures of completed world views by the teleological relationship which characterizes the life of the soul.[33] Dilthey believes there are three major possible world views: Naturalism, the Idealism of Freedom, and Objective Idealism.

The relativism of Dilthey's theory arises from the fact that any item of historical or social science knowledge consists in an estimate of significance in terms of one or other of the world views. Social science knowledge, thus, is assimilated to the pattern of ethical judgment.

Karl Mannheim (1893–1947) also approached the problem of social science knowledge from the standpoint of the collectivist traditions associated with objective idealism, though this time the Marxian tradition. It is false, Mannheim maintains, to say the single individual thinks; "rather it is more correct to insist that he participate in thinking further what other men have thought before him."[34] The individual orients himself in a ready-made situation and preexistent patterns of thought.

In accord with the Marxian tradition, Karl Mannheim takes it for granted that thought can have no other importance than to assist individuals and pluralities in the adjustment to their vital (materialistic) life interests. Moreover, also in accord with the Marxian tradition, he assumes that these life interests are differentiated by class. The ideas of pluralities of individuals must be

11

analyzed from this point of view. "From whatever source we get our meanings, whether they be true or false, they have a certain sociological function, namely, to fix attention of those men who wish to do something in common upon a certain 'definition of the situation.' "[35]

In their function of serving vital interests and assisting the organization of action, the complexes of ideas formed by men in accord with their peculiar class situations are described by Mannheim as falling into two broad types: ideologies and utopia. Ideologies are conservative idea-complexes oriented to the present and to the preservation of vested interests; utopias are the idea-complexes of underprivileged classes and are oriented with revolutionary import toward the future.

> Every epoch has its fundamental new approach and its characteristic point of view, and consequently sees the "same" object from a new perspective. . . . The history of art has fairly conclusively shown that art forms may be definitely dated according to their style, since each form is only possible under given historical conditions and reveals characteristics of that epoch. What is true of art also holds *mutatia mutandis* good for knowledge.[36]

The breakup of the medieval theological world and world view released masses of individuals for vertical and horizontal mobility. This in turn encouraged the rapid proliferation of different class situations and hence the confrontation of contrasting styles of thought. The confrontation of thought styles, in turn, brought the problem of knowledge to self-consciousness. All social knowledge is relative to a particular class-based style of thought, except for the case of the intellectuals who, Mannheim believes, are recruited from all classes and hence supply the foundation for a *relational* (rather than relativistic) approach to knowledge.[37]

As in the case of Dilthey, Mannheim's approach assimilates all social science knowledge to the type of ethical or aesthetic knowledge. Relativism is an unavoidable consequence of the approach to knowledge by objective idealism (and its materialistic counterpart, Marxism) flowing from this very assimilation of nonethical (logical and factual) forms of knowledge to the forms of ethical (or aesthetic) knowledge. Thus "relativism" is the form the problem of values assumes from the standpoint of objective idealism in the same manner as reductionism (of ethical to nonethical forms) is the form the value problem assumes for positivistic sociology.

Mandelbaum insists that even such eminent American historians as Carl Becker and Charles Beard espouse relativism.[38] Such relativism maintains that whatever "truth" a work in history of the human science contains is relative to the process under which it arose and without reference to which it cannot be understood.[39] Central to the relativistic position is the notion also that the student of human affairs constructs his account under the dominance of his particular values.[40] Moreover, these evaluations are not simply personal but reflect societal conditions and hence change from age to age.[41]

Ideological Convergence of Historicism and Scientism

Both positivistic sociology and objective idealism (and its materialistic counterpart, Marxism) erased the line between values and facts. Their different ways of accomplishing this fusion, as has been noted, led to reductionism and relativism, respectively. Both procedures had consequences unanticipated by their exponents; their systems were in fact in considerable measure ideologies—arguments in promotion of a specific value program.

By its critics positivistic sociology is frequently described as scientism; by its critics objective idealism (and its materialistic counterpart) is frequently described as historicism. In the post-World War II period scientism was brought under attack by Hayek,[42] historicism by Popper.[43] In the course of Hayak's attack on the positivistic position in sociology, he developed an antipositivistic conception of social science subject matter and method. Popper, on the other hand, brought the antipositivistic tradition under attack and developed an up-to-date positivistic conception of social science method. It would seem that Hayek and Popper were at opposite poles. However, upon inspection it may be seen that Popper and Hayek are opposed to an identical ideological program. Historicism, Popper observes, regards the ends of human activities as dependent on historical forces and so within its province.

> Holistic or utopian social engineering . . . is . . . always of a "public" character. It aims at remodelling the "whole of society" in accordance with a definite plan or blueprint; it aims at "seizing the key positions" and at extending "the power of the State . . . until the state becomes nearly identical with society" and it aims, furthermore, at controlling from these "key positions" the

historical forces that mould the future of the developing society.[44]

Having decided in advance that the complete reconstruction of society is necessary, the historicist, according to Popper, is projected against sociological hypotheses which state the limits of institutional control.

By a rejection *a priori* of such hypotheses, the utopian approach violates the principles of scientific method. On the other hand, the problems connected with the uncertainty of the human factor must force the utopianist, whether he likes it or not, to try to control the human factor by institutional means, and to extend his program so as to embrace not only the transformation of society, according to plan, but also the transformation of man. "The political problem, therefore, is to *organize human impulses* in such a way that they will direct their energy to the right strategic points, and will steer the total process of development in the desired direction."[45]

Hayek's objection to scientism takes a form quite similar to Popper's objection to historicism.

Closely connected with the "objectivism" of the scientists' approach is its methodological collectivism, its tendency to treat "wholes" like "society" or the "economy," "capitalism" (as a given historical phase) or a particular "industry" or "class" or "country" as definitely given objects about which we can discover laws by observing their behavior as wholes.[46]

Among persons illustrating this tendency Hayek lists Hegel and Comte, Marx and various twentieth-century counterparts, such as Sombart and Spengler.[47] All such theorists, in Hayek's opinion, elevate the requirements of the collective to priority over those of the individual. Even when the collectivist extols individual reason, it is not, he believes, in the promotion of true individuality.

In practice it is regularly the theoretical collectivist who extols individual reason, "who demands that all the forces of society be made subject to the direction of a single master mind."[48]

In the end objective idealism (historicism) and positivistic sociology (scientism) turn out to be ideologies of a similar type. They systematically reduce the question of values and ethics to the requirements of society, which is conceived as the source and vindication of all ethical principles. They as systematically deny the claims of individuality except insofar as it furthers the requirements of the collective. While it would be going rather too far to assume that Comte or Hegel or Marx would have been happy with Hitler's, Mussolini's, or Stalin's brand of totalitarianism in the twentieth century, it is not unfair to see their ideologies (in the opinion of Hayek and Popper) as the forerunners of totalitarianism.

Not only did the nineteenth-century unitary systems blur the lines theoretically between fact and value, but they offered systems of thought with ideological implications. The arguments of Popper and Hayek, who respectively trace similar ideological motives to the abuse of history and the abuse of science, may be taken to confirm that neither positivist nor antipositivistic epistemology and methodology has a necessary relation to wholistic or elementaristic forms of substantial theory.

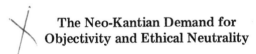

The Neo-Kantian Demand for Objectivity and Ethical Neutrality

Coming at the end of the first great period of contemporary philosophical development, which had been marked by a series of failures to integrate all types of knowledge into a single system, Kant formally abandoned as in principle unattainable all attempts to fuse ethical and empirical knowledge into a single system. Science was concerned with phenomena; morality with operations of the will as a thing in itself. The principle central to phenomenal order was mechanical causality; the rule ordering the sphere of morality was the "act of conscience" presupposing the principle of freedom (and responsibility). Moral judgment, however, was not unordered. It was oriented toward values which formed an axiological order, the key to which was the good will. The fundamental rule of conscience was to act in such manner that one would be willing to permit his action to become a universal law for all men. This meant, in the first place, to act in such manner as to presuppose the good will itself to be the highest good. Hence one should act in such manner never to treat another person as a means, only as an end.

Two fundamental contrasts appear between Kantian thought and the great unitary systems of the nineteenth century: Kant's thought presupposes the primacy of the individual rather than the

15

collective; and in contrast to the holistic systems it drew a sharp distinction in principle between judgments of fact and judgments of value. Kant assumed that human nature was universal and hence the foundation of a universal value system. While the builders of the unitary system attempted to restore the relation between fact and value, values were relativized. Partly in response to such relativisation, some social scientists were drawn to the Kantian position once more.

The neo-Kantians subscribed to an individualistic ethical orientation which made them especially sensitive to the contrasting ethical suppositions of the collectivists. However, inasmuch as the neo-Kantians took over the distinction between ethical and empirical judgments and felt that only the latter properly belonged to the sphere of science, they were disinclined to transform social science into a forum of rival ideologies. Moreover, since with Kant they were convinced that all phenomena are proper subject matter of scientific study, so far as human social and psychological materials entered the sphere of phenomenal experience (the empirical self and its actions in contrast to the phenomenal self), they were also proper materials of science.

When a person acts as a moral agent, thus, from a neo-Kantian perspective, his actions are subject to consideration on two levels: so far as they are phenomenally experienced they are proper objects of scientific study; so far as they arise from the pure ego they are subject to ethical evaluation. Acts based on an individual's valuations, thus, are among the "facts" of the social situation which the social scientist studies.

Alvin Gouldner, who adjudges the attempt by sociologists to maintain a distinction between judgments of fact and judgments of value to be vain, attributes the aspiration to Max Weber.

> This is an account of a myth created by and about a magnificent minotaur named Max—Max Weber, to be exact; his myth was that social science should and could be value-free. . . . The myth of a value-free sociology has been a conquering one. Today, all the powers of sociology from Parsons to Lundberg, have entered into a tacit alliance to bind us to the dogma that "Thou shalt not commit a value judgment," especially as sociologists. . . . Weber's brief for a value-free sociology is a right one and, some say, logically unassailable. Yet it is also absurd.[49]

Despite Weber's attempt to sharpen the distinction between judgments of value and judgments of fact and his exhortation to his fellow social scientists not to permit their judgments of fact to be distorted by their values, he was neither the inventor of the distinction nor the formulator of this particular version of the problem: Weber only presented a particular interpretation of the Kantian position.

The Kantian suppositions in his position are evident in Weber's methodological essay on " 'Objectivity' in Social Science." [50] Weber observed that when the combination of ethical evolutionism and historical relativism became dominant in the social sciences its exponents sought to deprive ethical norms of their formal character and to raise the social sciences to the status of ethical discipline with empirical foundations. For example, "even today the confused opinion that economics does and should derive value-judgments from a specifically 'economic' point of view has not disappeared." [51]

The task of the social sciences, Weber urges, is not to ignore the valuations of men. "It is self-evident that one of the most important tasks of every science of cultural life is to arrive at a rational understanding of these 'ideas' for which men either really or allegedly struggle." [52] The scientific study of value judgments is not only empathically to understand and analyze them, but to examine their function in conduct. However:

> As to whether the person expressing these value judgments *should* adhere to these ultimate standards is his personal affair; it involves will and conscience, not empirical knowledge. An empirical science cannot tell anyone what he *should* do—but rather what he can do—and under certain circumstances what he wishes to do. [53]

In these formulations made in 1904 Weber summed up and made incisive the applications to social science of the neo-Kantian critique of current practices with respect to values. In his essay on "The Meaning of 'Ethical Neutrality' in Sociology and Economics," [54] written in 1907, Weber elaborated and extended his position. The social scientist in his role as a university teacher, Weber insists, has an obligation to keep his value judgments to a minimum when he is unable to eliminate them. And if he must make value judgments, he should make relentlessly clear to his audience and to himself which of his statements are logically deduced or empirically observed facts and which are judgments of value. [55]

If one once admits value judgments in the classroom, Weber believes the only acceptable stand is to admit all possible value positions to be heard. To turn the college into a training institution for loyal administrators of the state is to transform it into the equivalent of a theological seminary but without the latter's dignity.[56] In the long run, Weber maintained a lecturer who stimulates interest by the insertion of his personal evaluations will "weaken the students' taste for sober empirical analysis."[57] Nor is scientific objectivity achieved, Weber urges, by a statesmanlike compromise between diverse evaluations. Some sort of "middle way" is not only just as undemonstrable scientifically as extreme evaluation, but "in the sphere of evaluations the extreme position is least unequivocal."[58] However, all this by no means implies that evaluations cannot become subject matter of scientific analysis. Rather, it means that not only must the empirical investigator keep his personal evaluation distinct from his empirical judgments, but he has no concern with the degrees of normative dignity of different evaluations. "These are problems in axiology, not in the methodology of the empirical disciplines."[59] When one investigates the empirical influence of an ethical or religious conviction, it is not necessary to share it.[60]

Studies of value judgments have the function of explicating internally consistent value-axioms, deducing implications which flow from them and determining their factual consequences. Moreover, the problems of empirical discipline must be solved nonevaluatively even if they are selected because of the value relevance of the phenomena treated. However, it is an illusion to suppose that value judgments can be derived from factual assertions about empirical trends.

> Nor do we see why empirical scientists should transform the adaptation to these "trends" from an ultimate value-problem, to be solved only by the individual as his conscience dictates with reference to each particular situation, into a principle ostensibly based on the authority of a "science."[61]

When an ethically neutral science analyzes some phenomena arising from an evaluative point of view such as, for example, syndicalism, its task is completed when it has reduced the syndicalist standpoint to its rationally most consistent form and has empirically investigated the preconditions for its existence and its practical consequences.[62] The only problem empirical analysis can solve is the prerequisites for adequately realizing an end which is once taken as unambiguously given.

Such considerations permit one to isolate the acceptable and unacceptable features of current concepts, for instance, as that of "progress." Progress can, to be sure, be defined purely in technical terms. "The use of the term 'progress' is legitimate in our disciplines when it refers to 'technical' problems, *i.e.*, to the 'means' of attaining an unambiguously given end. It can never elevate itself into the sphere of 'ultimate' evaluations."[63] Whenever these distinctions are not observed, the quality of analysis quickly degenerates.

> A careful examination of historical works quickly shows that when the historian begins to "evaluate," causal analysis almost always ceases—to the prejudice of the scientific results. He runs the risk, for example, of "explaining" as the result of a "mistake" or of a "decline" what is perhaps the consequence of ideals different from his own.[64]

A contemporary form of the neo-Kantian approach to values was developed by Felix Kaufmann. Comparison between epistemological, ethical, and aesthetic doctrines, he insists, discloses a parallelism between them and their supporting arguments. Feelings play a role in value theory comparable to sensations in epistemology.[65] Value judgments and propositions asserting emotional states (loving, hating, desiring, and fearing) must be distinguished. To say that a man is admired is to designate an emotional state; to say he is not worthy of admiration is to express a value judgment. Just as correct belief is defined in terms of the rules of scientific procedure, Kaufmann urges, correct preference is defined in terms of axiological rules or rules of valuation.[66] Value judgments are obtained by an analysis of axiological rules and presuppose that the object referred to is of a kind to which the value judgment applies. Only in terms of such axiological rules are preferences qualifiable as "correct." Hence, Kaufmann rejects the notion (endorsed by G. E. Moore among others) that values are intrinsic properties of the object. Judgments of values are from his perspective capable of being formulated as analytical propositions.

Differences in actual preference are no proof of differences in axiological rules. Moreover, most people do not always behave in accord with the axiological rules. However, it is in the nature of axiological rules that even when people do not behave in accord with them, they think they should. "Kant's categorical imperative demands that they should behave in accordance with these standards. *Moral will* is the will to do so."[67]

There are, Kaufmann observes, undoubtedly differences in standards, "but this should not lead to the hasty conclusion that there are no invariant properties characteristic of all systems of moral rules."[68] Loyalty of a person to his group, readiness to cooperate in important group concerns, compliance with group taboos, veracity in giving information, reliability in keeping pledges to group members are universal or nearly so. Hence secondary reflection on axiological rules tends to set in motion tendencies to rectify them, to eliminate inconsistencies and bring all mankind under a single system. The rationalists were convinced that rectifications of the axiological rules would result in full consensus about the meaning of goodness, happiness, and beauty. While this claim cannot be upheld, the amount of implicit consensus should, in Kaufmann's opinion, not be underrated either.[69]

Kaufmann's comments on the rectification of the rules is directly comparable to Weber's observation that while the empirical sociologist must rest content with noting the origins and consequences of evaluations, "philosophical disciplines can perhaps go further and seek to clarify the 'meaning' of evaluations; that is, they can indicate their place and spheres of meaningful validity within the totality of all possible ultimate evaluations."[70]

Kaufmann's analysis of the value problem of the social sciences rests on the same grounds as Weber's, proposing only to eliminate some ambiguities due to the elliptical character of some of Weber's formulations. Value judgments, he maintains, are analytical propositions, as may be seen whenever their elliptical formulation is replaced by a complete formulation. It becomes evident that value judgments do not belong to the body of empirical science. However, there is no objection to the acceptance of sentences containing value terms, provided their meaning is unambiguously established by axiological rules.

The New Priesthood

The neo-Kantians provided sociology with the conceptual tools to combat the endless disputes of a discipline with the self-appointed mission of bringing moral and religious unity to mankind. However, the cleavage in sociology which tends to divide its undergraduate from its graduate and professional orientation also encourages a division over the value issue. Graduate and professional sociology is, by and large, exemplary in seeking to cling to the program of ethical neutrality laid down for the social scientists by the neo-Kantians.

However, the undergraduate student, who is drawn to sociology by motives other than the desire for snap courses, usually looks to the field for orientation to the contemporary world. Orientation to the world, however, involves more than objective knowledge; it entails interpretation and notions of significance. The requirements of undergraduate sociology, thus, tend to pull the teacher down the primrose path of evaluation. Similarly, those sociologists who orient their attention primarily to nonprofessionals quickly discover that the quickest way to win an audience, as Weber was aware, is to throw caution to the winds and pass value judgments upon everything in sight.

C. Wright Mills: The approach of C. Wright Mills to the problem of values has special interest in view of the judgment still often advanced that he is the most important American sociologist of the post-World War II period. In *The Sociological Imagination* Mills confronted the problem directly. On the one hand he made extravagant claims for sociology,[71] the like of which have not been heard since Comte, while at the same time denouncing science as "a false and pretentious Messiah" and a "highly ambiguous element in modern civilization."[72]

Subscribing to the more extreme features of antipositivistic historicism ("all sociology worthy of the name is 'historical sociology' ")[73] Mills accepts as unquestioned the relativistic thesis that "There is, I believe, no 'law' stated by any social scientist that is trans-historical, that must not be understood as having to do with the specific structure of some period."[74]

Mills not only sought to unmask all trends in current sociology as ideologies but made quite explicit that for his own part he felt that social science can have no other function than to render value judgments. "To say that 'the real and final aim of . . . social science' is to predict is to substitute a technocratic slogan for what ought to be a reasoned moral choice."[75] Moreover, he conceives social science generalization as the passing of moral judgments. "What a man calls moral judgment is merely his desire to generalize, and to make available for others those values he has come to choose."[76]

For his own part Mills insists that "the political task of the social scientist" is to address himself to three types of men: those with power and are aware of it, those with power but unaware of it, and those without power. To those with power he "imputes responsibility," to those with power but unaware of it he "attempts to educate and then, again, he imputes responsibility," to those without power he reveals what the other two types of men are up to.[77]

This is identical with the function of Comte's sociologist priests who were to be entrusted with responsibilities as critics and ethical educators. And quite in accord with his own principles Mills' works after *The Sociological Imagination* (such as *Listen Yankee, The Causes of World War III*) were propaganda tracts.

Edward Shils: Mills made his arguments for the return of sociology to the role of ethical counseling in 1959. In an essay published two years later, Edward Shils takes up a similar position from the standpoint of the functionalistic theory Mills hated thoroughly. The sociological position of the functionalists is treated by Shils as the last stage in the development of the moral progress of the race.[78] Sociological traditions, contrary to functionalism, are described by Shils as marxist, quasi-marxist, alienated, and oppositional.[79]

> Both the manipulative and alienated forms of sociological research, and theories associated with them, are afflicted by intellectual deformity. Neither is capable, given their traditions and present dispositions, of producing a coherent and comprehensive sociological theory. Neither can meet the requirements of a polity that respects human dignity and is, therefore, adequate to aspirations of universal validity. Consensual sociology alone is capable of satisfying the requirements of an adequate theory and a proper relationship with policy.[80]

Max Weber had observed that where evaluation enters the picture a rapid deterioration of empirical responsibility is usually evident. In his passionate attack on what he describes as the alienated tradition in American sociology, Shills provides it with the following example:

> The coming of the Great Depression gave a stronger impulsion to the native American sociological critique. A variety of currents of Marxism began to flow through the intellectual classes in the United States in the second half of the 1930's. Stalinist sociologists, fellow-traveling sociologists, Trotskyite sociologists, ex-Trotskyite sociologists, and others who were none of these were attracted by the large perspectives and the humanitarian pretensions of Marxism. By the end of the Second World War, dissident Marxism, renewed and reclothed by Max Weber, was ready to take up where liberal and populist alienation had left off. Psychoanalysis was added to the armament of criticism, especially through the writings of Horney and Fromm.[81]

22

It can only be a matter of special regret that this outburst should be delivered by a notable scholar of considerable renown. Even if it were true (as it is not) that the majority of the nonfunctionalists were "reds" or ex-reds, the question would be irrelevant to the scientific adequacy of their studies. Since Max Weber died in 1920, Shils' attribution to him of various forms of continued deviltry even after World War II is rather curious. Weber's suggestion that where values dominate the discussion, scientific responsibility declines, seems authenticated.

Alvin W. Gouldner: Also in 1961 a passionate attack on the position of objectivity and ethical neutrality dating from Max Weber and the neo-Kantians was delivered by Alvin W. Gouldner in his presidential address to the annual meeting of the Society for the Study of Social Problems, August, 1961. The address was reprinted in *Sociology on Trial*[82] and the *New Sociology*,[83] suggesting widespread agreement with or at least interest in his thesis. The tradition of ethical neutrality, Gouldner argues, is itself ideology.[84] To Gouldner the sociologist's special technical competence entitles him to make value judgments. He asks rhetorically: "If technical competence provides no warrant for making value judgments, then what does?"[85] The argument for objectivity and ethical neutrality is taken to be a "trivial token of professional respectability"[86] which arose to facilitate the autonomy of the modern university. "Weber's hope seems to have been that the value-free principle would serve as a kind of 'Fair Trades Act' to restrain . . . competition."[87]

As a result of the principle of ethical neutrality Gouldner insists that "the timorous and the venal may now claim the protection of a high professional principle and, in so doing, can continue to hold themselves in decent regard."[88]

A major institutional and theoretical division in American sociology was for a long time drawn between the Harvard-Columbia and the Chicago outlook.[89] However, despite various differences in theoretical and methodological approach to social science subject matter, both subscribed to a value-neutral approach. In the course of his analysis of the problem of values, Gouldner performs an interesting bit of ideological "unmasking" with respect to both camps.

Gouldner observes that when the Columbia-Harvard and the Chicago trained men turned to the study of the sociology of medicine, the work of the former was "more respectful of the medical establishment," the work of the latter "more inclined

toward debunking forays into the seamier side of medical prac-
tise."[90] This ideological bias was even manifest in the titles of
important works by each group, and while the Columbia-Harvard
group named their most important works *The Student Physician*
and *Experiment Perilous*, the Chicago group irreverently named
their study of medical students the *Boys in White.*

The ideological bias of the classicists (which appears to be
Gouldner's identification of the Columbia-Harvard tradition) inclines them toward "ritualism, in which conformity to the formal
canons of the craft is pursued compulsively to a point where it
warps work, emptying it of insight, significant truth, and intellec-
tually viable substance."[91] The orientation of the Chicago style
intellectual, Gouldner urges, leads to a form of "naturalistic romanticism" that prefers the offbeat to the familiar."[92] Gouldner
urges that the two leading exponents of the Chicago style are
Howard S. Becker and Irving Goffman.

> As a case in point, Goffman's subtle study, "Cooling the Mark
> Out," takes its point of departure from an examination of the
> strategy of the confidence rackets. In the con game . . . after the
> mark's loot has been taken, one of the con men remains behind
> "to cool the mark out," seeking to persuade him to accept his
> loss of face rather than squeal to the police. Goffman then uses
> this stratagem as a model to explode a great variety of legitimate
> groups and roles—the restaurant hostess who cools out the impa-
> tient customer, the psychoanalyst who cools out those who have
> lost in love. The point is insinuated that the whole world may be
> seen as one of marks and operators and that, in the final analysis,
> we are all marks to be cooled out by the clergy, the operator left
> behind the job. This, it would seem, is a metaphysics of the
> underworld, in which conventional society is seen from the stand-
> point of a group outside of its own respectable social structures.
> This group of Chicagoans finds itself at home in the world of hip,
> Norman Mailer, drug addicts, jazz musicians, cab drivers, prosti-
> tutes, night people, drifters, grifters, and skidders, the cool cats
> and their kicks.[93]

However, if one expected Gouldner, after such brilliant demonstration of the manner in which covert value judgment and ideological bias may distort sociological study and lead to a selective
bias, to plead for objectivity, one would be disillusioned. Rather,
he saw ethical neutrality as a modern version of the medieval
conflict between faith and reason, "seeking to erect compartments
between the two as a way of keeping the peace between them."[94]

Peter L. Berger: While Gouldner is extraordinarily anxious to assume the mantle of the prophet, Berger, in a much more timid and circumspect manner, also assigns sociology a moral mission.

> This humanism to which sociology can contribute is one that does not easily wave banners, that is suspicious of too much enthusiasm and too much certainty. It is an uneasy, uncertain, hesitant thing, aware of its own precariousness, circumspect in its moral assertions. . . . The sociological humanism that we are suggesting is likely to adopt a . . . ironic stance.[95]

Berger seems to lack much of the self-assurance of Mills, or Shils, or Gouldner. To Berger, humanistic sociology seems to be a form of faint-hearted morality.

Sociology has, it seems, raised up a new generation of would-be priests and prophets. In a variety of ways they distort Weber's position. Weber did not think it possible or even desirable for a scholar to attempt to avoid value judgments outside his scholarly role. He sought to prevent the cynical exploitation of one's professional role for partisan purposes, nor did he believe one could adequately account for social life without taking into consideration the evaluations of people studied, which in no way suggests that one should only attend to what the people studied conceive to be insignificant. It is not unfair to apply Weber's analysis to contemporary would-be priests and prophets.

> Every teacher has observed that the faces of his students light up and they become more attentive when he begins to set forth his personal evaluations and the attendance at his lectures is greatly increased by the expectation that he will. Everyone knows furthermore that in the competition for students, universities in making recommendations for advancement will often give a prophet, however minor, who can fill the lecture halls, the upper hand over a much superior scholar who does not present his own preferences. Of course, it is understood in those cases that the prophecy should leave sufficiently untouched the political or conventional preferences which are generally accepted at the time. The pseudo-"ethically-neutral" prophet who speaks for the dominant interests has, of course, better opportunities for ascent due to the influence which these have on the political powers-that-be. . . . For my own part, in any case, I fear that the lecturer who makes his lectures stimulating by the insertion of personal evaluations will, in the long run, weaken the student's taste for sober empirical analysis.[96]

NOTES

1. August Comte, *System of Positive Reality* (London: Longmans, Green, 1877), vol. 4, p. 4.

2. Ibid., p. 6.

3. Ibid., p. 7.

4. Ibid., pp. 22-23.

5. Ibid., p. 27.

6. Ibid., p. 28.

7. Ibid., p. 70.

8. Ibid., p. 223.

9. Ibid., p. 225.

10. Ibid., p. 96.

11. Ibid., p. 141.

12. Count Leo N. Tolstoy, *What to Do?* trans. Isabel F. Hapgood (New York: Thomas Y. Crowell, 1887), p. 176.

13. Ibid., p. 175.

14. Ibid., pp. 188-89.

15. Ibid., p. 179.

16. Emile Durkheim, *The Elementary Forms of the Religious Life*, trans. Joseph Ward Swain (Glencoe, Ill.: The Free Press, 1947).

17. Ibid., pp. 87 ff.

18. Ibid., p. 9.

19. Durkheim may possibly have had Bergson in mind.

20. Ibid., p. 110.

21. Ibid., p. 12.

22. Ibid., p. 13.

23. Ibid., pp. 15-17.

24. Ibid., p. 16.

25. Ibid., p. 19.

26. Felix Kaufmann, *Methodology of the Social Sciences* (New York: Oxford University Press, 1944), p. 151.

27. See, for example, O. Neurath, "Physicalism," *Monist*, vol. 41 (1931), and "Radical Physicalism and Reality," *Erkenntnis*, vol. 4 (1934).

28. Wilhelm Dilthey, *Pattern and Meaning in History*, trans. and ed. H. P. Hickman (New York: Harper & Bros., 1962).

29. Ibid., pp. 67, 68, 69, 72, 74.

30. Maurice Mandelbaum, *The Problem of Historical Knowledge* (New York: Liveright, 1938), pp. 92-93.

31. *Dilthey's Philosophy of Existence*, trans. William Klubak and Martin Weinbaum (New York: Bookman Associates, 1957), pp. 25-26.

32. Ibid., p. 26.

33. Ibid., p. 28.

34. Karl Mannheim, *Ideology and Utopia*, trans. Louis Wirth (New York: Harcourt, Brace & Co., 1949), p. 3.

35. Ibid., p. 19.

36. Ibid., p. 243.——

37. Ibid., pp. 70 ff.

38. Mandelbaum, *The Problem of Historical Knowledge*, pp. 17 ff.

39. Ibid., p. 19.

40. Ibid., p. 31.

41. Ibid., pp. 34 ff.

42. F. A. Hayek, *The Counter-Revolution of Science* (Glencoe, Ill.: The Free Press, 1952).

43. Karl R. Popper, *The Poverty of Historicism* (New York: Harper & Row, 1954).

44. Ibid., p. 67. Popper's quotations are drawn from Karl Mannheim's *Man and Society in an Age of Reconstruction* (New York: Harcourt, Brace & Co., 1949).

45. Ibid., p. 70. Quotes from Mannheim's *Man and Society*, p. 199.

46. Hayek, *The Counter-Revolution of Science*, p. 53.

47. Ibid., p. 74.

48. Ibid., p. 86.

49. Alvin Gouldner, "Anti-Minotaur: The Myth of a Value-Free Sociology," in *Sociology on Trial*, ed. Maurice Stein and Arthur Vidich (Englewood Cliffs, N.J.: Prentice Hall, 1963), pp. 35-36.

50. *Max Weber on the Methodology of the Social Sciences*, trans. Edward A. Shils and Henry A. Finch (Glencoe, Ill.: The Free Press, 1949).

51. Ibid., p. 52.

52. Ibid., pp. 53-54.

53. Ibid., p. 54.

54. Ibid., pp. 1 ff.

55. Ibid., p. 2.

56. Ibid., p. 7.

57. Ibid., p. 9.

58. Ibid., p. 10.

59. Ibid., p. 12.

60. Ibid., p. 13.

61. Ibid., p. 23.

62. Ibid., p. 24.

63. Ibid., p. 38.

64. Ibid., p. 33.

65. Kaufmann, *Methodology of the Social Sciences*, p. 128.

66. Ibid., pp. 131 ff.

67. Ibid., p. 134.

68. Ibid., p. 134.

69. Ibid., p. 135.

70. Weber, *On the Methodology of the Social Sciences*, p. 18.

71. C. Wright Mills, *The Sociological Imagination* (New York: Oxford University Press, 1959), p. 14.

72. Ibid., p. 16.

73. Ibid., p. 146.

74. Ibid., p. 150.

75. Ibid., p. 117.

76. Ibid., p. 178.

77. Ibid., p. 185.

78. Edward Shils, "The Calling of Sociology," in *Theories of Society*, ed. Talcott Parsons, Edward Shils, Kaspar D. Naegle, Jesse R. Pitts (New York: The Free Press of Glencoe, 1961), vol. 2, p. 1430.

79. Ibid., p. 1422.

80. Ibid., p. 1440.

81. Ibid., p. 1439.

82. Maurice Stein and Arthur Vidich, eds., *Sociology on Trial* (Englewood Cliffs, N.J.: Prentice Hall, 1963), pp. 35-52.

83. Irving Louis Horowitz, *The New Sociology* (New York: Oxford University Press, 1964), pp. 196-217.

84. Ibid., p. 197.

85. Ibid., p. 198.

86. Ibid., p. 198.

87. Ibid., p. 199.

88. Ibid., p. 206.

89. This polarization is no longer maintained.

90. Ibid., p. 46.

91. Ibid., p. 47.

92. Ibid., p. 47.

93. Ibid., pp. 46-47.

94. Ibid., p. 211.

95. Peter L. Berger, *Invitation to Sociology* (Garden City, N.Y.: Doubleday, 1963), p. 162.

96. Weber, *On the Methodology of the Social Sciences*, p. 9.

SELECTED BIBLIOGRAPHY

Berger, Peter L. *Invitation to Sociology.* Garden City, N.Y.: Doubleday, 1963.

Comte, Auguste. *System of Positive Polity or Treatise on Sociology, Instituting the Religion of Humanity.* Paris: Carilian-Goeury, and Ver Dalmont, 1854.

Gouldner, Alvin W. "Anti-Minotaur: The Myth of a Value-Free Sociology." In *Sociology on Trial*, edited by Maurice Stein and Arthur Vidich. Englewood Cliffs, N.J.: Prentice-Hall, 1963.

Hayek, F. A. *The Counter-Revolution of Science*. Glencoe, Ill.: The Free Press, 1952.

Kaufmann, Felix. *Methodology of the Social Sciences*. New York: Oxford University Press, 1944.

Mills, C. Wright. *The Sociological Imagination*. New York: Oxford University Press, 1959.

Popper, Karl R. *The Poverty of Historicism*. New York: Harper & Row, 1954.

Shils, Edward. "The Calling of Sociology." In *Theories of Society*, edited by Talcott Parsons, Edward Shils, Kaspar D. Naegele, Jesse R. Pitts, pp. 1405-48. New York: The Free Press of Glencoe, 1961.

Weber, Max. *Max Weber on the Methodology of the Social Sciences*. Translated by Edward A. Shils and Henry A. Finch. Glencoe, Ill.: The Free Press, 1949.

CHAPTER 2

Branches of the Sociology
of Culture

The two major nineteenth-century collectivistic traditions of positivistic sociology and objective idealism (together with its prodigal son, dialectical materialism) treated the human collectivity itself as the primary cause of whatever happened within it. No clear line was drawn between society and culture (between interpersonal activities and socially acquired forms, between instrumentalities and ideas). Durkheim's collective representations and Dilthey's forms of the objective mind were items of culture; both were thought to be the core of society. No distinction was initially drawn between the problems presented by behavior and cultural items which arise in human behavior but which are capable of analysis in isolation from it.

However, the programs of positivistic sociology and objective idealism soon turned out to be faced by problems more complicated than establishing a few great epochs in the history of society and culture (such as Hegel's contrast between Oriental Despotism, with one man free; Greek Democracy, with some free; and Nineteenth-Century Germany, when all were free—or Comte's Theological, Metaphysical, and Positivistic Eras) in which to a given stage in the development of social institutions there corresponded a typical system of knowledge, ethics, and art.

The critical considerations that drove positivism toward reductionism and objective idealism toward relativism soon forced realization of the fact that the relation between society and the various categories of culture (intellectual systems, the arts, ethical systems) was more complicated than initially assumed. There seems to be little question that the early forms of the sociology of culture (the sociology of knowledge and sociology of art, for example) were intended to salvage the program of the collectivistic social science at a time when it seemed to be breaking down. The program of establishing a few great epochs in society and culture was abandoned, and the detailed examination of the relation between various specific social institutional states (pressure groups, classes, and so on) and cultural forms was substituted in its place. However, many of the early students of the sociology of knowledge made the same basic assumptions as their predecessors and found themselves in a similar predicament, as illustrated by Karl Mannheim's relationism.

However, when it is seen that the relativistic predicament of the collectivist arises from the. assimilation of logical and empirical knowledge to the pattern of ethical or aesthetic knowledge, a new attack on the problem is possible. The structure of various areas of culture (such as play, ideology, the arts) is provided by men's preferences and the axiological principles by which they judge them to be correct. Axiological principles cannot be derived from empirical events. They are free creations by which men secure to themselves a range of values. One may examine various interrelationships between a cultural sphere and its axiological principles and institutional forms without being entrapped in the reductionistic or relativistic predicaments. One consequence is the establishment of the sociology of culture as an area of investigation for social science.

Among the unsolved problems of this area is the relation of various special subareas of the sociology of culture to one another. In the following the place of the theory of civilization to other aspects of the sociology of culture is reviewed as a step toward bringing integration to the area.

The Concept of Civilization

The term "civilization" referring to an advanced state of society characterized by developed arts, science, and religion did not come into currency until recent times. In 1772 Doctor Johnson still declined to include it in his dictionary. However, with the increased interaction between Europeans and peoples with less complex social orders, the term came widely into use in the nineteenth century. Moreover, when information was assembled on so-called barbaric and primitive peoples, some ethnographers began to insist that many peoples without cities were nevertheless highly "civilized." Alongside the older meaning of "civilization" as an advanced state of society appeared another: the unique type of culture of a people—as in the case of Polynesian or Maori civilization.

As the term "culture" also came into general use, the need was felt to distinguish between the two terms. Some German writers began to employ the term "civilization" for the technical apparatus of human society (for science, technology, and material equipment) and the term "culture" for the nonmaterial apparatus of human society (art, religion, phiolosophy), but this never became universal. Also, at times, the term "culture" has been restricted to the society and social forms of preliterate peoples, and the term "civilization" has been retained for the society and social forms of literate peoples. This usage still appears, as in the writings of Spengler and Toynbee.

In addition to these special usages is the practice of a large number of students employing the term "culture" in a generic sense for the sum total of man's social heritage, whether material or nonmaterial. The term "civilization" then is taken to refer to a specific organized system of culture of a comprehensive and enduring sort. This usage will be followed here.

Only in the nineteenth century did the sum of man's social heritage, his culture, fall under the purview of science. As the science of culture began to assume its present form, two events of major importance marked its progress: (1) the establishment of the existence of comprehensive systems of culture—of civilizations; and (2) the investigation of the principles of civilization formation. The first of these events occurred in the course of the transition from eighteenth-century rationalism to nineteenth-century romanticism. The second has only recently begun.

In the following pages the rise of the contemporary theory of civilization will be traced and a provisional attempt will be made to locate it, together with closely related disciplines, in the general science of culture.

Rationalism, Romanticism, and the Concept of Civilization

The eighteenth century has special importance for all students of the western world, for it sustained a series of revolutions which ushered in the contemporary national state. Prior to these revolutions, under the absolute monarchies which proved to be transitional between the feudal and modern worlds, an advanced section of the intellectual spokesmen of the times was inspired by deep confidence in the possibilities of human progress. In the name of human rationality and progress, these opinion leaders sought to clear away the debris of the Middle Ages. In the words of Cassirer, "reason" had become "the unifying and central point of this century, expressing all that it longs and strives for, and all that it achieves."[1]

The enlightenment thinkers were firmly convinced that the essence of man was his rationality. The world, moreover, had a natural order which, while independent of his mind, was discoverable by reason.

> One should not seek order, law, and "reason" as a rule that may
> be grasped and expressed prior to the phenomena, as their *a
> priori*; one should rather discover such regularity in the phenomena themselves, as the form of their imminent connection.[2]

In one of the major products of eighteenth-century psychology, Condillac's *Treatise on Sensation*, the spheres of material and mental phenomena were reduced to common elements subject to the same laws.

> The third sphere of reality is that which we find in the structure
> of the state and of society.... Society must submit to being
> treated like a physical reality under investigation.... The general
> will of the state is treated as if it were composed of the wills of
> individuals and had come into being as a result of the union of
> these wills.[3]

These suppositions laid the foundation for a modern science of culture by naturalizing man and his works, making them a fit subject of scientific study.

It follows from the presuppositions of rationalism—the rationality of man and the lawfulness of nature and society—that human culture is not only natural but universal. However, the universality of human culture must be squared with the fact that it manifests itself in different ways from place to place. Montesquieu analyzed these variations as different expressions of the general spirit of mankind.

> Mankind is influenced by various causes: by the climate, by religion, by the laws, by the maximus of government, by precedents, morals, and customs; when is formed a general spirit of nations. . . . In proportion as, in every country, any one of these causes acts with more force, the others in the same degree are weakened. Nature and the climate rule almost alone over the savages; customs govern the Chinese; the laws tyrannize in Japan; morals had formerly all their influence at Sparta; maxims of government, and the ancient simplicity of manners, once prevailed at Rome.[4]

As a result of the differential operation of such facts, the character of peoples is a composition of good and bad qualities. The Spanish, Montesquieu believed, join honesty with indolence; the Chinese combine prodigious industry with greed. Other societies have other compositions.

Within the framework of universal culture, Montesquieu began to isolate local drifts and eddies produced by special circumstances. He and other rationalists nevertheless held out the possibility that by the manipulation of local training and circumstances cultural contrast could be modified or eliminated, for in the background was a common, rational, human nature which responded in the same manner to similar conditions. The isolation of systems of culture (civilization) was always subordinated to the universality of man.

While the presuppositions of rationalism dominated an advanced section of European opinion, from around the middle of the seventeen century a rival point of view—eventually to be described as "romantic"—began to gain currency.[5]

The romantic point of view was first evident in literature. When it first gained currency in aesthetic criticism, the term "romanticism" referred to the "imaginative," "extraordinary," and "visionary" elements of works of art which in some literary circles were beginning to be appreciated more highly than form, classical balance, and logical clarity—the prized literary qualities of the enlightenment.[6] During the course of the eighteenth century the term "romantic" ceased to be merely aesthetic, coming to designate a group of experiences, emotions, and sentiments which lay outside the rationalistic conception of rational human nature: fantasy, unrepressed passion, and deep feeling. As the romantic conception of man, nature, and society gained coherent form, basic contrasts to rationalism became apparent. In place of the concept that the essence of man was his reason, the romantics found man's most significant characteristics in inspiration and demonic frenzy; in place of the rationalistic evaluation of order, the romantic doctrines of the infinite variation and progress were posed; in place of the rationalistic preference for the methods of reason, there appeared the romantic evaluation of irrational, superrational, mystical, occultist, magical, and intuitive procedures; in religion in place of the Deism of the rationalists, there arose new cults of emotionalism and enthusiasm (English Methodism, German Pietism, the mystic fervor of Johann Hamann and Swedenborg); in place of the rationalistic conception of the superiority of civilization to primitive society there appeared the romantic doctrine of the natural poetic genius of primitive peoples; in place of the rationalistic conception of the rational equality of men there appeared the romantic cult of genius; and finally, in place of the primacy of the individual to the group there appeared the romantic conception of society as a super-individual organism and the glorification of the state. These changes of supposition had important consequences for the theory of civilization.

The romantic conception of civilization (that is, of total systems or culture) came to fruition in Hegel's *Philosophy of History.* The starting point for his formulation seems to bear superficial similarities to those of the rationalists, inasmuch as like them he places the problem of reason in central focus in his analysis of social life.

> The only thought which Philosophy brings with it to the contemplation of History, is the simple conception of Reason; that Reason is the Sovereign of the World; that the history of the world, therefore, presents us with a rational process.[7]

However, Hegel's Reason bears little resemblance to the Reason of the Rationalists. Reason for the rationalists was the universally distributed faculty for logical and rational thinking of individual man. This did not necessarily imply that human history followed a rational course. Hegel's Reason, by contrast, is not a property of the individual mind, but of collective experience. It is the "World-Spirit" that is rational; its "nature is always one and the same, but which unfolds its one nature in the phenomena of the World's existence."[8] The *individuals* in whom Hegel's Reason is manifest are not single persons, but peoples: "In the history of the World, the *Individuals* we have to do with are *Peoples*; Totalities that are states."[9]

While the rationalists were convinced that reason (individual good sense) is approximately equally distributed in all individual persons, making one man as important as any other, Hegel was convinced that only a restricted category of men manifest the Reason of the World-Spirit, making them historically important. "Historical men—World-Historical Individuals—are those in whose aims . . . a general principle lies."[10] Such historical men are driven by private purposes which involve the great issues of the World-Spirit.

> They may be called Heroes, inasmuch as they have derived their purposes and their vocation, not from the calm, regular course of things, sanctioned by the existing order, but from a concealed fount . . . from that inner spirit, still hidden beneath the surface. . . . Such individuals had no consciousness of the general idea they were unfolding, while prosecuting those aims of theirs; on the contrary, they were practical, political men. But at the same time they were thinking men, who had an insight into the requirements of the time—*what was ripe for development.*[11]

When the mission of such heroes of history is accomplished, they "fall off like empty hulls from the kernel. They die early, like Alexander; they are murdered, like Caesar; transported to St. Helena, like Napoleon."[12]

Individual persons are merely the subjective aspects of the world-spirit which is objectively manifest in the State. Morality and Truth are properties of the collective and not of the individual person.

> The State is the actually existing realized moral life. For it is the Unity of the Universal, essential Will, with that of the Individual; and this is "Morality."

> Truth is the Unity of the universal and subjective Will; and the Universal is to be found in the State, in its laws, its universal and rational arrangements. The State is the Divine Idea as it exists on Earth.[13]

Only that individual person is free who conforms to the order of the State.

> Freedom of a law and limited order is mere caprice, which finds its exercise in the sphere of particular and limited desires. . . . When the State or our country constitutes a community of existence; when the subjective will of man submits to its laws—the contradiction between Liberty and Necessity vanishes.[14]

In short, individual freedom is conformance to collective necessity.

If we take the term "civilization" to refer to a comprehensive system of culture, it is evident that both the rationalists (as evidenced by Montesquieu) and the romantics (as evidenced by Hegel) have recognized the existence of civilizations and have assigned importance to them for the understanding of social and historical life. However, the rationalists and the romantics offer quite different estimates of the nature and importance of civilization. To the rationalists, any particular civilization (Montesquieu would describe it as a special spirit of a nation) is a local eddy in universal human culture. To the romantics, any particular civilization (Hegel would describe it as the integrated spirit of a people or a State) is a special embodiment of the objective Reason or the World-Spirit. For the rationalists, a civilization is a by-product of individual activity; for the romantics, a civilization is the primary cause of individual activity. For the rationalist, causal priority lies with the individual; for the romantics, causal priority is assigned to the collective.

In the course of the development of western thought from the eighteenth to the nineteenth century, the modern concept of civilization was born. The enlightenment thinkers recognized civilizations as local eddies in the general drift of universal human culture. Such local eddies were secondary rather than primary social phenomena. The romantics of the nineteenth century seized upon these phenomena that their predecessors had described as "the spirit of particular nations" and transformed them into the primary manifestations of the World-Spirit in human history. More was involved in this new analysis than a mere change of emphasis. To the rationalist the individual is primary, the collective (and the spirit of the collective) is secondary; to the romantic the collective is primary, and the individual is only the local and subjective aspect of the collective mind.

The mutual exchange of criticism by adherents of these two approaches to the problem of civilization led to the increasing disrepute of their key terms. One rarely finds in scholarly discourse the individualistic concept of the "spirit of the particular nation" or the collectivistic concept of *Volksgeist* any longer employed. However, the positions have persisted under new euphemisms. The term "climate of opinion" is widely employed by contemporary adherents of the individualistic approach to civilization. The term *"milieu,"* on the other hand, is widely used by adherents of the collectivistic approach to civilization. The concept of civilization (designating general systems of culture) thus has been fixed as part of the intellectual heritage of western man, and through various euphemisms individualistic and collectivistic theories of civilization have been pursued.

Three Twentieth-Century Analyses of Civilization

In the twentieth century, collectivistic analyses of civilization have generally been pursued more systematically and vigorously than individualistic analyses. The three most dramatic of these are the studies of Spengler, Toynbee, and Sorokin.

Oswald Spengler carried out his analysis of civilization from the standpoint of the same basic contrast of spirit and nature as Hegel. "The *world-as-history*, conceived, viewed, and given form from out of its opposite, the *world-as-nature*, here is a new aspect of human existence on this earth."[15] In Spengler's view, different methods of thought are required for understanding each of these spheres. History is understood on the basis of analogy; nature on the basis of Mathematical Law.

> There is, besides, a necessity of cause and effect—which I may call the *logic of space*—another necessity, an organic necessity in life, that of Destiny—the *logic of time*.[16]

Organic necessity (Destiny) characterizes religion, art, in fact the whole of history. What diaries and autobiographies are to individuals, histories are to the development of people as a whole. History studies the soul of a culture.[17]

Based upon these contrasts, Spengler lined up his concepts in a number of peculiar ways. A culture was taken to be an organic system of collective life born in the soul of a peasant folk bound to the soil and sustaining a peculiar conception of man and nature. The evolution of this culture begins when a people attempts to realize itself in objective form. Every culture gives rise to its own peculiar civilization. A peculiar civilization thus is the destiny of a culture.

Civilizations are the most external and artificial states of which a species of developed humanity is capable. They are a conclusion, the thing-become succeeding the thing-becoming, death following life, rigidity following expansion, intellectual age and the stone-built, petrifying world-city following mother-earth and the spiritual childhood of Doric and Gothic. They are an end, irrevocable, yet by inward necessity reached again and again.[18]

Pure civilization consists in the objectification of forms that by this very process have become inorganic and dead. In place of a folk born of the soil, there appears a restless, nomadic civic mass. In place of the epic (the literature of the soil), there appears the drama and the novel (the literature of the city). In place of the genuine folk song, there is civic lyricism. In place of peasant art, there appear urban painting and architecture.[19]

The stone Colossus "Cosmopolis" stands at the end of the life's course of every great Culture. The Culture-man whom the land has spiritually formed is seized and possessed by his own creation, the city, and is made into its creature, its executive organ, and finally, its victim. This stony mass is the *absolute* city. Its image, as it appears with all its grandiose beauty . . . contains the whole noble death-symbolism of the definitive thing-become.[20]

Spengler published his *Decline of the West* in 1918. The problem of civilization central to it was taken up once again by Toynbee in his *Study of History*, the first volume of which appeared in 1934. Like Spengler, Toynbee proposed that the basic unit of historical study is neither mankind as a whole nor the nation-state, but the society (the civilization). The central characteristic of any given society, Toynbee believes, is the direction taken by *mimesis* or imitation. Societies of the past and present were divided into two species: primitive societies characterized by a mimesis directed toward the past, ancestors, and tradition, giving the society a static structure; civilizations are societies in which mimesis is directed toward creative personalities. We can, Toynbee maintains, identify twenty specimens of civilizations and around 650 primitive societies.[21]

In a manner suggestive of Spengler, Toynbee sees civilization as an evolution out of primitive society.

Primitive societies . . . may be likened to a people lying torpid upon a ledge on a mountainside, with a precipice below and a precipice above; civilizations may be likened to companions of these "Sleepers of Ephesus" who have just risen to their feet and have started to climb up the face of the cliff.[22]

Toynbee argues that though we may rely on the ordinary methods of science and search the various external factors (such as race and environment) for the origins of civilization, we are disappointed. The genesis of civilizations is not the result of biological or geographical factors acting singly or jointly. If we are to discover the true genesis of civilizations, we will find it necessary to "shut our eyes, for the moment, to the formulae of Science in order to open our ears to the language of Mythology."[23] In a methodological parallel to Spengler, Toynbee suggests that methods appropriate to the study of physical things are inappropriate to the study of human social affairs.

> We have the choice of conceiving this relation either as an interaction between two inhuman forces . . . or as an encounter between two super-human personalities. . . . Let us yield our minds to the second of these two conceptions. Perhaps it will lead us toward the light.
>
> An encounter between two super-human personalities is the plot of some of the greatest satires and dramas that the human imagination has conceived. An encounter between Yahweh and the Serpent is the plot of the story of the Fall of Man in the Book of Genesis; a second encounter between the same antagonists . . . is the plot of the New Testament which tells the story of Redemption; an encounter between the Lord and Satan is the plot of the Book of Job; an encounter between the Lord and Methistopheles is the plot of Goethe's *Faust*; an encounter between Gods and Demons is the plot of the Scandinavian *Voluspa*; an encounter between Artemis and Aphrodite is the plot of Euripides Hippolytus.[24]

These and a host of similar examples suggest to Toynbee that the essential event in the birth of civilization out of primitive society, mythologically mirrored in the story of the temptation of man by the devil, is a challenge and a response. The most immediate result of this temptation is the casting of man from the Garden of Eden.

> The first stage . . . in the human protagonist's ordeal is a transition from Yin to Yang through a dynamic act—performed by God's creature under temptation from the adversary. . . . The second stage in the human protagonist's ordeal is the crisis. He realizes that his dynamic act, which had re-liberated the creative power of his Master and Maker, has set his own feet on a course which is leading him to suffering and death.[25]

Toynbee appears determined to restore the Biblical story of Genesis at the core of contemporary social science. The birth of "civilization" is found in "a challenge from the human environment." This challenge "begins with a differentiation and culminates in a succession."[26]

There are major similarities between the analyses of civilization by Toynbee and Spengler. Even Spengler's notion that a unique type of method is necessary for the analysis of history finds a parallel in Toynbee's recourse to the "language of mythology." In both cases, the spiritual act which gives birth to new development externalizes itself as a civilization which turns, in the end, into an empty shell.

A few years after the appearance of the first volume of Toynbee's *Study of History*, the third major twentieth-century study of civilization, Sorokin's *Social and Cultural Dynamics*, appeared.

Sorokin accepted the concept of culture in the general sense understood by social scientists since Tylor as "the sum total of everything which is created or modified by the conscious or unconscious activity of two or more individuals."[27] Man's culture can, he argues, be organized in four basic ways: (1) spatially or mechanically, (2) by association with an external factor, (3) causally or functionally, and (4) internally or logico-meaningfully.[28] The spatial or mechanical relation of the elements of culture is illustrated by any collection of cultural items through a common external factor (but without functional or logical connection), as illustrated by the collection of items brought together in a ski lodge (winter clothes, liquor, skis, and other equipment, fireplaces, and the like). The common factor of a winter climate is critical for bringing them together. Causal or functional integration of cultural elements may be illustrated by the various parts of an internal combusion engine assembled into a working combination.

> Any cultural synthesis is to be regarded as functional when, on the one hand, the elimination of one of its important elements perceptibly influences the rest of the synthesis in its functions (and usually in its structure).[29]

The logico-meaningful integration is illustrated by the unity of elements of a poem, or of the arguments of a book of philosophy (such as Kant's *Critique of Pure Reason*) or the passages of a musical score (such as Beethoven's *Third Symphony*).

> If we know the proper patterns of meaning and value, we can put these passages or parts together into a significant unity in which each page or fragment takes its proper place, acquires a meaning,

and in which all together give the supremely integrated effect that was intended. . . . Their unification is far closer than that of mere functional association.[30]

It is quite possible, Sorokin argues, to discover the same kind of intimate logico-meaningful integration as is present in a poem or a piece of music between a large number of the details of an entire culture. In terms of whether ultimate reality is conceived to be super-sensory or sensory, two profoundly different cultural super-systems may be isolated.

First Culture	*Second Culture*
Dominance of	Dominance of
Nationalism, Mysticism	Empiricism
Idealism	Materialism
Eternalism	Temporalism
Indeterminism	Determinism
Realism	Nominalism
Sociological Universalism	Sociological Singularism
The conception of corporation or juridical personality as a primary reality	The concepts of corporation or juridical personality as an expedient fiction
Ethics of Absolute Principles	Ethics of Happiness (Hedonism, Utilitarianism, Eudaemonism)
Few discoveries in the natural sciences and few inventions	Many discoveries and inventions
Static character of social life with a slow rate of change	Dynamic character of social life with a rapid rate of change
Ideational style of painting	Visual style of painting
"Scripture" as the main form of literature	Secular realism and naturalism in literature, with sensualism and even sexualism
Pure or diluted theocracy	Pure or diluted secular power
"Expiation" as the basic prin-	"Adjustment," re-education

First Culture	*Second Culture*
ciple of punishment and of criminal law	mixed with extermination of the "unadjusted" and "socially dangerous persons."[31]

The two great cultural super-systems (civilization) arising on the basis of these contrasting forms of logico-meaningful integration are described by Sorokin as Ideational and Sensate.

> Each had its own mentality; its own system of truth and knowledge; its own philosophy and *Weltenschauung*; its own type of religion and standards of "holiness"; its own system of right and wrong; its own forms of art and literature; its own mores, laws, code of conduct; its own predominant forms of social relationships; its own economic and political organization; and, finally, its own type of *human personality*, with a peculiar mentality and conduct. The values which correspond to one another throughout these cultures are irreconcilably at variance in their nature; but with each culture all the values fit closely together, belong to one another logically, often functionally.
>
> Of these two systems one may be termed *Ideational* culture, the other *Sensate*. And as these names characterize the cultures as a whole, so do they indicate the nature of each of the component parts.[32]

Between Ideational and Sensate civilizations appears only one stable compromise form of civilization, the Idealistic.

The major premises of these great super-systems concern the nature of reality, the nature of the needs and ends to be satisfied, the extent to which they are to be satisfied, and the methods of their satisfaction. Ideational culture conceives reality to be spiritual, its needs and ends are spiritual, highest priority is given to the satisfaction of spiritual needs which are fulfilled by the self-imposed minimization or elimination of physical needs. Sensate culture assumes reality to be sensual, it gives hedonistic needs priority, and attempts to satisfy them physically by modifying the external world. Idealistic culture represented a balanced unification of the Ideational and Sensate types with a predominance of Ideational elements. For if reality is both spiritual and material, its needs and ends are also both spiritual and material (predominantly spiritual), and it seeks to satisfy them by modification both of the self and the external world.

Sorokin's types of reality retain the medieval distinctions between the three faculties of man—the senses, faith, and reason, and their corresponding objects. Corresponding to these realities are three types of men and three types of society. The faculties through which these three types of reality are known are said to yield three types of truth: truths of the senses, truths of reason (logical truth), and truths of faith (intuition). However, in the end Sorokin postulates the existence of a synthetic type of *integral truth* which is said to be the highest of all, inasmuch as it fuses the truths of sense, reason, and intuition.[33]

To Spengler and Toynbee civilizations represented the consequences of spiritual impulses arising in primitive or peasant societies which externalized themselves at least in vast structures of steel and stone from which all life had vanished. Civilizations were great individualized systems of culture in the overall draft of history. At least in Toynbee's case each of these civilizations ran the kind of course described in Genesis. Man was tempted out of his original state of primitive bliss (his Garden of Eden) by some challenge (the temptation of his Satan) to face dreadful ordeals in the course of which his civilization evolved as he struggled his way along a dark path which terminates in suffering and death. Spengler and Toynbee, thus, had largely taken over St. Augustine's theory of history, merely generalizing it to apply to all the great civilizations rather than to Western civilization alone.

Sorokin, on the other hand, turned his face against both the doctrines of evolution and progress (which Spengler and Toynbee also contested) and the doctrine of decline (which they sponsored). The types of civilization have been reduced to three and were conceived as an eternal cycle of these forms.

While Spengler's and Toynbee's conceptions of history represent rather direct extensions of the Christian theory of history as found in St. Augustine, Sorokin's theories superficially seem distinct.

In the fourteenth book of Augustine's *Civitas Dei* we read: "Epicurean philosophers lived after the flesh because they placed man's highest good in *bodily pleasure;* and . . . those others do so who have been of opinion that in some form or other bodily good is man's supreme good." According to Augustine, the next higher level of life is represented by the Stoics, "who place the supreme good of man in the soul." Since "both the soul and the flesh, the component parts of man, can be used to signify the whole man," both Epicureans and Stoics (and Platonists) live "according to man." Or one may say that they live according to *reason,* if reason can be divorced from faith. Only the Christian, in his *faith*, lives according to God.[34]

However, Speier indicates that Sorokin's basic distinctions between sensate, idealistic, and ideational are modeled after the early Christian notions of sense, reason, and faith. The chief differences between Sorokin's ideas and these early Christian notions is the blurring of the hierarchization of values and the substitution of a kind of relativism for the absolute standards implied in Christian thinking.[35] These considerations led Speier to describe Sorokin's position as a "modern vulgarization of early Christian thinking."[36]

Concepts similar to those of Spengler, Toynbee, and Sorokin have continued to attract contemporary students despite the extensive criticisms leveled against all three of these thinkers. For example, in his *Evolution of Civilizations* Carroll Quigley employs a distinction between collections, groups, and societies which is reminiscent of Sorokin's distinction between the kinds of cultural integration. Societies which are defined as aggregates which have more relations with insiders than outsiders are, in turn, divided into simple tribes or bands and civilizations in a manner somewhat similar to Toynbee.[37]

Aggregates of Persons

A. Collections

B. Groups

C. Societies

    1. Parasitic societies

    2. Producing societies

        a. Simple tribes or bands

        b. Civilizations[38]

Moreover, every civilization was argued to pass through seven stages:

1. Mixture

2. Gestation

3. Expansion

4. Age of Conflict

5. Universal empire

6. Decay

7. Invasion[39]

Quigley's stages of civilizational development are a compact summary of those earlier presented by Toynbee. The great and continuing interest in analyses of civilization such as those of Spengler, Toynbee, and Sorokin is striking testimony of the importance of the concept for contemporary social science. However, the many criticisms to which these works have been subject testifies to the ambiguity with which the principles of civilization have been established. If, in the face of the criticisms, one abandons the task of analyzing civilization, it is still necessary to take account of the fact that various euphemisms for civilization such as *milieu* and *climate of opinion* continue to be employed in social science analysis, even where the concept of "civilization" is studiously avoided.

One of the major problems of contemporary social science is to establish a more adequate theory of civilization than appears in the works of Spengler, Toynbee, and Sorokin and to isolate the principles of civilization on a more adequate foundation than has been achieved hitherto.

Community and Civilization

Scientifically the major twentieth-century analyses of civilization suffer from a number of defects: they make inadequate use of the concepts developed by social science; they employ methods lacking scientific standing; and they are riddled with value judgments. Nonscientific methods (Sorokin's truths of faith and integral truth, Toynbee's method of mythology, and Spengler's logic of Destiny) and ethical evaluation have no place in a scientific theory of civilization. Moreover, the study of systems of culture can be enriched by the employment of concepts more precise than mimesis (Toynbee), logico-meaningful integration (Sorokin), or organic succession (Spengler). A first step in increasing the precision of the theory of civilization is to introduce clear distinctions between civilization and society (or community). Moreover, once this distinction is carried through, the contrast can be drawn between the principles of community formation and civilization formation.

Community and civilization are distinct but related products of social life for the understanding of which two major characteristics of human social life are critical: (1) man's lack of instincts and (2) his possession of language. Because of his lack of instincts (biologically pre-fixed solutions to the basic problems of life), man is compelled to learn or invent the solutions to his life problems. Language arms man with an instrument of unusual power for such invention and learning. When the individual solves his problems, language makes it possible to bring to bear all the experience of his associates upon them. By means of language the experience of men remote in time and space can be introduced into the sphere of the present. By means of language individuals can influence each other in ways of unusual precision.

Behavior that is linguistically restructured acquires a polarity not possible to instinct-based, language-free behavior. A creature responding to his problems instinctively "does what comes naturally." When he has solved his problems in the instinctively prescribed manner, he is "satisfied." No sharp division appears between behavior performed for instrumental reasons and behavior for sheer enjoyment.

All of this is quite changed in a creature without instincts and armed with language. Language introduces into present behavior a field of possibilities. Instinctive behavior arises in response to what is at hand; language-mediated behavior is always oriented in some measure to things not at hand. Among other things, a division appears between behavior which is instrumental (designed for survival) and behavior which is pursued for its own sake (intrinsically).

Not only does human social behavior, thus, differ from nonhuman social behavior in the appearance within it of the contrast between instrumental and intrinsically pursued activities, but complex systems of instrumental and intrinsic activities become possible. This distinction is of fundamental significance for the contrast between community (or society) and civilization.

Communities as Systems
of Instrumental Activities

The fact that man is without instinctive solutions to his problems and that he possesses language does not mean that he can permit his problems to go unsolved. Man must learn or invent his solutions. The learned or invented solutions to human problems are *institutions*. Institutions play the role among men performed by instincts in nonhuman beings. They do not have the certainty of instincts, but they have a plasticity which is absent in instincts.

The creatures dependent on instincts must have a set sufficiently comprehensive to keep it alive and perpetuate its kind. The institutions which men invent to replace their lost instincts must perform the same functions. At least three major categories of institutions are necessary for any plurality of people if they are to survive in nature and get along with one another: (1) they must solve the problems of their material existence (*mastery of nature*); (2) they must transform individuals and situations which are not per se social into social realities (*socialization*); and (3) they must secure sufficient discipline to carry out collective tasks (*social control*).

Strong forces are at work to bring the institutions of pluralities of people into working relation with one another. The manner in which a plurality of persons makes a living (its mastery of nature) has direct and indirect influences upon its institutions of socialization (family, religion, education, and so on). The realization of a plurality's economic and socialization objectives, moreover, is bound up with its institutions of social control. Three principles may be discerned operating on and between a people's institutions to bring them into stable interrelation with one another: *stabilization* (the fixing of solutions to interhuman problems), *consistency* (the adaptation of the solutions to the problems in one area of life to those in another), and *closure* (the fusion of the series into an interrelated set).

A community (or a society) is a total way of life consisting of a set of institutions (drawn from all of the major spheres of institutions) formed into a system sufficient to bring the plurality of individuals through the cycles of a normal year and an average life. A community (or society) thus is a behavioral system.[40]

Civilizations as Products of
Intrinsically Valued Activities

Every human community is an instrumental-behavioral system of activities designed to secure the survival of its component groups and individuals. By its nature such a system of behavior can only explore a few of the many possible alternative groups which could be designed to secure similar and related ends. Since the men who establish these communities are language-using, thinking creatures, they are quite capable of envisioning alternatives to their groups and their communities. A field of possibilities tends to arise around every system of societal life.

When frustrations arise in the behavioral-instrumental system, men automatically turn to the symbolic system. When they are bored or weary, they may find temporary relief from the pressure of everyday anxieties in the world of fantasy or in the world of play. If their frustrations are more deep, they may draw from the world of fantasy new suggestions for the arrangement of the everyday. In any case, alongside the behavioral-instrumental system of human activities there arises a symbolic-intrinsic system of potential activities. If they look to the behavioral system for survival, men look to the symbolic system for enrichment. While men shape their behavioral-instrumental activities into communities, they shape their symbolic-intrinsic activities into civilizations.

In contrast to all theories which draw no distinction between society (or community) and civilization, these two types of systems of human activity are here taken to be of intrinsically different types. When some students argue that civilizations pass through stages such as mixture, gestation, expansion, an age of conflict, universal empire, and so on, the lines between society (community) and civilization become hopelessly blurred. As an intrinsic-symbolic system a civilization cannot have a universal empire—a category applicable to society or community, to a behavioral complex, but not to a symbolic one. The arbitrariness this application of categories causes is illustrated by the argument that the Mogul domination represented the Universal Empire of Hinduism. However, the Mogul Empire was never a part of Hindu civilization at all; it was, rather, a behavioral event. To be sure, Hindu civilization underwent some changes when the Mogul domination was clamped down on Hindu communities after the tenth century, but that is something quite different from the reification of Hindu civilization and the assignment of a foreign domination to it as one of its components.

Primary Subdivisions
of the Sociology of Culture

The sociology of culture is the study of the social implications of the intrinsic-symbolic forms of interhuman activity. The most comprehensive branch of the sociology of culture is the study of the formation of civilizations. However, there are a number of sub-branches of lesser scope: the sociology of play, the sociology of art, and the sociology of knowledge. There is some advantage in approaching the sociology of civilization by way of them.

The Sociology of Play

Without multiplying the definitions of play, it may be observed that most students recognize its properties as forms of activity in which the center of interest lies in the activity itself. In these terms, play has an intrinsic-symbolic character. Huizinga sums up the formal characteristics of play as:

> A free activity standing quite consciously outside "ordinary" life as being "not spurious," but at the same time absorbing the player intensely and utterly. It is an activity connected with no material interest, and no profit can be gained by it. It proceeds within its own proper boundaries of time and space according to fixed rules and in an orderly manner. It promotes the formation of social groupings which tend to surround themselves with secrecy and to stress their difference from the common world by disguise of other means.[41]

Mitchell and Mason characterize play in similar terms:

> *Play* is effort in which the satisfactions are in and a part of the activity itself. The goals are immediate, and they are accomplishable. It is activity scaled down to the capacity of the performer, so as to provide a balance of success and failure possibilities, with the result that there is always hope of achievement. Play is its own reward and no other inducement is needed. *Play is self-expression for its own sake.*[42]

A number of theories of play were advanced in the course of the nineteenth century. It was argued, for example, that play in the higher animals is a device for ridding the organism of surplus energy, not required for survival.[43] It has been theorized that play serves the purpose of recreation[44] or relaxation from the instrumental activities of life.[45] Play has been said to be an activity performing a role in the practice of the instincts,[46] and that play represents the survival of past behavior which the individual recapitulates in the course of his individual development.[47] However, Huizinga's comment disposes of all such approaches to play:

> All these hypotheses have one thing in common: they all start from the assumption that play must serve something which is not play, that it must have some kind of biological purpose.[48]

50

This (that is, the biological reduction of play to the instincts) eclipses the very properties that give play its distinctive character, its intrinsic-symbolic character. All theories which attempt to reduce play to an instinct or to subordinate it to instrumental activities distort its basic character.[49] In all the higher animals play increases in importance as the sphere of instincts narrows. It occurs most frequently in man, who is most lacking in instincts. Playfulness is best viewed as a nonreducible property of the behavior of all higher creatures. When the range of instincts is narrowed while the energy for action still remains, there is placed at the disposal of the creature a sphere of activity within which free experimentalism becomes the rule.

The same problem also may be approached by way of the distinction between instrumental and intrinsic activity. As indicated above, there is no reason to presume that creatures acting on the basis of instinct do not experience a state of well-being when the activity is successful, and a state of frustration when it is unsuccessful. However, the distinction between activities which are instrumental (but not particularly enjoyable) and activities which are enjoyed for their own sake or intrinsically (but which serve no exterior purpose outside themselves) can hardly arise. However, the bifurcation between instrumental and intrinsically enjoyable activities does become possible in all creatures in whom instincts weaken and disappear. In such creatures spontaneous, intrinsically enjoyed activities, among them *play*, occur.

Huizinga has made one of the comparatively few general attempts to explore the significance of play for civilization. He maintains that "genuine, pure play is one of the main bases of civilization."[50] He was of the opinion that the basic elements of play which he lists as "contests, performances, exhibitions, challenges, preenings, struttings, and showings-off" are already present in the animal world.[51] There is a Hobbesian element in Huizinga's thought: the assumption that in his original state man tended toward a war of each against all. From this point of view civilization arises when man's spirit of hostility is fused with a spirit of friendliness, permitting him to operate in the framework of agreed-upon rules.[52] Civilization is born in the instant when conflict is harnessed in the interest of collective life. Far from being an incidental by-product of human activity, play is taken to be the form of activity which makes culture possible.

The view we take in the following pages is that culture arises in the form of play, that it is played from the very beginning.[53]

51

Once established, however, culture acquires an autonomy of its own, and the play element recedes into the background, being absorbed by the sacred sphere. In general:

> The function of play in the higher forms . . . can largely be derived from the two basic aspects under which we meet it: as a contest *for* something or as a representation *of* something. These two functions can unite in such a way that the game "represents" a contest, or else becomes a contest for the best representation of something.[54]

In Huizinga's opinion civilization cannot exist in the absence of a play element.[55] Hence he was plunged into gloom by what he saw as the decline of Western civilization.

> More and more the sad conclusion forces itself upon us that the play element in culture has been on the wane ever since the eighteenth century, when it was in full flower. Civilization to-day is no longer played, and even where it seems to play it is false play.[56]

There is little doubt that in play Huizinga isolated one of the most fundamental of all civilization-forming processes. However, like many discoverers, Huizinga sharpens his distinctions (between play and nonplay) into stereotypes. In ongoing social life the lines between an activity valued instrumentally and intrinsically are not always sharply drawn. Work sometimes has many of the properties of play. Moreover, one need not assume a kind of presocial war of each against all or assign minor significance to individual play forms as against the social play of the contest, as does Huizinga. One may, nevertheless, assign to play indispensable civilizational significance.

In both individual and collective forms, the play activities of mankind continually move out into the world of the possible. Play submits this world of possibilities to a set of rules of its own, in terms of which it explores their properties. As a by-product play continually casts up new cultural forms. A surprising number of man's basic tools first made their appearance as the toys of earlier periods.

As a continuous joyous exploration of the world of the possible, play pioneers the routes of civilization.

The Sociology of Art

As in the case of play, a variety of theories has been developed which would reduce art to biological and instrumental status. According to Weitz, instrumental explanations dominate the recent approaches to art.

> The functions of art have been much discussed in aesthetic theory. . . . If there is a dominant one today it is, . . . some kind of instrumentalism. The Marxists, humanists, Thomists, and pragmatists, perhaps quite inadvertently, have joined forces in the condemnation of any doctrine of art for art's sake.[57]

However, the formalist theory of art, introduced by Kant and Herbert, developed by Zimmerman, voiced in musical criticism by Hanslick, and promoted by such art critics as Clive Bell and Roger Fry, locates art as a category of cultural activities concerned with intrinsic values.[58]

In the attempt to establish the character of art as an autonomous activity which in Kant's phrases was characterized by "disinterested interest," the formalists have even tended to reject as essential to art the various forms of representation which have appeared in the arts. The representational elements of art are most immediately subject to instrumental (propagandistic or sentimental) interpretation. On the other hand, if one withdraws all representational elements from the arts, many of them are impoverished. The literary arts suffer especially from the withdrawal of representational elements, for they are transformed into semimusical gibberish.

To avoid impoverished types of formalism (which result when representation is banished from the arts) without abandoning the character of art as a form of activity pursued for its own sake (for the intrinsic values it contains), Weitz develops what he describes as an "organic theory" of the arts. This theory rejects the distinction between form and content which was basic to the repudiation of means, subjects, and representations in arts. "It refuses to rule out the nonplastic spiritual values for the very simple reason that these can contribute as much to art as line and color."[59] Weitz construed "organic" approach as an "expanded formalist theory." "In art . . . *how something is expressed is what is expressed*. Both the how and the what, like the form and the content, refer to the totality of the work, not to any set of separate constituents."[60]

This seems to bring the theory of art into correspondence with actual practice of most times and places.

The characterization of the doctrine of art for art's sake as effete and reactionary and evaluation of it as sick and decadent arises from a restricted moralistic view of life which cannot tolerate the concept of a sphere of activity pursued for the love of it without need.

> The advocate of the doctrine of art for art's sake, . . . like the theoretical physicist in relation to the construction of his mathematical formulations, or the religious mystic in relation to his God, wishes only to call attention to the initially and primarily intrinsic character of his experience with art. He wishes to distinguish sharply between art as an end and art as a means; and he wishes to affirm that whatever experiences there are that are intrinsic, the aesthetic is among them. It is in this sense that he wishes to say that art either exists for its own sake or not at all, for without the recognition and acceptance of this intrinsic dimension of art, it becomes a handmaiden of something else and in that way is destroyed as an independent activity.[61]

The core of the aesthetic is located in man's capacity for the discernment of form and pattern in experience and his capacity for specialized response to this pattern.[62] Just as play activities may exist in varying degrees of separation from instrumental activities, so too may aesthetic activities.

The aesthetic experience first makes its appearance as a special kind of emphasis within the context of every day activity. At all times, the decorative arts seem to precede the rise of the pure arts. The border of a pot or basket is seized upon to be outlined in black or decorated with a rhythmic pattern. A stone surface is finished in a rhythmic pattern, or polished until it shines, though this in no way increases the efficiency of the tool. An open space on the side of an object is decorated with a design or picture. In all these cases, various properties of the form, color, and texture of tools and objects of ordinary use are isolated, emphasized, or modified in such manner that, be it ever so slightly, interest has been withdrawn for a few moments from the sheer practical purposes of the tool or object and riveted on form or pattern for its own sake.

A further stage in the emergence of the aesthetic in isolation from the instrumental appears in peasant art. Here an object of everyday use (a dish, tool, or even an item of food such as an egg or a cake) is frequently subjected to so much decorative treatment as to make it unusable. The tribal metalsmith decorates a dish to a point where it is hung on the wall and contemplated rather than used as a food container. The Ukranian Easter egg is so glorified with decoration as to become inedible. A Polynesian war club is carved into an object of delicate beauty, making it quite unusable for purposes of war. In all such cases aesthetic concerns which have arisen in the heart of the practical have reversed the direction of interest, and the practical utility of the object has been thrust aside.

Every development of technique, technology, and knowledge of materials potentially increases man's capacity for aesthetic discernment and for artistic execution. Moreover, since both abstract formal and contentual (representational-symbolic) elements may be present, two great style-forming possibilities are given from the beginning. Artistic stylization may move primarily in terms of abstract formal or symbolic elements, or it may seek some kind of balanced integration of each. There is no a priori reason for assuming that either abstract or symbolic styles are more primitive than the other, though both theses have been argued.

The abstract-formal and representational-symbolic dimensions of art arise originally in activities in which the distinction between instrumental and intrinsic requirements is not sharply drawn. Hence, art originally emerges as the decoration of a practical object, an embellishment of practical activity or as the symbolic supercharge objects or activities. However, once the distinction is drawn, art is free to go its own way. There is no more reason why artistic activities should have one-to-one correspondence with the nonaesthetic activities than that play should have a one-to-one correspondence with work. This is important for evaluating instrumentalist theories of art.

Plekhanov, who presented one of the original Marxian (instrumentalist) theories of the relation between art and social life, formulated the propositions concerning this relation:

> The tendency of artists, and of those who have a lively interest in art, towards art for art's sake, arises when they are in hopeless disaccord with the social environment in which they live.
> The so-called utilitarian view of art ... the inclination to attribute to works of art the significance of judgment on the phenomena of life, and its constant accompaniment of glad readiness to participate in social struggles, arises and becomes stronger wherever a mutual sympathy exists between the individuals more or less actively interested in artistic creation and some considerable part of society.[63]

Both of these formulations, the first of which would reduce art to the status of a retrograde utopia and the second of which would reduce it to propaganda, radically distort the character of art and oversimplify the relation of the aesthetic to ordinary life. These are formulations of a man who can only live life for a moral purpose, never for its own sake. One need not be in disaccord with his society to enjoy art or even try to transform life into a work of art.

The aesthetic, even when imbedded in the actual, is an adventure into the world of the possible. It is the development of man's capacity for discernment and discriminating response, for the intensified sense of life this entails without the necessity of shackling this sense to practical or moralistic requirements. In various ways the world of art may embellish, complement, or even call to critical account the world of the everyday, and those certainly are great periods when a heightened sense of style may flow from the arts to everyday life and back again. However, wherever they develop, the arts are always a school of uniquely human capacities for discernment and discriminating response.

Some of the ways in which an art may develop a system of forms adapted to the requirements of the social stratum which primarily bears it and change when this stratum changes or when the art moves to the sphere of a new stratum have been indicated by Mukerji in his studies of the sociology of Indian music.[64] He believes that both European and Indian music arose out of folk and religious music, developing their classical specialization in the interests of the upper classes and renewing themselves by contact with the music of the people in times of class crisis.

> In both regions religious and folk music has been the inevitable context of classical music; in both, classical music at moments of crisis had drawn from people's music for fresh life, elaborated it at leisure, and imposed sophisticated forms upon it in return. Music was equally intimate with the functions of collective living and equally susceptible to the genuine influences that worked upon the culture-pattern. So long as the princely courts, the priestly dignitaries, and the strongly entrenched guilds fixed the rules of living, Indian and European music alike betrayed the rudiments of melody and harmony. Since then, the tempo of change has been slower in India than in Europe, accounting partly, at least, for the so-called "spirituality" of her music.[65]

Hindustani classical music, Mukerji maintains, is about four hundred years old. It arose as a cultural synthesis during the period when the Muslims were in power. It incorporated folk, regional, and non-Indian types of music into its system, and refined them to the taste requirements of courtly and priestly strata.

> Our classical music has always served two masters, religion and the court. *Dhrupad* is defined in the texts as songs of praise of the gods and kings. Gradually, the kings prevailed, and the gods were sung in the *deshi* fashion. By the eighteenth century, when it became a courtly affair, music gained in sweetness and subtlety, but it lost its pristine simple vigour. Eventually, it became vocal gymnastics, until the romantics in the provincial *durbars* started protesting.[66]

Until the 1880s, according to Mukerji, Hindustani music led a sheltered existence in the courts of princes and the circles of musicians' guilds. However, when the princes were replaced by the *Zamindars* and merchant-princes, a change occurred The *Zamindars* left their estates and settled in the cities, where the merchants had always been located. Left without a rural stratum to support them, the musicians poured into the cities from the decaying *durbars.*

> There was hardly a muscian of note who in that period did not come to the then Imperical City of Calcutta to try his fortune. Bengal got a taste of classical Hindustani music from that date.[67]

Hindustani music, which had once been primarily an art of priests, was first turned into an art of princes and finally was transformed into an art of the middle classes. This final transition was completed by the 1930s, by which time the old musical traditions had begun to decay.

> By the thirties of this century, when the middle class suddenly awoke to culture, they had to import musicians from Maharashtra to teach music to their sons and daughters. To-day, the Marris College, renamed the Shatkhande University, has become the premier institution in Northern India with about 800 boys and girls, nearly all belonging to respectable middle class families.[68]

In the hands of the middle class, the decay of the classical music tradition has continued.

> Bengali music, while it is good enough for the new *bourgeoisie* in other provinces, is insufferable for its cloying sweetness, its proto-

plasmic invertebrateness. Art can no more be raised above its context than you can lift yourself by the ears.[69]

Both the revivalist and creative tendencies of classical Indian music are gone. "The revolutionary potencies of both seem to have lost themselves in the sands which separate the middle class from the rest of the people."[70]

The changing relation between an art and the social order is illustrated in Mukerji's review of the development of Hindustani music. The developmental course of the art was shaped by a combination of instrumental and intrinsic (expressive) needs which differed from class to class. Hindustani music was born in the circles of priests; it was transmitted on to courtly circles of nobles and princes; it migrated to the halls of the *Zamidars* and merchant princes in the cities; it is pursued today in circles of the middle classes. The instrumental requirements imposed on classical music varied: the priests subordinated it to ritualistic and religious requirements; the princes employed it as an occasion for sumptuous display; the *Zamindars* and merchants exploited it for bizarre and exotic properties; and in the middle classes which cultivated it, such music was a mark of prestige, identification, and emotional, sentimental experiences (see table 1).

If one takes the high point in the Hindustani classical music tradition to be the period of the princes and musicians' guilds and the low point to be the present musical culture of the middle

Table 1

*Class Anchorage of Hindustani Classical Music
and Instrumental-Intrinsic Properties*

Class	Instrumental Requirements	Intrinsic-Expressive Forms
Priests	As a ritualistic and religious aid	Limited, closed forms, like magical formulas
Princes and Musical Guilds	As an item in the opulent display of courts	Open forms, dramatically developed but under control
Zamindars and Merchant Princes	An item in status competition of the *Nouveau Riche*	Theatrical and Melodramatic elements emphasized with loss of formal control
Middle Classes	A prestige item of the newly cultured	Exploitation of emotional and sentimental elements

classes, and if we admit that from an aesthetic standpoint recent forms are inferior to those of the great period, it still does not follow that art has vitality only when it is borne by a class with a social purpose with the implication that the contemporary Indian middle classes are without social purpose.

It would most certainly be a curious definition of social purpose which would identify the objectives of the princes—who exploited their societies for their own requirements—as constituting a true social purpose, while the objectives of the contemporary middle classes who struggle for the best possible life for themselves and their children are not. In fact, since classical Indian music reached its highest point under the princes rather than under the priests, one would have to demonstrate why the social purpose of the princes was higher than that of the priests.

It is true, on the other hand, that the conditions necessary for the development of high art were maximumized under the princes: Indian music at the time was in the hands of professional musicians able to consolidate and amplify every new gain in technique and every new insight into aesthetic forms; these musical guilds had no worry about their support, since they were patronized by the princely courts; in the society of the court such musicians had stable, cultivated audiences with leisure to devote time to cultural pursuits—ironically, for all instrumentalist theories the princely court was precisely in the position to pursue art for art's sake. Under such propitious circumstances it was quite possible—as in fact occurred—for Indian music to undergo constructive cycles of aesthetic development in which the skills of the artists and their new experiments in musical form could win immediate understanding and appreciation in courtly circles whose musical tastes were being refined by this very process.

By contrast, when Indian music was practiced for religious purposes by priestly musicians, conditions were favorable for the development of only limited musical traditions. So long as musical expression was subordinated to religious ritual, musical forms were limited to magically interpreted formulas. While religious music was dominated by instrumental requirements, the court freed it for expressive experimentalism always, however, under the control of skilled professionals on the one hand, and audiences with trained musical tastes on the other.

When the social situation of the princes and their courts was destroyed, so, too, was the foundation for this kind of musical practice. The *Zamindars* did not support the musical guilds as the princes had done. Nor did they form a homogeneous status group whose musical tastes could be continually refined. Finally, the social situation of the classical musician deteriorated still further, when he was cast on the open market to compete for the tastes of newly cultured strata. While the *Zamindars* looked to classical music for bizarre and exotic musical effects, the new middle classes looked to it for emotional and sentimental experience. It takes time for the situation of the musician to stabilize and for audiences to be trained, until the foundation has been established for the emergence of a high art. Neither the *Zamindars* nor the middle classes in India have had this time.

There is, finally, another imponderable in the development of a high art. Art, like play, lays down the ground rules for performance (forms and styles) in the world of possibilities. However, unlike play, where interest primarily resides in the individual performance—making it possible for the same basic games to be played by men from endless generations—in an art interest' attaches to the perfection of form realization. Art is, so to speak, a special kind of cultural game. The emergence of an artistic style follows the upward curve of exploration and perfection of a limited series of forms. Any single work of art is unique property. It is executed once and for all time. One may do other things like it, but it is never re-done. Hence the form possibilities of any given art are gradually exhausted. It becomes increasingly difficult to produce more perfect works in the same style.

When one asks of the Indian middle classes that they create more perfect examples of classical Indian music, one is asking the impossible. It is like asking a modern dramatist to write plays in the style of the Greek tragedy, but more perfect than those of the Greeks.

A striking property of a work of art—defying the instrumental interpretations in another way—is that once created it may be enjoyed by societies which had nothing to do with its creation. There is nothing necessarily retrogressive in the contemporary Indian middle classes enjoying the forms of classical Indian music. The greatest of the arts tends, in fact, to become part of the cultural richness, not simply of the circle in which such arts originated, but potentially of all mankind.

However all this may be, the proposition stands beyond all doubt that the sociology of art is one of the fundamental areas of the sociology of culture and a high road to the theory of civilization.

The Sociology of Knowledge

The third major sub-area of the sociology of culture, the sociology of knowledge, deals with the relation between idea and belief systems and behavioral systems. The rise of knowledge systems in every community is an unavoidable aspect of human social life. Having lost their instincts, men must learn or invent their social forms. By the development of language, men acquired an instrument of unusual power for inventing numerous possible solutions to their problems.

Language (a shared system of symbols and rules for their use) by its very nature introduces a series of possibilities into the field of the actual. At any moment language may introduce into the context of present reference things quite remote or even things that never existed at all. Thus language shatters the usual limitations of time and space which fix most animal behaviors to an immediate present focus. Through language men may discuss the thoughts and experiences of men thousands of years remote in time or thousands of miles distant in space. By way of language, possibilities may be considered in the solution of present problems which are not part of the actual existent scene.

All men employ language in the establishment of their communities. However, such communities represent the selection and fixing of a particular series of solutions which are embodied in a working system. The body of ideas essential to the behavioral system may be described as the *standard operating notions* of the society in question. However, the given community represents the fixing on its participants of only a limited set of the possible solutions to the problems of collective life. Alternatives to the *standard operating notions* (the body of social instrumental knowledge) of the community do not automatically disappear—they live on in the knowledge systems of the community as dreams, as ideals, as traditions, and as criticisms of the standard operating notions.

The fact that men continually tend to explore in their ideas alternatives to their standard operating notions is of great potential importance to their societies. When conditions change or unexpected problems develop, new solutions to collective problems may be available, needing only to be put into practice. The fanciful notion of the present may become part of the standard operating knowledge of the future. One of the most significant of all forms of play is that occurring in the world of ideas—the play

61

of imagination. Problems may be lifted out of the context of everyday complications, clarified, and resolved in the world of thought.

The manner in which the literary productions a people may explore, underlying problems which go beyond the everyday, is brilliantly illustrated by Leo Lowenthal's study of the changing image of man in relation to society, as revealed in the literature of the Western world from the end of the sixteenth to the beginning of the twentieth century. Lowenthal traces the image of man through such writers as Cervantes and Shakespeare, the French classical dramatists (Corneille, Racine, and Molière), through Goethe, to Henrik Isben and Knut Hamsun.

The classical Spanish writers (particularly Cervantes) present the picture of a highly mobile and competitive society in a world losing its theological interpretation and acquiring a secular orientation. Shakespeare's *The Tempest* is said to present a paradigm of the condition of man at the beginning of the modern era in an age still characterized by the adventurous mercantile economy which preceded the consolidation of the middle class. "He provides the most complete picture of the Renaissance individual who interprets the world almost exclusively in the light of his own needs and to whom outward events appear as tests of an inward adequacy and dynamism."[71]

The French writers are said to analyze the individual at a later stage of social development in which the monarchy is firmly established and the middle classes have begun to consolidate. The stages in the consolidation of the middle classes are reflected in their ethos. "The *bourgeois* ethos is more apparent in Racine than in Corneille, and in Molière it is virtually all-pervasive."[72] Goethe's writings present further stages in the growth of the middle class. His own development progresses from his Storm and Stress period to an acceptance of middle-class responsibility in *Wilhelm Meister's Travels.*

This curve of development in the situation of Western man, which began with the ideal of free individuality, emerged in the late Renaissance, and was first thought to be boundless, ends with Ibsen and Hamsun. Ibsen is the critic of middle-class society. "In every sphere of life he found the results of competition and specialization to be pernicious. In all of their personal and social encounters, his characters emerge as losers." And while Ibsen presents the dilemma of liberalism, Knut Hamsun presents "its authoritarian resolution. There is, in all his novels, an anticipation of the Nazi ideology."[73] He rejects urban industrial society and submits to forces beyond human control, such as the Nazi "blood, race, and soil."

One relation that the world of ideas may have for social practice, as Lowenthal's study shows, is to clarify strategic issues. To reverse the formula, the world of social practice may cast up themes which are explored in the world of thought. Alternative hypotheses as to the specific character of social influences on knowledge have been presented by sociology of knowledge theorists.

The major positions in the sociology of knowledge were advanced by nineteenth-century thinkers. The Marxists treated knowledge systems as reflections of man's material existence.

> Consciousness can never be anything else than conscious existence, and the existence of men is their life process. . . . In all ideology men and their circumstances appear upside down as in a *camera obscura*. . . . The phantoms formed in the human brain are . . . sublimates of their material life-process. . . . Morality, religion, metaphysics, all the rest of ideology . . . no longer retain the semblance of independence. . . . Life is not determined by consciousness, but consciousness by life.[74]

A modified form of the Marxian sociology of knowledge was developed in the twentieth century by Karl Mannheim.[75] A second major nineteenth-century position treated idea and belief systems as rationalizations of biological and psychological forces. This was formulated clearly by Nietzsche:

> The falseness of an opinion is not for us any objection to it. . . . The question is, how far an opinion is life furthering, life preserving, species preserving, perhaps species rearing. . . . That which causes philosophers to be regarded half-distrustfully and half-mockingly, is . . . that there is not enough honest dealing with them. . . . They all pose as though their real opinions had been discovered and attained through the self-evolving of a cold, pure, divinely indifferent dialetic. . . . They are all advocates who do not wish to be regarded as such, generally astute defenders, also, of their prejudices. . . . The spectacle of the Tartuffery of old Kant, equally stiff and decent, with which he entices us into the dialectic by-ways that lead (more correctly mislead) to his "categorical imperative"—makes us fastidious ones smile. We find no small amusement in spying out the subtle tracks of old moralists and ethical preachers. Or, still more so, the hocus-pocus in mathematical form, by means of which Spinoza has, as it were, clad his philosophy in mail and mask . . . how much of personal timidity

and vulnerability does this masquerade of a sickly recluse betray![76]

The determination of knowledge by biological and psychological forces has been held in the twentieth century by sociologists such as Pareto and a host of psychologists such as Freud. These two positions on the sociology of knowledge in the nineteenth century stood in contrast to the view that man's material life was determined by his ideas—a position held by idealistic philosophers such as Hegel and sociologists such as Comte and Durkheim. However, as the nineteenth century wore on, some thinkers attempted to establish a compromise between those positions which attempted to derive knowledge from man's material or psychological life and those which attempted to derive man's material existence from his ideas. In philosophy such a compromise was advanced by neo-Kantians such as Wilhelm Windelband and Heinrich Rickert. In sociology a compromise position of this sort was advocated by Max Weber. As Weber saw the matter, social and psychological influences react back on men's idea and belief systems, but men's ideas also have causal significance for their material and social life. It is often more correct to describe the relation between knowledge systems and social systems as a kind of *selective affinity* rather than to assign exclusive causal significance to either one. In the twentieth century the most original extension of the position found in the works of Rickert and Weber appears in the studies of Werner Stark.

Stark maintains that every society establishes a value system which operates at the foundations of the judgment of its members, including their judgments of intellectual matters. He describes this value system as a social a priori or axiological system.

> This social *a priori* or axiological system is the value-system of the society in which the historian, the seeker after human knowledge, lives. The pre-judgments or prior evaluations with which he works, and which enable him to do his work, are not prejudices or value-judgments in the current sense of the word. The latter unfortunately creep in from time to time, but they are as illegitimate as they are avoidable. His pre-judgments, however, are the value-facts at the basis of the contemporary social set-up which encloses him and has shaped his mind.[77]

This position advanced by Stark has at least the advantage of considerable flexibility over reduction of knowledge to the rationalization of biological and psychological impulses or to instruments of class warfare.

There are, Stark believes, three major aspects to the analysis of knowledge from the standpoint of his social a priori: (1) the values basic to any given world view are objective, given by the structure of the given society; (2) though the axiological system determines what is selected as important from the facts, it does not determine how it is selected (values determine what questions are formulated, but do not require that we falsify the facts in answering them); finally, Stark maintains, (3) "our sociology of knowledge . . . can lead to an objectivity in the treatment of social and historical reality . . . deeper than any . . . attainable by those who deny the existence and the influence of a basic axiological layer in the human mind."[78]

Marx and Mannheim felt that class interests formed the basic substructure of knowledge systems; Pareto and Nietzsche located the substructure of systems of knowledge in biological impulses; Stark locates the substructure in a basic axiological layer in the human mind supplied by the particular society. By testing hypotheses as to the relations between this substructure and the superstructure of knowledge systems, Stark believes it is possible to develop a general typology of societies with associated types of thought and feeling. Such a typology permits new analyses of concrete historical societies and the realm of facts considered important by each. On such a foundation Stark wishes to erect a metasociology, a "supra-historical doctrine of man" which would deal "with the results of man's search for knowledge as well as the different directions which it has taken. It would have to coordinate these results."[79]

Such a coordination of the elements of fact and truth contained in discordant world views is said to require a new method.[80] It is unnecessary to assume that any specific world view is false. Each has access to a part of the truth, though "the truth in its entirety escaped them all because they had each limited themselves to a specific line of vision."[81] However, the strategy of systematic discrimination and coordination of world views could easily "degenerate into an empty scholasticism" unless implemented "by the discrimination and coordination of research methods" in order to "escape the impasse of cultural relativity."[82] And the ultimate escape from cultural relativity is approximated, though it cannot be finally reached. "The true Archimedan point would lie beyond the end of history, beyond the last day. It cannot be reached by us, however much we stretch and strain."[83]

Stark presents a modified Kantian conception of mind and a Newtonian conception of the objective world. His paradigm of the elements involved in cognition and in the location of the sociology of knowledge is as follows:

The subject and his approach	The categorical layer of the mind The physical apparatus of perception The axiological layer of the mind	The concern of the sociology of knowledge
The objective world	The objects of knowledge The materials of knowledge[84]	

In accord with the special character of the axiological layer of the mind unique to them, the individuals of any given society have a special world view based on a selection of the materials of knowledge. Each of these is a partial truth. The total truth, possible only from the standpoint of all possible perspectives, is evidently available only to the mind of God.

While Stark's "axiological layer of the mind" may appear similar to the *standard operating notions* of a given society, they should not be confused. The total stock of ideas of a society cannot be assigned to all members. To attribute to them a single shared system of values is a rather questionable practice. In every known society there is an unequal distribution of ideas and a variety of value perspectives. The intimate relation presupposed between the knowledge systems of a society and the axiological layer in the mind of its members implies a unity in the idea systems of a society which they do not in fact show. The Platonic dialogues were continuously occupied with the controversies of the Greek world. The ancient Chinese, Indians, and Jews similarly report duels of their intellectuals. Our own times are torn by controversies. Moreover, not only are alternative evaluations present in a society projected into the knowledge schemes of a people, but divisions appear between those who attack and those who defend the social order, between those who would complement or extend some aspects of the social order and those who would controvert them. At times the intellectuals develop alternatives to current social practice which have so little immediate bearing on social issues as to be ignored, only to be discovered later as harbingers of a social order yet unborn. The world of ideas finally is explored as a realm of intrinsic-symbolic activity in considerable measure for its own sake.

The Theory of Civilization
as the Culmination of the
Sociology of Culture

It is unfortunate that the study of civilization has so often been conducted directly rather than by way of a preliminary study of the findings of the less comprehensive branches of the sociology of culture. The sociology of play, of art, and of knowledge as major sub-branches of the intrinsic-symbolic activities of men are the logical avenues to a general theory of civilization. In science it is always sound strategy to establish a beachhead on a limited front, consolidating one's position and working out from there rather than dissipating one's activities by a simultaneous attack on all positions at once. As things stand, the more ambitious theories of civilization too often have collapsed because of the failure to observe the findings of specialists in sub-areas of culture.

The theory of civilization is the logical culmination of the sociology of culture, for it is concerned with the more comprehensive integrations of culture that men have achieved. The theory of civilization occupies a place in the sociology of culture comparable to the theory of community in the sociology of behavior. The theory of the sub-areas of culture is the counterpart of the theory of special institutional areas (socialization, the mastery of nature, and social control) of social behavior. Moreover, like any given community, a civilization is not a seamless web but is made up of component parts.

Just as communities do not spring into being fully constituted but arise out of the operation of basic principles, so civilizations

Table 2

*Comparisons between the Sociology of Behavior
and the Sociology of Culture*

Discipline	Sociology of Behavior	Sociology of Culture
Activity Studied	Behavioral-Instrumental	Symbolic-Intrinsic
Smallest unit studied	Social action	Cultural form or trait
Intermediate units studied	Groups	Styles
Most comprehensive units studied	Communities or Societies	Civilizations

67

arise on the basis of processes operative throughout social life. In the case of communities, acts are stabilized into interindividual or group forms, and the group solutions to the problems of collective life are modified to accommodate one another. This has led to the isolation of the primary principles of community formation as: *stabilization* (the fixing of the collective solutions to problems), *consistency* (the modification of the solutions to one set of problems to facilitate the solutions of others), and *completeness* (the establishment of a set sufficient to carry the plurality through its basic life cycles). In a comparable manner, the principles of civilization must account for the formation of cultural forms or traits, the working out of style-integrations of cultural forms and traits, and the formation of comprehensive style integrations which key basic cultural styles to behavioral problems. The three primary principles of civilization formation are *playfulness* (the enjoyment of the intrinsic-instrumental activities for their own sake and the invention of cultural forms or traits which extend and complement the forms of everyday life), *aesthetic receptivity* (the human capacity for and delight in the integration of cultural forms into comprehensive systems or styles), and *sublimation* (the tendency to cast unsolved problems and tensions of the behavioral system into the cultural sphere, where they are sublimated and transformed into nuclear points around which cultural styles may be comprehensively integrated).[85] This is seen in summary form in table 3.

In every sphere of cultural activity the three principles of civilization-formation are operative. However, the special value of the subdivisions of the sociology of culture is that they deal with

Table 3

Comparative Principles of
Community and Civilization Formation

Basic Process	Community Formation	Civilization Formation
Forming of basic units	Stabilization	Playfulness, invention of forms
Interadjustment of units	Consistency	Aesthetic receptivity Development of styles
Formation of comprehensive systems	Completeness and behavioral closure	Sublimation and symbolic closure

areas of experience where one or other of the principles is predominant. Hence, though the play activities of a people reveal the operation of playfulness, aesthetic receptivity, and sublimation, the invention and exploration of form possibilities is the dominant feature of play. On the other hand, while an invention of forms everywhere plays a role in the arts, it always strikes one as achieving its proper sphere in the development of styles. Artistic practice in which the sheer invention of forms is dominant strikes one as falling short of high art—such a practice strikes one as merely "playful" rather than as serious art. Just as the sphere of play presents itself as an ideal situation for the study of the invention of forms, the arts present themselves as ideal situations for the study of stylization.

The productions of literary culture also show the operation of all three principles. However, in contrast to play and art, literary activities (including both literature and philosophy) are characterized by the predominance of the principle of sublimation. The literary products of a people by their very nature deal directly with the stock of expressed ideas, opinions, and sentiments of a people. To these literary products people turn for orientation, for interpretation and guidance from the tensions and contradictions that their social life casts up. Theorists of art as a catharsis from the days of Aristotle to Hirn[86] have usually looked to the dramatic and literary arts for their examples of the function of cultural products as purgations of the emotions and that attainment of serenity. Such emotional explosions are often created by contradictions or shortcomings of the society in which they appear. Literary culture, in short, is perhaps somewhat more dominated by the process of sublimation than the sphere of play or of the nonliterary arts, even though the other civilization-processes are also at work in it.

These reflections seem to lead to the following tentative conclusion: The sociology of culture is the study of the intrinsic-symbolic activities of man, in contrast to the sociology of behavior which deals with his instrumental-behavioral activities. The sociology of culture need not have recourse to astrological predictions of the doom of mankind or to nonscientific methods. It has a number of recognized branches (the sociology of play, the sociology of art, and the sociology of knowledge) for the study of which the accepted methods of investigation of the sciences and humanities appears to be quite adequate. The culminating discipline of the sociology of culture is the study of the formation of civilizations (of cultural systems which accompany social systems). Civilizations are analyzable in terms of their component cultural traits and forms and their integrating styles. The basic civilization-forming principles of playfulness, aesthetic receptivity, and sublimation account for the invention of cultural traits or forms, the synthesis of these into styles, and the keying of cultural styles to their system of social behavior. The subdisciplines of the sociology of culture present spheres in which detailed study is possible of these civilization-forming principles.

NOTES

1. Ernst Cassirer, *The Philosophy of the Enlightenment*, trans. Fritz C. A. Koelin and James P. Pettegrove (Boston: Beacon Press, 1951), p. 5.

2. Ibid., p. 9.

3. Ibid., pp. 18-19.

4. Baron de Montesquieu, *The Spirit of the Laws*, trans. Thomas Nugent (New York: Hafner, 1949), pp. 293-94.

5. G. A. Borgese, "Romanticism," in the *Encyclopedia of the Social Sciences* (New York: Macmillan, 1948), vol. XIII, p. 426.

6. Arthur O. Lovejoy, *Essays in the History of Ideas* (Baltimore: Johns Hopkins, 1948), pp. 183 ff.

7. G. W. F. Hegel, *The Philosophy of History*, trans. J. Sibree (New York: Wiley, 1944), p. 9.

8. Ibid., p. 10.

9. Ibid., p. 14.

10. Ibid., p. 29.

11. Ibid., p. 31.

12. Ibid.

13. Ibid., pp. 38-39.

14. Ibid.

15. Oswald Spengler, *The Decline of the West* (New York: Alfred A. Knopf, 1928), vol. I, p. 6. The opening pages of Hegel's *Philosophy of History* contain similar formulations.

16. Ibid., p. 7.

17. Ibid., p. 9.

18. Ibid., p. 31.

19. Ibid., vol. II, p. 193.

20. Ibid., p. 99.

21. Arnold J. Toynbee, *A Study of History* (London: Oxford University Press, 1934), vol. I, p. 148.

22. Ibid., pp. 192-93. The "precipice above" is, perhaps, a hole in the sky.

23. Ibid., p. 271.

24. Ibid., pp. 271-72.

25. Ibid., p. 293.

26. Ibid., p. 336.

27. Pitirim A. Sorokin, *Social and Cultural Dynamics* (New York: American Book Co., 1937), vol. I, p. 3.

28. Ibid., p. 10.

29. Ibid., p. 15.

30. Ibid., p. 19.

31. Ibid., p. 33.

32. Ibid., p. 67.

33. For a critique of Sorokin's ideas, see Hans Speier, *Social Order and the Risks of War* (New York: George Stewart, 1952), pp. 202 ff.

34. Ibid., p. 211.

35. Ibid., p. 212.

36. Ibid., p. 211.

37. Carroll Quigley, *The Evolution of Civilizations* (New York: Macmillan, 1961), p. 31.

38. Ibid., p. 32.

39. Ibid, p. 79.

40. These concepts are discussed at length for various special purposes in a number of contexts. See Don Martindale, *American Social Structure* (New York: Appleton-Century-Crofts, 1960), *American Society* (Princeton: D. Van Nostrand, 1960), and *Social Life and Cultural Change* (Princeton: D. Van Nostrand, 1962).

41. Johan Huizinga, *Homo Ludens: A Study of the Play-Element in Culture* (Boston: Beacon Press, 1950), p. 13.

42. Elmer D. Mitchell and Bernard S. Mason, *The Theory of Play* (New York: A. S. Barnes, 1948), p. 116.

43. Argued by Fredrich Schiller, *Essays, Aesthetical and Philosophical* (London: Bell & Sons, 1875), among others.

44. Moritz Lazarus, *Ueber die Reize des Spiels* (Berlin: F. Dummler, 1883).

45. G. T. W. Patrick, *The Psychology of Relaxation* (New York: Houghton Mifflin, 1916).

46. K. Groos, *The Play of Animals* (New York: D. Appleton, 1904).

47. G. Stanley Hall, *Youth* (New York: D. Appleton, 1906).

48. Huizinga, *Homo Ludens*, p. 2.

49. See the discussion in Martindale, *Social Life and Cultural Change*, pp. 49-50.

50. Huizinga, *Homo Ludens*, p. 5.

51. Ibid., p. 47.

52. Ibid., p. 58.

53. Ibid., p. 46.

54. Ibid., p. 13.

55. Ibid., p. 211.

56. Ibid., p. 206.

57. Morris Weitz, *Philosophy of the Arts* (Cambridge: Harvard University Press, 1950), pp. 202-3.

58. Ibid., p. 1.

59. Ibid., p. 62.

60. Ibid., p. 63.

61. Ibid., p. 204.

62. Martindale, *Social Life and Cultural Change*, p. 51.

63. George V. Plekhanov, *Art and Social Life* (London: Lawrence & Wishart, 1953), p. 177.

64. Dhurjati Prasad Mukerji, *Indian Music* (Poona: Kutub, 1945).

65. Ibid., p. 18.

66. Dhurjati Prasad Mukerji, *Modern Indian Culture* (Bombay: Hind Kitaba, 1938), p. 150.

67. Ibid., p. 153.

68. Ibid., p. 155.

69. Ibid., p. 173.

70. Ibid., p. 175.

71. Leo Lowenthal, *Literature and the Image of Man* (Boston: Beacon Press, 1957), p. vi.

72. Ibid.

73. Ibid., p. vii.

74. Karl Marx and Friedrich Engels, *The German Ideology* (New York: International Publishers, 1947), pp. 14-15.

75. Karl Mannheim, *Ideology and Utopia* (New York: Harcourt, Brace, 1949).

76. Friedrich Nietzsche, *The Philosophy of Nietzsche* (New York: Modern Library, 1954), pp. 384-85.

77. Werner Stark, *The Sociology of Knowledge* (Glencoe, Ill.: The Free Press, 1958), p. 106.

78. Ibid., p. 127.

79. Ibid., pp. 206-7.

80. Ibid., p. 207.

81. Ibid., p. 208.

82. Ibid., p. 209.

83. Ibid., p. 210.

84. Ibid., p. 108.

85. Martindale, *Social Life and Cultural Change*, pp. 50-54.

86. Yrjö Hirn, *The Origins of Art* (New York: Macmillan, 1931).

SELECTED BIBLIOGRAPHY

Howell, Arthur R. *The Meaning and Purpose of Art.* London: A. Zwemmer, 1945.

Huizinga, Johan. *Homo Ludens: A Study of the Play-Element in Culture.* Boston: Beacon Press, 1950.

Lowenthal, Leo. *Literature and the Image of Man.* Boston: Beacon Press, 1957.

Mannheim, Karl. *Ideology and Utopia.* New York: Harcourt, Brace, 1949.

_____. *Essays on the Sociology of Knowledge.* New York: Oxford University Press, 1952.

Martindale, Don. *American Society.* Princeton: D. Van Nostrand, 1960.

_____. *Social Life and Cultural Change.* Princeton: D. Van Nostrand, 1962.

Mukerji, Dhurjati Prasad. *Indian Music.* Poona: Kutub, 1945.

_____. *Modern Indian Culture.* Bombay: Hind Kitaba, Ltd., 1938.

Mukerjee, Radhakamal. *The Social Function of Art.* Bombay: Hind Kitaba, Ltd., 1948.

Plekhanov, George V. *Art and Social Life.* London: Lawrence & Wishart, Ltd., 1953.

Sorokin, Pitirim. *Social and Cultural Dynamics.* New York: American Book Co., 1937.

Spengler, Oswald. *The Decline of the West.* New York: Alfred A. Knopf, 1928.

Stark, Werner. *The Sociology of Knowledge.* Glencoe, Ill.: The Free Press, 1958.

Toynbee, Arnold J. *A Study of History.* London: Oxford University Press, 1934.

Weitz, Morris. *Philosophy of the Arts.* Cambridge: Harvard University Press, 1950.

PART II

The Theory of
Social Reality

The various problems reviewed so far have direct bearing upon the empirical concerns of sociology other than the sociology of culture. Aside from the sociology of culture with its various subdisciplines (the sociology of knowledge, the sociology of art, the sociology of play and leisure and theory of civilization), the empirical concerns of sociology are usually grouped into three categories: social persons, social structures, and social change.

For historical reasons the theory of social persons was slow to form and has developed unevenly. Social structure and social change, however, were recognized as major branches of sociology from the beginning. Both have been elaborated in considerable detail. Social structure and social changes are ordinarily taught as special courses in most sociology departments, while social persons is not. Moreover, not only is social structure examined in general, but various special institutions (the family, economic, political, and religious institutions) are subject to special study. General courses also are taught on the community as well as on special communities such as rural, urban, and ethnic. All in all, social structure is the most developed area of sociology. From time to time various special forms of social changes also are brought under detailed study—revolution, war, industrialization, urbanization, bureaucratization, and the like. However, there is widespread agreement that this area of sociology has been in crisis.

The shaping and major problems of sociology's substantive areas are traceable in some measure to its philosophic heritage. However, a variety of other factors also play a role.

CHAPTER 3

Social Persons

Sociology took form as a new movement in philosophy in the nineteenth century, differing from its predecessors in part by a submergence of the individual in the collective. When at last it came to accept the theory of social persons as one of its branches, the concepts of individuality contained in the wave of intellectual developments from Descartes to Kant were drawn upon.

The Origin of
Contemporary Individuality

When people invent new communities, they also explore new resources of their natures. Such periods are marred by anxieties and a sense of crisis alternating with a euphoric sense of self-realization, for individuals operate in a free field for social and self-creation. Eventually some of the institutional expedients and forms of selfhood with which they experiment will be discarded.

But the sense of peace this may bring is marked with regret. In the late medieval world the founding of civic communities constituted such an open period. Only half a step behind the formation of the cities was the formation of new territorial configurations which were to evolve into nations of a contemporary type. Under these circumstances the personality of Western man was formed.

Though Jacob Burckhardt's classical study *The Civilization of the Renaissance in Italy* was addressed to the period when the city-states reached their full development, his observations hold for the entire period. Burckhardt notes that in the new cities men ceased to evaluate themselves in terms of some social category, as race, people, party, or family, and began to estimate their significance as individuals. Objective analyses of social institutions became necessary as new subjective self-consciousness developed. Already, by the close of the thirteenth century, Burckhardt observed that in Italy a great differentiation of personality had taken place, and a multiplicity of personal forms confront us, each with its peculiarities.[1] Among the factors which Burckhardt believed particularly important for the flowering of individuality was despotism, not only in the person of tyrant or condottiere, but in the men protected and used by the despots—the secretary, minister, and poet. Wealth and culture became bases of self-development. The politics of the cities evoked new talent and founded new social types including even the man indifferent to politics. The rapid changes of fortune of political parties encouraged the exploitation of situations of temporary ascendancy and flexibility in misfortune. The banishment of members of defeated parties cast them upon their personal resources, weeding out the weak and developing forms of autonomous individuality.

These changes in the outward situation of individuals transformed their psychology and aspirations, and the new aspiration, in time, re-cast the significance of the outer world. "To this inward development of the individual corresponds a new sort of outward distinction—the modern form of glory."[2] Men began to desire recognition for their purely personal achievements, and to award recognition (fame) to others on the same basis. The artist ceased being an anonymous craftsman. Honors which formerly had been granted only to saints and heroes now came to be awarded to writers and artists. The cult of the birthplace of famous men developed: pilgrimages were made to the graves of the famous; cities rivaled one another as the birthplace of notables.[3] Autobiographical and biographical literature of great richness appeared in response to the new interest in personality. Accompanying the adulation of great men and the often extravagant claims to individual importance, the development of ridicule and wit occurred, in part itself a manifestation of individuality, in part as a corrective to its excesses.[4]

The context for the new flowering of individuality was primarily supplied by the upper political, economic, military, and professional circles of the cities. However, the destruction of traditional institutions and the need to create new ones also affected every man down to the lowest strata. The change in religion in civic contexts was particularly important. Religion was addressed to life's crisis situations, dealing with such matters as birth, death, marriage, illness, and misfortune. In the new social contexts of the city and, later, the nation, these crises assumed a form for which pre-civic institutions were inadequate. In the course of adaptation of religion to his new requirements, contemporary man transformed his individuality as well.

Two general forms and theories of individuality took shape: the humanistic and the religious. In the upper status circles of the cities and states, individuals were called upon primarily for intellectual and artistic skills of various sorts. Persons in these situations quickly discovered that the culture of antiquity was a valuable source for ideas on problems very similar to their own. They placed increasing value on the skills that gave them access to the classical culture. They pillaged these sources for models of style and personal deportment as well as for solutions to the problems they faced. The personal ideal that emerged at the pinnacle of humanistic circles placed highest value on the man of letters, the man of taste and of scholarly judgment. The humanistic conception of man was optimistic, rationalistic, and urbane.

The Christian religious tradition of old, by contrast, was firmly wedded to the notion of the basic sinfulness of man: to his burden of original sin was added his fallibility. However, the medieval conception of the church as an island of the faithful destined for salvation in a decaying world no longer corresponded to experience. The conception of the sacraments and the mediation of the priesthood, once viewed as absolute essentials for salvation, were experienced as archaic restraints of traditionalism. The new individualism grew restive under such authoritarianism. The partial failure of the Church to keep abreast of social changes turned the demand for reform toward revolution.

The Protestant revolts spearheaded the drive toward a more

individualized religious orientation, reducing the significance of the sacraments and the priesthood. The individualization of salvation striving shifted the arena of religious responsibility to the individual conscience. Now the individual was forced to look only into his own heart for his worthiness. A special dramatic irony accompanied this change. With the simultaneous retention of the notion of original sin and the corruptibility of human nature, and the simultaneous assignment of ultimate responsibility to the individual for himself, personalities were formed with built-in tension-producing mechanisms. The ultimate arena for proof of individual worthiness ceased to be the retreat from the world, and became the world itself in all its variations. Almost any area of life now potentially supplied the fuel for the individual's personal tensions. When various life areas are turned in this fashion into a testing ground of personal worth, revolutionary transformations may be brought about, for occupations now may acquire a religious intensity. Though the religious view of man was particularly strong in Protestant circles, it was by no means confined to them but distributed widely throughout the Christian world. Moreover, not simply the experience of the elite, but of every man down to the most humble creature, was being re-cast.

There were many contrasts both in their character and social anchorage between the humanistic and religious views of man. The humanist was optimistic about man and his prospects; the religious devotee was pessimistic, concerned with his sinfulness and weakness. The humanistic view placed the emphasis on man's literary skills and social graces; the religious view placed the emphasis on man's conscientiousness in all life spheres. The humanistic view was addressed to the requirements of upper strata; the religious view was addressed primarily to the middle strata, in time tending to sink down to the lower strata. Both orientations, however, were individualistic in emphasizing man's capacity for autonomous self-realization. Both located the control mechanism of social as well as personal affairs in the individual. The humanistic view established the ideal of the man of taste; the religious view established the ideal of the man of conscience.

The Individualism of Contemporary Philosophy: Descartes to Kant

Both the humanistic and religious views of man played a part in individualism presupposed by the great wave of philosophic development from Descartes to Kant. Most thinkers did not draw a sharp line between the two positions but rather inclined more toward one or the other. Descartes (1596–1650), for example, preferred the humanistic position.

> Good sense or reason, is by nature equal in all men. Hence . . . the diversity of our opinions does not proceed from some men being more rational than others, but solely from the fact that our thoughts pass through diverse channels and the same objects are not considered by all. For to be possessed of good mental powers is not sufficient; the principal matter is to apply them well. The greatest minds are capable of the greatest vices as well as of the greatest virtues, and those who proceed very slowly may . . . really advance much faster than those who, though they run, forsake it.[5]

Reason, which Descartes thought was the only thing that distinguishes men from the brutes, is found complete in all men. All that is needed is a proper method for all persons to arrive at the same point. Because of his fundamental optimism Descartes does not hesitate to elevate doubt into a systematic procedure for arriving at certain principles from which one then may proceed with mathematical certainty. And the most fundamental principle supplied by the method of doubt is the existence of the individual mind.

> I noticed that while I thus wished to think all things false, it was absolutely essential that the "I" who thought this should be somewhat, and remarking that this truth "I think, therefore I am" was so certain and so assured that all the most extravagant suppositions brought forward by the sceptics were incapable of shaking it, I came to the conclusion that I could receive it without scruple as the first principle of the Philosophy for which I was seeking.[6]

While Descartes was close to the humanistic view of man, his contemporary, Lord Herbert of Cherbury (1583-1648), showed somewhat greater influence from the religious view of man. More or less in the same manner as Descartes, Lord Herbert assumed that human nature is more or less the same everywhere. Human beings act, Lord Herbert thought, on the basis of various capacities or faculties of which there were argued to be four classes: natural instincts, faculties of the internal sense (powers of the mind concerning good, evil, pleasure, and displeasure), faculties of the external senses, and faculties of discursive thought or reason.

While Descartes elevated the reason to primary importance, Lord Herbert viewed discursive thought or reason as the capacity of man most subject to error. Reason works with the materials supplied by the other faculties: immediate intuition, moral and spiritual ideas, and perceptions. Lord Herbert was particularly concerned with the spiritual certainties supplied by the faculties of internal sense (capacity for moral and spiritual judgment). Among the common notions which supply the universal basis of religion supplied by the faculty of the internal sense are: that there is a supreme God; that He should be worshipped; that virtue and piety are the most important part of religious practice; that men must expiate their sins by repentance; and that there is reward and also punishment in the after life.[7]

In their accent on reason and the faculties of the internal sense, respectively, Descartes and Lord Herbert of Cherbury display the influence of the humanistic and religious views of man. The ultimate appeal of Descartes to reason and of Lord Herbert to the faculties of the internal sense (conscience), which he presumed to be more basic than reason, is typical of the two views.

It is of no special value here to trace the career of the humanistic and religious views of man through the philosophers. The significant point for present purposes is the inseparable linkage of the program of achieving a unified system of knowledge with individualism. The heroic quality of the first great wave of contemporary philosophy derives in no little measure from its character as a series of attempts to encompass the world in the scope of the lone individual's personality. The Classical Greek, too, knew the ideal of the many-sided man, taking all things in their measure with nothing in excess. But the Greek poets and dramatists had a message for their fellows. The hubris (arrogance or insolence) that led man to attempt to embrace the very heavens in their plans and invade spheres proper only to the gods brought inevitable disaster. One could not unfairly treat the successive brave attempts to establish the rational unity of the world from the standpoint of the individual and their repeated collapse as episodes in an old drama. In classical ways it would surely have been the subject of a tragedy. The revenge of the gods would, as in ancient drama, have been overwhelming, for the price of failure of the enterprise of the philosophers seemed to be the unity of the individual self. For in the end, it appeared, the individual's capacity for reason, for feeling and sensitivity, for moral experience, seemed to present so many insuperable difficulties for one another that they could not possibly be aspects of a single person.

If the triumph of man's reason was taken as his capacity for empirical science, and if, as Hume suggested, one applied the test of experience to man's own self, it did not present itself at all as a unified agent with the axiomatic certainty ascribed to it by Descartes. Empirically one was confronted only with a vague flux of feelings and sensations; the "I" was not given at all.

There are some philosophers, who imagine we are every moment intimately conscious of what we call our Self; that we feel its existence and its continuance in existence; and are certain, beyond the evidence of a demonstration, both of its perfect identity and simplicity.... Unluckily all these positive assertions are contrary to that very experience, which is pleaded for them, nor have we any idea of *self*, after the manner it is here explained.

For my part, when I enter most intimately into what I call *myself*, I always stumble on some particular perception or other of heat or cold, light or shade, love or hatred, pain or pleasure. I never can catch myself at any time without a perception, and never can observe anything but the perception.... If anyone upon serious and unprejudic'd reflexion, thinks he has a different notion of *himself*, I must confess I can reason no longer with him.... But setting aside some metaphysicians of this kind I may venture to affirm of the rest of mankind, that they are nothing but a bundle or collection of different perceptions, which succeed each other with an inconceivable rapidity, and are in a perpetual flux and movement. Our eyes cannot turn in their sockets without varying our perceptions. Our thought is still more variable than our sight; and all our other senses and faculties contribute to this change; nor is there any single power of the soul, which remains unalterably the same, perhaps for one moment.[8]

The clear firm notion of personal identity, Hume suggests, is a product of the imagination operating on the variations of experience, the parts of which the memory links by relations of cause and effect.

Had we no memory, we never shou'd have any notion of causation, nor consequently of that chain of causes and effects, which constitute our self or person.[9]

Nevertheless, Hume observes, memory is notoriously unreliable.

Who can tell me, for instance, what were his thoughts and actions on the first of January, 1715, the 11th of March, 1719, and the 3d of August, 1733? Or will he affirm, because he has entirely forgot the incidents of these days, that the present self is not the same person with the self of that time; and by that means overturn all the most establish'd notions of personal identity? . . . . The whole of this doctrine leads us to a conclusion, which is of great importance in the present affair, viz., that all the nice and subtile questions concerning personal identity can never possibly be decided.[10]

With regard to the physical world, Hume observed that philosophers had begun to be reconciled to the notion that they had no idea of eternal substances distinct from particular qualities. The same reasoning that established this applies to the mind. The notion of personal identity is only an article of faith.

> We only *feel* a connexion or determination of the thought, to pass from one object to another. . . . Thought alone finds personal identity, when reflecting on the train of past perceptions, that compose a mind, the ideas of them are felt to be connected together, and naturally introduce each other.[11]

The indubitable principle with which Descartes had opened contemporary philosophy was shattered on the rocks of Hume's empiricism.

It was inevitable that when Kant undertook to save the philosophic tradition of the West from shipwreck, he turned his attention to the hero of the piece: the individuality of Western man. Moreover, Kant embraced in his program not only the rationalist and empiricist traditions but the humanistic and religious views of man.

The existence of the self Kant takes not as a necessary demonstration from experience with Descartes, but as a necessary prerequisite of experience. "Without our being conscious that what we are thinking now is the same as what we thought a moment before, all reproduction in the series of representations would be vain."[12] Kant did not re-state Descartes' principle, "I think, therefore I am," but presumed that unless there is a mind there can be no continuity of thought. However, Kant agrees with Hume, this unified self is not presented to consciousness: "The consciousness of oneself, according to the determination of our state, is, with all our internal perceptions, empirical only, and always transient. There can be no fixed or permanent self in the stream of internal phenomena."[13]

Kant made use of a distinction he had established earlier between phenomena (things as experienced) and noumena (things in themselves) to provide the anchorage for the self.

What is necessarily to be represented as numerically identical with itself, cannot be thought as such by means of empirical data only. It must be a condition which precedes all experience, and in fact renders it possible, for thus only could such a transcendental supposition acquire validity.[14]

Thus Kant draws a fundamental distinction between the empirical self and the transcendental self which is presumed to make empirical self-consciousness possible.

The contrast between the empirical self and pure ego was useful to Kant in establishing the character of ethics as a distinct sphere of activity from science.

We may call all philosophy *empirical*, so far as it is based on grounds of experience: on the other hand, that which delivers its doctrines from *a priori* principles alone we may call *pure* philosophy. When the latter is merely formal, it is *logic*; if it is restricted to definite objects of the understanding it is metaphysics. . . . In this way there arises the idea of a twofold metaphysic—a *metaphysic of nature* and a *metaphysic of morals*. Physics will thus have an empirical and also a rational part. It is the same with ethics; but here the empirical part might have the special name of *practical anthropology*, the name *morality* being appropriated to the rational part.[15]

Fundamental to Kant's ethics was the individualistic tradition of the preceding period. "Nothing can possibly be conceived in the world, or even out of it, which can be called good without qualification, except a Good Will."[16] Moreover, in looking for universal principles applicable to moral experience, Kant subscribes to ideas inseparably bound up with the religious view of man. Kant thrust the notion of *duty* forward as criterion of ethical correctness. "Duty is the necessity of acting from respect for the law."[17] The law which rules the world of ethical activities is "I am never to act otherwise than *so that I could also Will that my maxim should become a universal law.*"[18] Moreover, since only "rational nature exists as an end in itself, one may also formulate the practical imperative as follows: "So act as to treat humanity, whether in thine own person or in that of any other, in every case as an end withal, never as means only."[19]

Moral activity in Kant's formulation thus rests upon the notions of individual autonomy and duty (actions according to conscience) central to the religious view of man. Moral activity presupposes the principle of freedom as the basis of the order of responsibility as certainly as the world of phenomena presupposes causality if it is to be treated scientifically. Man's moral responsibility is a property of man as transcendental self.

However, Kant also embraced the humanistic view of man in his personal synthesis. To decide whether anything is beautiful or not, Kant insists, we must estimate its properties neither empirically nor ethically, but in terms of the feelings of pleasure or pain associated with it. There are three kinds of judgments of representations with regard to pleasure and pain: the pleasant, the beautiful, and the good. "That which gratifies a man is called pleasant; that which merely pleases him is beautiful; that which is esteemed or approved by him, *i.e.*, that to which he accords an objective worth, is good."[20] Taste in the beautiful is a disinterested and free satisfaction.

> *Taste* is the faculty of judging of an object or a method of representing it by an *entirely disinterested* satisfaction or dissatisfaction. The object of such satisfaction is called *beautiful.*[21]

Thus Kant sought to bring the humanistic as well as the religious principles into some sort of synthesis in his own uncompromising individualism.

Elimination of Individualism
by the Unitary System

The great unitary systems of the nineteenth century illustrated by positivistic sociology and objective idealism marked a revolutionary break from the first period of contemporary philosophy in their abandonment of individuality as the primary philosophic and social principle.

Comte dismissed the individualistic doctrines of the eighteenth century as metaphysical fancies, and far from deriving society from man's rational nature, he derived man's rationality from society.

> Gall's cerebral theory has destroyed forever the metaphysical fancies of the last century about the origin of Man's social tendencies, which are now proved to be inherent in his nature, and not the result of utilitarian considerations. The true theory has exploded the mistakes through which the false doctrine arose—the fanciful supposition that intellectual combinations govern the general conduct of human life, and the exaggerated

notion of the degree in which wants can create faculties. Independently of the guidance afforded by Gall's theory, there is a
conclusive evidence against the utilitarian origin of society in the
fact that the utility did not, and could not, manifest itself till
after a long preparatory development of the society which it was
supposed to have created.[22]

In Comte's view individuals are only the raw materials of society.

As every system must be composed of elements of the same
nature with itself, the scientific spirit forbids us to regard society
as composed of individuals. The true social unit is certainly the
family—reduced, if necessary, to the elementary couple which
forms its basis.[23]

In the family "man comes forth from his mere personality, and
learns to live in another, while obeying his most powerful instincts. No other association can be so intimate as this primary
combination, which causes a complete fusion of two natures in
one."[24]

Comte was impressed not with the universality of human nature
and its perfection but with its imperfection and variety. Even the
most restricted society, he thought, presupposes not similarities
and equality, but diversities and inequality.[25] Man displays an
unequal distribution of talent and capacity to reason. The large
majority are born to follow, and only a few are born to reason and
to command. The most basic of all social groups, the family, rests
solidly on the biological inequality. "Sociology will prove that the
equality of the sexes, of which so much is said, is incompatible
with all social existence, by showing that each sex has special and
permanent functions which it must fulfill in the natural economy
of the human family."[26] Women, to be specific, are inferior in
their capacity for mental labor, but superior in capacity for
affection. Women belong not in intellectual and political pursuits,
but in the home. And, in general,

The main cause of the superiority of the social to the individual
organism is, according to an established law, the more marked
specialty of the various functions fulfilled by organs more and
more distinct, but interconnected; so that unity of aim is more
and more combined with diversity of means.[27]

Comte never retreated from this position. When he formulated
the theory of society as the Great Being, as the only proper
substitute for God in an age of science, he again asserted the

superiority of society to the individual and saw the primary threat to social order in an excess of individuality.

> The peculiar difficulties attendant on its acceptance once fairly overcome, the hardest point remaining in the theory of the Great Being is the right estimate of individuals as its ministers. An uninterrupted service on their part, either as agents or even as representatives, is a necessary condition of collective existence in any form. No association could act, or make itself felt, except through individuals. As this is clear for the Family and the Country; *à fortiori* must it hold good of Humanity. In this condition we find the primary source of the attributes and the difficulties which alike inhere in the very idea of a composite existence.
>
> To combine, and that persistently, concert with independence is the capital problem of society, a problem which religion alone can solve, by love primarily, then by faith as the basis of love. The superiority of Humanity lies mainly in this: that its immediate instruments are beings in nature similar to itself, though at a lower stage of development, and apparently capable of standing alone. On the other hand, as such, they tend to separate, losing sight, in an exaggerated sense of their own importance, of the absolute dependence of the parts on the whole. The danger exists in the best constituted society; in periods of anarchy it takes such proportions as at the present time to be the main hindrance to the advent of the Great Being. And yet the danger to society would be equally great if concert could ever succeed in stifling independence. Distinctness then no less than convergence of effort, being an essential condition of human cooperation, the great problem ultimately comes to this, how to reconcile Order and Progress, universally held by Antiquity to be incompatible. Of the two dangers, however, the greater is, it must be allowed, the excess of independence: with few and transient exceptions that from excess of concert is less urgent.[28]

Since one of the first major sources of criticism of positivistic sociology came from adherents of German traditions of objective idealism stemming from Hegel, it is important to note that such criticism was not directed against positivistic sociology's treatment of individualism.

The soul, according to Hegel, is the awakening of the mind from the sleep of nature. It is a center of being emerging from the world of silence and night. This first entelechy goes through a process of self-detachment in the course of which it becomes self-conscious as the spectacle of the world without unrolls before it. As such it is as yet a mere ego or logical self, on which the play of ideas occurs.[29]

In Knowledge which is reason's perception, and in Will which is Reason's impulse, "there is a king's highway, a public forum where souls meet and . . . perform a collective work."[30] In public contests mere individuality is relatively inconsequential. Individuality and personality acquire significance only so far as they are bound to the laws of development and history. The ethical community such as the family, the state, or mankind is maintained by "a spirit which transcends and includes alike the outward shell of civil law and the inward law of conscience."[31] Individuals and society live and grow when they are continuous and one. Language supplies the machinery for a meeting ground in which the development of knowledge is possible; ethical and political forms supply the machinery for the development of freedom.

> It is in these collective and objective structures that we get the expression of the law of human development. . . . The individual in these attains his relative truth: for they show the weakness of the individuality of the mere individual.[32]

Authentic personality and individuality presupposes the social state or organic community. "The individuals whose aggregation makes the community are themselves products of the social union."[33] True and complete individuality for Hegel are euphemisms for the community.

> A true and real personality, a complete individuality is something which so transmutes all that we are most accustomed to call by that name that it is hardly any use clinging to it.[34]

Social organizations, not the individuals, are animated by moral ideas and constitute the arena "on which the true union of mind and matter, of idea and nature, of thought and fact, may be worked for."[35]

The true individuals of history are not persons, but peoples.[36] The vast congeries of volitions, interests, and activities of specific persons are only the instruments and means of the World Spirit for realizing itself.[37] History is so little concerned with persons that Hegel rejects any notion that it is a "theatre of happiness."[38] The contingencies of private life have no bearing on what is good or bad for history.

Historical men or world-historical individuals are those in whose private aims a general principle lies.[39] Such men, heroes in that they derive their purpose and aim, their vocation, not from the regular course of things sanctioned by the existing order, but, as it were, from a concealed fount. They usually have no consciousness of the general idea they are unfolding but are motivated by private passions. Their importance, however, comes from unfolding a trend that moves history on its course.

> When their object is attained they fall off like empty hulls from the kernel. They die early, like Alexander; they are murdered, like Caesar; transported to St. Helena, like Napoleon.[40]

Hegel's basic doctrines on the place of the individual were followed with virtually no change by the Marxians. Here the true agents of history were classes. Actual individuals achieve their historical importance in their roles in class-based action.

Nineteenth-Century Theories of the Individual

Although the great unitary systems of thought of the nineteenth century (positivistic sociology, objective idealism, and dialectical materialism) agreed in estimating the individual to be of minor importance compared to the collective, many students were by no means ready to go this route. Schopenhauer, for example, who addressed himself to problems in Kantian philosophy as did the founders of objective idealism came to quite different conclusions.

Kant had drawn a distinction between phenomena (the world as experience and object of science) and noumena (the world of things in themselves which included the problems of morals). This seemed to lead to a conception of man divided into separate compartments such that his intellectual and ethical life were in principle different. The objective idealists restored the organic unity of ethics and reason but did so by assigning them to the so-called objective mind, banishing the individual as a mere moment of it.

Schopenhauer examined Kantian philosophy and came to quite different conclusions. Accepting the division of phenomenon and noumena, he notes that the former is the sphere of ideas and reason, the latter of ethics and will. "Phenomenal existence is idea and nothing more. All idea, of whatever kind it may be, all *object*, is *phenomenal* existence but the *will* alone is a *thing in itself.*"[41] Schopenhauer notes that one experiences his own actions as free and uncaused. It is only through reflection on experience that he finds to his astonishment that he is subject to necessity.[42] Hence, he proposes a major modification of the Kantian view. In self-consciousness the will itself, which Kant assured was free, is directly known.

In contrast to the Hegelians with Kant, Schopenhauer takes the individual to be the primary reality. However, in contrast to Kant he assumes the essence of the individual is his will, not his reason. Reason, in fact, and all its operations are mere "objectifications of the will." The critical problems of personality are located by Schopenhauer in the various tensions between reason and will.

In his essay on "Personality, or What a Man Is," Schopenhauer argued that personality is the most powerful of all factors in his happiness and welfare.

> A noble nature, a capable head, a joyful temperament, bright spirits, a well constituted, perfectly sound physique, in a word, *mens sana in corpore sano*, are the first and most important elements in happiness; so that we should be more intent on promoting and preserving such qualities than on the possession of external wealth and external honor.[43]

The central problems of personality were located by Schopenhauer in the operations of consciousness. What is important is not so much the way things are objectively in fact, but how they appear.[44] Schopenhauer followed Aristotle in the view that happiness means self-sufficiency and the free exercise of man's highest faculties. Moreover, also in agreement with this ancient humanistic tradition he conceived self-fulfillment as the well-rounded development of all man's capacities and particularly cultivation of his intellectual capacities.

> Now, our mental powers are forms of sensibility, and therefore a preponderating amount of it makes us capable of that kind of pleasure which has to do with mind, so-called intellectual pleasure; and the more sensibility predominates, the greater the pleasure will be.[45]

His preference for this rationalistic tradition of Western humanism seems to have been a major reason for Schopenhauer's pessimism. His answer to the Kantian problem had led him to place will at the core of the self. However, in preserving the rationalistic ideal he is led to see reason and will as in tension and the conception of the necessity for the suppression of the will.

> A man of powerful intellect is capable of taking a vivid interest in things in the way of mere *knowledge*, with no admixture of *Will*; nay, such an interest is a necessity to him. It places him in a sphere where pain is an alien,—a diviner air, where the gods live serene.[46]

Man's hope for genuine satisfaction, thus, depends on the suppression of what Schopenhauer's analysis had concluded to be his essential nature—his will.

The objective idealism of Hegel and his followers had appropriated the concept of reason and assigned it to the collective, reducing the individual to insignificance. In salvaging individuality Schopenhauer had located its essence, not in the reason, but in the emotions and will. Kierkegaard had a somewhat similar response to the objective idealists who, as he saw it, in cancelling individuality had negated man's traditional religious significance. In his *Journals* he exclaimed:

> How often have I shown that fundamentally Hegel makes men into heathens, *into a race of animals gifted with reason*. For in the animal world "the individual" is always less important than the race. But it is the peculiarity of the human race that just because the individual is created in the image of God "the individual" is above the race.[47]

If Hegel makes reason a collective process, the essence of individuality must lie, Kierkegaard maintained, in the nonreasonable aspects of man.

> The "in-and-for-itself" and reason are related to one another inversely; where the one is the other is not. When reason has completely penetrated all relationships and everything the "in-and-for-itself" will have disappeared entirely from life.
> That is more or less where we stand now. Reason is everywhere; instead of love—a *mariage de convenance*, instead of unconditional obedience—obedience as a result of reasoning, instead of faith—reasonable knowledge, instead of confidence—guarantees, instead of daring—probability, clever calculation, instead of action—events, instead of "the individual"—several people, instead of personality—impersonal objectivity, etc.[48]

Kierkegaard's attempt to salvage individuality from collectivism bears major parallels to Schopenhauer's.

Also among the nineteenth-century attempts to salvage individualism in the teeth of the unitary philosophies and the decline in

faith in the rationality of the common man was the emerging cult
of genius. Eric Bentley has attempted to trace the cult of hero
worship through the writings of Thomas Carlyle, Friedrich Nietzsche, Richard Wagner, Bernard Shaw, Oswald Spengler, Stefan
George, and D. H. Lawrence. Heroic vitalism, as he describes the
cult of the unusual individual, has "its roots . . . in the deep sense
of individuality which has been growing since the Renaissance. But
it assails the idea of human equality and issues a warning against
the belief that the crew should control the captain."[49]

However, whether or not the nineteenth-century approach to
individuality took the form of a cult of the hero as against both
the collective and the common man, the new emphasis on the
emotions and will as the essence of the individual as against reason
is everywhere apparent. As noted, since Schopenhauer accomplished this relocation while retaining the earlier idea of rationality, his reflections on the individual assumed a pessimistic turn.
However, if one ceased to value the emotional life of the individual negatively, such pessimism was not inevitable. This is already
apparent in Nietzsche's first major work, *The Birth of Tragedy*.
Depending on which of man's faculties were brought into integration, there were two possible types of self-realization in art or in
life: the world of ideas and the world of emotions (the world of
dreams and drunkenness, of Appolonian and Dionysian self-
expression).[50] Nietzsche envisioned a form of aesthetic consciousness and of life orientation which would surmount the opposition
of these two forms of self-realization and bring them into higher
synthesis. It was the conviction that the attainment of this synthesis lay outside the powers of the mass man that led Nietzsche in
his later work to the cult of the hero.

The many sided re-evaluation in the course of the nineteenth
century of the various components of the individual's nature was a
major factor in the rise of the various depth psychologies of which
that of Freud and his followers became most famous.

Sociology and the Social Person

As long as sociology was dominated by the holistic systems the
problem of social persons could not arise. However, accompanying
the neo-idealistic and neo-Kantian revivals in the social sciences,
the study of social persons became an integral part of the discipline. George Simmel, who was one of the major agents of the

neo-Kantian reaction in sociology, may illustrate the manner in which, once an elementaristic perspective had been assumed, the problem of social persons became inevitable.

Society, the collective to Simmel, was not an independent entity separate from individuals. Nevertheless, we do symbolize it as an entity as if it were separate from individuals, though properly speaking, life is attributable only to individuals. At the same time, Simmel observes, "the really practical problem of society is the relation between its forces and forms and the individual's own life."[51] This problem can only arise because men have the capacity to divide their behaviors into parts and to act and feel themselves to be social beings in tension with various interests and impulses not experienced as part of their social character.

> Society asks of the individual that he employ all his strength in the service of the special function which he has to exercise as a member of it; that he so modify himself as to become the most suitable vehicle for this function. Yet the drive toward unity and wholeness that is characteristic of the individual himself rebels against this role. The individual strives to be rounded out in himself, not merely to help to round out society.[52]

The group is assigned by individuals in the course of their interaction a kind of life of its own with characteristics and laws of its own. These characteristics of groups differ from those of individual existence. Moreover, Simmel believed that to the groups to which they belong individuals tend to assign their lower and more primitive impulses, while the properties which are more refined and differentiated cease to be the property of all and become more or less exclusively the property of the individual. The similarities of men's nature, in short, form the collective; their dissimilarities are perceived as individual. Thus "considered in his entirety, the individual appears to possess much higher qualities than those he contributes to the collective unit."[53] This difference between individual and collective accounts for the frequency with which the mass corrupts the individual and pulls him down to the level of all.

Mass actions being founded on the primitive and elemental aspects of all tend to be simple and radical and to avoid detours. "The mass neither lies nor simulates . . . it also lacks consciousness of responsibility."[54] The development of the intellect according to Simmel illustrates the lag of the social behind the individual.

Whoever wishes to move the masses appeals to feeling, to collective emotion and passion, which are important here as in all herds.

> We can bring the formation of the social level under the following valuational formula: what is common to all can be the property of only those who possess least.[55]

It is a mistake, Simmel believes, even to assign to the mass what is the "average." "In reality, the level of society is very *close* to that of its lowest components, since it must be possible for all to participate in it with identical valuation and effectiveness."[56]

As Simmel sees it, men vary in their capacity to suppress their most valuable powers and interests in favor of their lower qualities. This is one of the reasons why certain noble personalities remain aloof from public life. At the same time the frequent avoidance by men of the highest intellectual caliber of contact with the mass delays the rise of the social level.

Simmel's approach to the problem of the individual departs in a fundamental sense from that of the nineteenth-century collectivists. Far from seeing the collective as the source of all value, Simmel sees society and its representative in the individual, the socioethical sense as often imposing a specialization which destroys his wholeness and even qualities which are general-human.[57] Society, from Simmel's point of view, is only one of the forms in which men shape the contents of their lives. And so far as human values are measured by ideal standards, a given form of society may have only an accidental relation to humanity.

In its ties to the Kantian position and the nineteenth-century romantic concern with individual uniqueness, Simmel's sociology would seem to require for its completion the development of a theory of social persons. Two things, however, prevented Simmel from taking this step; his conviction that a science of the individual was the proper sphere of psychology, and his conception of sociology as the study of social forms in abstraction from content. However, when one conceives sociology from an elementaristic point of view as concerned with the content of social life, and not simply with social forms, the bearing of individuality upon social interaction cannot be left to psychology.

Max Weber, like Simmel, was strongly influenced by the neo-Kantian and neo-idealistic revivals. Like Simmel he set aside holistic analyses of interactive life as little more than a provisional orientation to sociological analysis. Society was merely a name for ways individuals interact, with no reality apart from this interaction. However, Weber did not confine sociological analysis to the study of social forms in abstraction from content. Hence, in the analysis of interaction the various ways individuals drew the lines between the self and other moved to the forefront of analysis.

In the first work to catapult Weber to fame, *The Protestant Ethic and Spirit of Capitalism*, Weber directed analysis to the formation of a peculiar type of individual psychology (an attitude of inner-worldly asceticism) which emerged hand-in-hand with a peculiar combination of economic institutions (capitalistic economic behavior). The formation of a type of personality orientation and a characteristic set of institutional relations were assumed, in reciprocal manner, to occur. In other works Weber explored other ties between institutions, cultural forms, and personal orientations: classical humanism and Confucian ethic and the imperial bureaucratic ethos in ancient China; ascetic otherworldliness and Brahmin religiosity in ancient India; emissary prophecy and the demogogic-political orientation in ancient Israel before the Exile.

While Weber never formally took up the task of developing a theory of social persons, many of his most penetrating sociological studies center on the relation between social and cultural forms and personality types.

In the one branch of sociological theory to develop a theory of social persons, symbolic interactionism, the neo-Kantian and neo-idealistic revivals again played a role. American pragmatism developing through Charles Pierce, William James, John Dewey, and George Herbert Mead, which reexamined the idealistic and positivistic traditions and reoriented them to more prominent conceptions of the individual, supplied the philosophic foundations of symbolic interactionism.

In William James' *Principles of Psychology*, the Kantian contrast between the pure and empirical ego formed the point of attack on the problems of personality. With some imagination James divided the individual into the pure and empirical ego and the empirical ego (the self as experienced) into three subcategories: the material self (those physical things a man experiences at his own such as body, clothes, and so on); the social self (the recognition one receives from others); and the spiritual self (one's inner subjective faculties and dispositions). The tone of man's self-feeling and self-esteem was seen by James as the ratio between his success and his pretensions (what he expects of his material, social, and spiritual self in conjunction with what he is able to achieve).[58] This bears many similarities to the conceptions by Kant and those idealists who followed him of the notion of man's moral essence as the projection of ethical claims on the empirical world and the attempt to realize them. James identified the pure ego as the self which serves as subject designated by the self word "I" and the empirical ego (the self as experienced) as designated by the self word "me."

In Charles Horton Cooley's *Human Nature and the Social Order* the same framework was preserved. The self as subject was treated as a basic core of self-feeling which, in turn, developed in response to various views of the self held by others. One's personal idea of one's self took shape in terms of one's response to one's notion of how one appeared to others and one's reaction to how he assumed he was being judged. Cooley described the empirical social self as the "looking glass self."[59]

George Herbert Mead generalized the theories of James and Cooley and tried to isolate the general process of self-formation (reflexivity), the elements of the self (reciprocally-shared attitudes) and the units of interactive life (roles).[60] For any given person, Mead argues, life is already a going concern at the time he is born. His self arises as a personal differentiation within the ongoing system of social life. The critical mechanism which permits this personal differentiation is language which consists of a shared system of symbols and of rules for their use which permit people to orient their actions to one another with great flexibility and precision.

Learning a language involves acquiring symbols from others and hence sharing parallel states of mind concerning them. To use a term is, from this perspective, to orient one's actions toward objects and behavior the way others do, hence to share comparable attitudes. To learn a language is to take over the role of the other. Language makes the self inevitable by forcing one to take up and respond to the attitude of others toward one's self. The "I" following the traditions extending from Kant through James and Cooley is the principle of response, the self as subject; the "me" consists in the internalized attitudes of others in terms of which the "I" acts.

The emphasis on the language as the mechanism of self-formation has led to the designation of this tradition as symbolic interactionism. Its concept of one's position in groups as a status and one's performance in terms of the reciprocal expectations of other group members as a "role" have become common currency of contemporary sociology. The symbolic interactionist theory of personality, in accord with its origin in Kantian and neo-idealistic philosophic traditions, was strongly humanistic.

As illustrated by W. I. Thomas and Florian Znaniecki, if one applied the symbolic interactionist position to the actual analysis of social experience, one was pressed toward a typology of social persons. In their analysis of the Polish peasant in Europe and North America Thomas and Znaniecki felt that it was necessary to examine the life record of an immigrant. Three concepts were deemed to be essential for that purpose: temperament (the individual's physiologically based inclinations), character (his socially reconstructed attitudes and inclinations), and his life organization (a set of rules for the definition of life situations).[61]

Personality development was believed to result from the formation of personality on the basis of temperament, the emergence of a life organization permitting objective expression of characterological attitudes, the adaptation of character to social demands, and the adaptation of individual life-organization to social organization.[62]

In the case of Polish peasants living in ethnic minority situations, in America three major forms of personality formation were theorized to express typical lines of genesis of life-organization: Bohemian, Philistine, and Creative man. The Bohemian is the kind of personality overwhelmed by the contrast and conflict of the two cultures and unable to internalize a personal formula based on one or other. Hence the Bohemian flows from situation to situation, responding to each situation on its own merits with no permanence. The Philistine is a personal type which solves the problems of dual cultural claims by clinging tenaciously to the traditional culture with little capacity for change. The Creative man is marked by the taking over of the best elements in the new and old culture.

It appeared for a time that the theory and empirical study of social persons had a most promising future. A considerable number of studies of social roles and forms of personal adaptation to social conditions and situations was undertaken under the influence of symbolic interactionism (such as Shaw and McKay's *The Jack Roller*, Sutherland's *The Professional Thief*, Nels Anderson's *The Hobo*) and the case and life history was for a time elevated to the status of a primary methodology. However, this impulse in sociology went into eclipse (for a variety of reasons) and the promise of the area is still relatively unexplored.

One reason for the eclipse of the study of social persons in American sociology appears to have been the rise of a new form of holism in structure-functionalism. Like all forms of holism, functionalism tends to minimize the significance of social persons. Nevertheless, once an area has been established, it becomes common property of all schools. The functionalists in contrast to the positivistic organicists did acknowledge the social significance of personality, though in much reduced manner than the elementarists. Moreover, as illustrated by the work of Talcott Parsons, the significance of some concepts was changed (for example, roles were visualized not as properties of individuals but of groups) and preference was shown for different personality theories (Parsons, for example, much prefers a modified version of Freudian personality theory to that of the symbolic interactionists).

Sociology still has only unsystematically exploited the resources of contemporary personality theory, and the empirical study of social persons on a systematic basis remains to be undertaken despite sporadic explorations of the relation between particular social roles, institutional and class situations, groups and personality such as the studies of the intellectual, the scientists, the bureaucrat, the academic man, and the like.

Community Type and Personality

Repeatedly the need is felt by contemporary men not only for a study of the interrelation between various special social conditions and personality formation, but the relation between total community formation and personality. While sociologists have dragged their heels in this phase of the study of social persons, various other social scientists (psychologists, psychiatrists, and ethnologists) have been drawn to it. Sufficient evidence has been assembled to indicate that there are affinities between total community formation and personality types.

Since the discernible establishment of human society there have been five major historical types of community: tribal communities, peasant villages, cities, feudal manors, and nations of a contemporary type. Each of these types of community has had peculiar consequences for personality. A review of some of the characteristic ties that have been found between personality and community types may illustrate the great richness that remains in the underdeveloped phase of the sociological study of social persons.

The Tribesman

Since men cannot build a community (a total system of collective life) without forming their own natures, it would seem to follow that if there are common features in tribal communities, they also should be manifest in what may be described as a tribal personality.

Tribal communities of hunters-gatherers-fishers are small. Their members have relatively complete knowledge of one another from birth to death. Mutual personal resources are known with great fullness. Since the economy rests upon the natural produce of a territory large enough to sustain the group, detailed knowledge of the total natural food resources of this territory is one of the unconscious possessions of each individual. The tribesman's food cupboard is his total natural environment. He lives on more intimate relations with a "natural" area (one not penetrated by human intervention) than any other type of man. He also has greater self-assurance upon being left alone than is possible for any other type of man.

In most tribal communities frequent occasions arise when the conditions of survival atomize the social group into very small social units. Sex must be ordered in such small groups if it is not to be a source of fatal conflict. Usually very firm incest taboos are present, but they obtain only within a narrow group. A division of labor follows sex lines. Kinship tends to be counted bilaterally when the group is so small. Exogamous marriage is a way of establishing peaceable relations with other groups.

If tribal personality may be isolated, such widespread features of tribal communities are its source. An example or two may illustrate this.

Social Structure and Personality among the Ammassalik Eskimos: A few observations on the Ammassalik Eskimos and their social structure permit isolation of relevant personality features of the community.

A strong sense of individualism that characterizes the Ammassalik technology and economy appears in their social structure. The Ammassalik possess no political unity, no organized leadership, no social stratification, no complicated relationships, no set residence. The biological family constitutes their only social bond. Children are cared for until able to set out on their own. With each new marriage, a new household is set up.[63] The Ammassalik do not have certain widespread Eskimo traits. There are no hospitality wrestling matches; there is no group ritual; they do not practice female infanticide; they do not substitute the murderer for the man he murdered; there are no *angakut* (shaman) contests. On the other hand, the Eskimo custom of wife exchange as a part of guest hospitality is carried out under the game of "Putting Out the Lamps" (under cover of darkness a man may take any woman as his sex partner, exclusive of daughters or sisters prohibited by the incest taboo).

While there is no organized leadership, there are recognized leaders. An outstanding hunter, a powerful angakok, and a skillful drum singer are honored. However, there is no best or most powerful, or most skillful leader, medicine man, or artist. There is room for many. Leadership is ephemeral, and the successful hunter of one season quickly loses his standing if his skill or luck fails during the next.

It is absolutely necessary for a man to marry, since the division of labor is essential to survival. As soon as he is able, a boy takes a wife to look after his things, dress his game, manufacture his clothes, and the like. A skillful and lucky hunter may need two wives, since one woman may be overwhelmed by the amount of work to be done. Complete sex freedom exists before and after marriage. Nevertheless, the economic necessity for a wife or wives makes women a focal point of competition, even though a man is at liberty to treat his wife as he pleases, from caressing to beating and stabbing, from devotion to desertion. Women are the primary source of quarrels which may lead to murder, to revenge by theft, or to a drum match.

Drum matches held both winter and summer are a juridical procedure for settling disputes which conform to a wider social pattern of singing songs for pleasure. Carried out before large audiences, they are major dramatic events in which the audience participates with keen enjoyment. A man may have several drum matches going on at the same time. Drum songs are never (as on the west coast of Greenland) sung to taunt a man with incompetence as a hunter or to accuse someone of laziness or cowardice. They arise when one man takes another's wife—which may be obscured under a charge of stealing food, poisoning, using a dead relative's name, or the like.

Murder is frequent. But there is no blood feud, no retaliation (physical or magical), no substitute procedure, or purification rites. The murderer remains in the group. Religion is a highly individual affair, carried on by angakok. It revolves around food-getting and curing the sick. Any person of either sex may become an angakok.

There is maximum cooperation only in times of famine. Famine occurs in winter, when the individualistic trends give way to cooperative settlement and behavior.

The Ammassalik ideal man is one who is outstanding in skill, in strength, in power. A man who expresses his personality fully without economic, social, or supernatural deterrence is most admired. Such a man may do what he wishes without fear, without opposition or ostracism. He is at once a terror and a pride. Prestige is a direct reflection of powerful personality expressed in self-assertion, violence, arrogance, aggressiveness. The honors go to those skillful in hunting, angakokism, or drum singing. The successful hunter or angakok may have two wives and be welcomed as a son-in-law, husband, and housemate. The skillful drum singer may steal, murder, and slander, but still win communal approval for his cleverness and artistry.

However, there is no competition for higher positions, for any number of persons may be acknowledged to be important. There is sufficient elasticity in the community to permit numerous persons simultaneously to be important. Bigness can even be displayed by a single individual, by taking his family and going away by himself. In the drum matches, when competition enters the picture, activity quickly assumes the properties of a game in which mutual enjoyment is more important than winning. "Success and the attainment of prestige depend directly on a person's skill and personality alone. Conversely a person who has neither is despised and "the butt of his fellows. Such a role is traditionally and factually taken by the orphan."[64]

Social Structure and Personality among the Kaska: Somewhat similar relations between personality and social structure appear among the Kaska Indians of Northern British Columbia and the Southern Yukon Territory in the area from the Continental Divide on the West to the Rocky Mountains on the East. This polar continental zone of warm summers and cold winters comprises a forest belt of spruce, jackpine, and poplar with relatively plentiful game: moose, bear, caribou, and a variety of small fur-bearing animals. The Kaska subsist by hunting, trapping, gathering, and trading.[65]

Lower Post, the trading center for the region, located on the Dease and Laird rivers, is composed of three trading stores, the families of the merchants, a policeman, and a game warden. During the summer months the settlement swells to around 2,000 persons. By September most of this population disperses for the trap lines.

Trap lines are owned by individuals (at times, by unattached women). Until spring, a single family or matrilocal group of three or four families lives in isolated winter cabins with only an occasional visitor. Women and children frequently are alone at home for days, while their husbands, sons, and sons-in-law tend their trap lines.

The Indian community in Lower Post is atomistic. No effort is made to set up a planned community. Each family pitches its tent where it pleases, though related families often set up adjacent tents. Sociability takes the form of groups of men, women, and children loitering around the trading store, exchanging visits, drinking, dancing together, and gambling. Most of these activities are casual and informal. Unless stimulated by alcohol, social interaction is rarely intense.

Individualism typifies the informal arrangements for dances, which are never planned in advance but arranged on the spot. Though there is a nominal chief, he exercises no authority. Criticism is the strongest sanction, even in cases of major misconduct. For example, promiscuity of the girls with visiting soldiers was severely disapproved by the older people, yet the girls were not ostracized or disrespected. Rorschach tests confirmed the impression of inversion and emotional aloofness observable in much Kaska behavior.

Kaska mothers withdraw from intense emotional involvement with their children. "Their attitudes may be described as being compounded of passive affection and emotional indifference. The result in the child appears to be an emotional aloofness which later manifests itself in the withdrawn, taciturn adult personality which we have described as introverted. The impetus to strong interaction having been removed from the developing individual, the child is thrown upon his own resources."[66]

Inclinations toward independence are positively manifest in the eagerness of the boy to accompany his father on the trap line. "To subsist in the adult culture the boy needs trapping experience and knowledge. A good hunter and trapper is respected, has a definite prestige with girls, and can reassure himself as to his self-sufficiency."[67] While trapping is a rigorous occupation, there are positive values in acquiring its skills, for the good trapper can support a wife and family without severe deprivation. Individualism is further promoted by the atomistic structure of the community. Discipline is lax, frustrations are minimal, and social sanctions little elaborated. The individual Kaska is quite free to develop his individuality along the lines of an emotional aloof personality.

Social Structure and Personality among the Comanche: The Comanche at present located in the area of the Texas Panhandle and southwestern Oklahoma illustrate a shift in personality emphasis from an autonomous individualism to a somewhat more cooperative personality formation, accompanying a change of community formula from more or less pure hunting and gathering to a community specialized for maruauding.[68]

Prior to 1680, the Comanche lived on the Montana plateau in close association with the Shoshone, to whom they are ethnically and linguistically related. On the Montana plateau with its arid sagebrush vegetation, they lived as hunters and gatherers on roots, seeds, deer, antelope, and small game. Throughout the winter they lived in sheltered valleys, where fuel and water were available. Each band had its own domain through which it traveled, though there was no punishment for trespass. Social organization was rudimentary. There was no political organization and no fixed order of camp groups or families into bands. They had no chiefs. Medicine men, however, sometimes achieved eminence. Though there was no fixed stratification system, there was considerable respect for the aged. There was no clan organization. A simple bilateral incest rule was observed. Fraternal wife-lending and polyandry were practiced as well as customary marriage of a deceased wife's sister. There was no bride price, and marriage was unstable with partners separating at will.

Families were matrilocal. There was little jealousy or mutilation of wives for faithlessness. A technique of birth control was practiced. Puberty ceremonies for both sexes were calculated to confirm skill in later occupations, such as to make good hunters out of the boys.

The Comanche at this time considered themselves to be humble and harmless, content to spend their time in hunting. They had a lively fear of ghosts, and thought death polluting, but their medicine lacked a malevolent magic. Animals were a source of power and a general force (*mana*) was thought to be behind all things.

At this time, in short, the Comanche displayed much of the atomistic individualism manifest in varying ways among the Ammassalik Eskimo and Kaska. Their personalities were closer to the latter.

Some time between 1680 and 1690 the Comanche moved from the Montana plateau to their present area. At the time of their move it was a no-man's land between New France and New Spain. Also at the time of the migration the Comanche shifted the emphasis of their communal life from hunting to raiding. They raided New Spain for horses and captives, selling both in the East, becoming one of the great suppliers of horses to the Plains. When they could no longer sell captives, they stole children whom they held for ransom. They also became efficient cattle rustlers, a practice which only ended when they were forced to live on reservations. The only trading they did was when wagon trains came from Mexico under a truce bringing ammunition, salt, and blankets. At other times they constantly raided the Mexicans, keeping in contact with them, however, through sheepherders who were unarmed neutrals and whom it was not sporting to kill.

Their subsistence economy consisted of a variety of vegetable foods (berries and roots) and buffalo, which were accessible in all seasons. Meat was rarely scarce for more than three or four days. Antelope hides were used for clothing. Deer, black bear, and smaller game were hunted chiefly for sport. Buffalo were hunted both individually and in communal hunts in which the men on horseback stampeded the herd and rode up behind the animals, driving their arrows home at short range. Food was shared freely. Several meals a day were eaten, and visitors were immediately offered food. The Comanche also raised horses and ate horse meat with relish. Horses were given as gifts, as fees for medicine, and used as a medium of exchange.

The material culture was simple and supplemented by an immense amount of loot. The chief industry was preparing hides for clothing and tipis. Men made their own bows and arrows and their own arrow heads (particularly favoring the bottom of a frying pan). Their clothing was designed simply and decorated with beadwork and a peculiar trident design with several points painted on the robe worn by the first wife. The number of points symbolized the number of men the husband had killed. Individual ownership of all objects was the rule, but hoarding was not practiced. Loot from raids was soon disbursed.

Comanche domestic establishments were fairly large. Polygynous families could have as many as five tipis: a dwelling tipi, a sacred tipi (if the owner was a medicine man), a separate tipi for the adolescent son. One tipi required ten buffalo hides. Inside the tipis were lazyback beds, a fireplace, and various possessions hung on frames. On the march the Comanche Indians needed four pack horses as a minimum in addition to the family horses. Buffalo and war horses were driven along with the herd.

The tribe was never a political unit. It varied in component bands. Bands came together or broke into separate camping units in response to the character of the food supply. Each band had a peace chief (a wise, gentle, older man) who had no real executive or police authority. The influential men in the bands were war chiefs or leaders of war parties. They held their positions as long as they were successful. The management of the tribe was in the hands of the war whip, who took charge of dances, but he exercised no formal civil authority. The war chiefs had supernatural power but practiced no negative magic. Top rank was attained by the fine warrior still fighting and able to lead war parties. Once he passed his prime, he quickly lost authority. Bilateral incest taboos obtained. Fraternal wife lending and sororate marriage remained over from plateau culture.

The critical changes in Comanche personality from the earlier period was the decline of humility and peaceableness. Individuality had to be strengthened if the Comanches were to be turned into bold raiders cooperating in the operations of war and raiding parties. They developed "a society in which death of the young is constant, but in which anxiety about death is minimal; a high degree of security notwithstanding the constant threat of annihilation."[69]

The security system of the individual, according to Kardiner, consisted in perfecting his resources for dealing with the outer world. There was a minimum appeal to deity except for what was involved in the concept of medicine or power. There was also reliance on forms of cooperation using the pooled manpower resources of the community. Such cooperation was facilitated by the notion of power which can be borrowed, loaned, pooled, and freely distributed through the entire group. Moreover, every man in the community profited by the exploits of the entire group. Only the accumulation of horses which could be used as currency and to enhance prestige did not flow in the usual course of distribution of property. Disruptive tendencies were primarily channeled into the struggle for women. However, this was modified by the practice of wife lending and the tendency to direct punishment at women. There was an absence of homosexuality and transvestitism—passive attitudes of any kind on the part of the males would have destroyed the society. However, the institution of friendship was highly cherished.

The society and ego structure, in Kardiner's opinion, "could exist only as long as there were slaves to steal and cattle to rustle. In other words, this fine ego structure of the Comanche was bought at the expense of criminality perpetuated on others and at the cost of complete collapse of the society once this criminality was incapable of being exercised."[70]

Examples such as the Ammassalik Eskimo, the Kaska, and the Comanche seem to indicate that the personality of the tribesman— of man in the pre-cultivating community—tended to gravitate with special frequency around a core of coherent, individualistic self-reliance.

The Peasant

There are many things about the cultivator's way of life which have consequence for his personality. Cultivation involved the penetration of nature rather than acceptance of it as an external fact and as a natural ally whose structure an individual would not dream of dissecting. The food plants are relatively few among the vast variety of the world. Most of them in a wild state are rapid growing, light loving, but relatively minor species without the active assistance of human cultivators. Man's association with them not only removed him from the daily association with a natural area and its produce but bound him to an endless sequence of toil over a small area. The moment he left his garden unattended he found it penetrated with horrifying speed by undesirable plant species.

Cultivating elevated the status of women; it increased the size of the group; it turned children into an economic asset. It led to an increase in the significance of property, and an integration and differentiation of social structure. These changes had consequences for personality formation.

The range of basic personalities which has been characteristic of cultivating communities and the features more or less common to them remains to be established. An example or two may illustrate personality configurations which seem to have emerged rather frequently with the cultivating community.

Social Structure and Personality among the Zuni: The largest of the pueblo communities of the North American southwest is Zuni, consisting of some 2,000 Indians living in the terraced adobe houses which form the typical pueblo unit. Many Zuni live in scattered farming villages, returning to Zuni for ceremonial observances held calendrically. The Zuni are dependent entirely on agriculture and sheep herding. The high New Mexican plateau is arid, much of it unsuitable for agriculture and grazing. The major concern of the husbandman is water. The main source of water is the Zuni river which for much of the year is a mere trickle except for flooding during cloudbursts. Prayers for rain are central to the religion of Zuni.[71]

Zuni's government under a priestly hierarchy is concerned with religion. Civil law is in the hands of a secular committee appointed by the priests. Social control is not centrally administered but dependent on public opinion. The individual life cycle is determined by the requirements of the matriarchal household. Food sharing is communally organized. Other activities are determined by the requirements of matrilineal clans and the religious and secret societies.

Zuni agriculture originally centered in maize, beans, and squash and was dependent on hand irrigation. Irrigation is now organized with respect to the government dam. Agriculture has been expanded to comprise fruit orchards, corn and wheat fields, and melon patches. The Zuni also tend sheep herds (introduced by the Spaniards). The social organization of the Zuni is opposed to excessive accumulation of a surplus in individual hands. The land is worked by cooperative group labor. Fields are owned by individuals or by matriarchal households but are worked by all men of the household. Wealthy families are expected to undertake special obligations, such as entertaining the masked god impersonators at the winter solstice ceremonies. Poor people who help out in a wealthy household are rewarded with gifts of food. "In general," Goldman observes, "the culture has removed all sting from a competition that might develop by giving little weight to the possession of material goods *per se.* The Zuni have no interest in accumulating more property than they can use, and when an individual does become wealthy he re-distributes his wealth in the great winter festival of the Shalako."[72]

The individual is fitted into a close knit social organization. A man is born with fixed kin and clan affiliations. At marriage he leaves the household of his mother to join the communal economic unit of his mother-in-law. At puberty the boy is initiated into one of the six dance groups constituting male society. The Zuni tribe is presently divided into thirteen matrilineal clans. The household is an economic unit cooperatively organized. In the house all share food equally or according to need. Divorce is simple, for the Zuni do not like bickering. However, for the same reason (a dislike of quarreling) most marriages are durable and peaceful. Within a Zuni family conflict is not possible over a possible mate. No woman would think of sleeping with a man who had slept with her sister, nor would two brothers conceivably have relations with the same woman. While sexual jealousies are a major cause of quarrels, divorce is simple (the woman simply packs the man's belongings). It is an adequate safety valve for any major troubles.

Zuni culture stresses sobriety and subordination to the group, a trait also apparent in Zuni religion. A large part of the waking life of the adult Zuni man is devoted to ritual: memorizing word-perfect formulas of elaborate ceremonies organized by calendar and integrating the various cults. The cult basic to all Zuni ceremonialism is that of the ancestors who guide, protect, and nourish human life. The ancestor cult touches every phase of Zuni life. Beside the ancestor cult there are six other major cults: of the sun, of the rain makers, of the katcinas (a mythological people living at the bottom of a lake), and of the medicine societies including those devoted to the beast gods, the most dangerous and violent in the Zuni pantheon, the bow priesthood, and those participating in a clowning cult. The katcinas society is organized in six sections conforming to the six directions recognized by the Zuni.

While aggression is suppressed in all Zuni relations, the bow priesthood, which deals with war and serves as the executive arm of the priestly hierarchy, channels such aggression as remains in Zuni. However, the priesthood offices carrying greatest responsibilities are not sought after. All ceremonials are collective. While on the plains individual visions were sought, among the Zuni only group ritual is effective. The masked katcina dances are group affairs which collectively bring rain.

The ideal man of the Zuni is not wealthy but ceremonially minded and willing to devote himself to ritual routines which bring supernatural blessings to the group. Though priestly office sets the individual apart, he must avoid manifestations of individuality and must not seem officious. The stress is ever on immersion of the individual in the group. The individual must cooperate in the work of the fields and with the men of the kiva in the religious performances. Competitiveness toward others must not be expressed. The ideal man is a person of dignity and affability who does not try to dominate and who has not called forth comment of his neighbors. Any conflict is held against him. In the days when war was still a reality, individualism was channeled into the bow priesthood. With the elimination of war even that outlet narrowed. Economic life also offers little room for individualism, for there are no great rewards to the rich. Wealthy men distribute their wealth in communal Shalako. The strong willed, culturally aberrant individual in Zuni faces the danger of being accused of sorcery. In Bunzel's words, the Zuni place little value on "initiative, ambition, an uncompromising sense of honor and justice," and "intense personal loyalties." Rather, the Zuni most value "a yielding disposition and a generous heart."[73]

The Balinese Temper: Bali is an island to the east of Java, where a culture anciently derived from India is domiciled. A four-year study of the arts, musical legends, and rituals of a Balinese agricultural village (centering in rice cultivation) was made by Jane Belo.[74] The Balinese present an interesting variation on the same general characteriological theme as the Zuni: the sacrifice of the aggressive forms of individuality to a life emphasizing smoothness of social coordination and even temper.

The most striking immediate characteristics of the ordinary behavior of the Balinese is his absolute poise of bearing, posture, movement, and gesture, a property noticeable in all mature men and women and even discernible in very small children. This poise arises from the fact that the Balinese is never unconscious of his position in space in relation to *kadja* (North, the direction of the mountains) and *kelod* (South, the direction of the sea) and of the relation of his position to the ground which must never be higher than his social superior. The position of the Balinese must constantly be adjusted to the laws of his cosmology and social group. He habitually avoids all impulsive movement which could destroy his sense of well-being. He walks slowly with studied poise but is capable of feats of sustained endurance (Belo reports the visit of an average family to a shrine and back, a distance of more than fifty miles, without showing the slightest signs of wear).

Much of the land of the island lies between the high mountains and the shore in an area formed by longitudinal ridges running parallel to each other. Between the ridges are steep ravines where flow the rivers and springs which the Balinese need for drinking and bathing. Since villages are located on the high ground, each member of the family must go down to the river one or more times a day for bathing, for water (women carry forty-pound jars on their heads but never waver in their slow erect pace) and for work in the rice terraces. Small boys escort ducks and water buffalo to the streams for their daily emersion. The desire for the daily bath is strong, sending people of all ages down to the streams for this purpose if for none other. In this incessant travel up and down the steep slopes there is a reluctance to display the slightest sign of effort or weakness or lack of ease. The refusal to admit weakness is evident also in the reluctance to spare the sick person. A woman, knocked unconscious with an axe, for example, was forced to walk home under her own power. She could not be carried home like a corpse.

The Balinese have an acute consciousness of position. A man may be in three positions—erect, seated, or incumbent. Even children do not stand on their heads or turn somersaults in play. Babies are never seen to crawl but are carried until old enough to stand alone, for only animals walk on all fours. White men who scamper down a hillside in an excess of good spirits evoke laughter in the Balinese. His physical orientation requires avoidance of shocks, pains, and disturbances of the circulation. The feeling of confusion, lack of sure-footedness and sense of disequilibrium are unpleasant. Directions are given by the Balinese in terms of north and south rather than right and left. If he is unsure of these directions the Balinese grows anxious and is unable to eat or sleep. Every Balinese sleeps only with his head to the north or to the east.

From their elders children soon learn on which "level" they should sit at formal gatherings. The Balinese house has a number of pavilions providing a hierarchy of sitting-places for its members. A guest of higher cast than the family of the host must be given the highest place. At weddings formal rules are observed in seating guests: on the floor of the highest pavilion sit the high priests; on a lower pavilion sit men of rank; across the court and still lower sit women of the family also of noble birth; and so on.

Strict etiquette holds even among small children who are so quiet as hardly to be noted. Babies are not heard to cry (at the slightest whimper they are given the breast). Quarrels, brusque words, and threatening gestures on the part of one child call forth attitudes of submission from the weaker. If one is humiliated by an elder, one may pass it on to a younger member of the group.

The strict order of the Balinese way of life and religion also appears in linguistic usage which obeys complex social rules. The language is rich in terms with minutely differentiated meanings and stratified into hierarchical orders. Low Balinese is a familiar language used between members of a family, friends, and intimates except where there is a disparity of rank between speakers. A man of low caste addresses his social superior in High Balinese and is answered in Low Balinese. Complex rules prescribe the way of sitting. A Balinese (from eight to eighty) lowers himself with the back held straight, at the same time pulling the loincloth with his two hands tight over the thighs to prevent exposure. In sitting, relative height is strictly observed. A high priest has the place of honor. Certain ascetics of noble caste are bound not to sit down or eat facing any direction other than north or east. In places of the nobility, men of humble rank may sit or walk but may not stand or walk when a noble is seated. When fulfilling an order, the menial advances in a half-crouching position. The Balinese normally eats alone and is forbidden to speak to anyone who is eating.

The Balinese fear the dark, and terror of the *lejaks* (living male and female sorcerers in supernatural form) is intensified between night and dawn. Adult boys and men will not visit unholy places such as cemeteries, crossroads, and certain trees and bridges at night. They fear to walk along the dark village streets at night. The housecourt of the Balinese is his haven, for it is protected by a magic strip of wall immediately within the gate.

A man may not touch a woman, even his wife, before others. He may not touch a woman's clothes, nor should his clothes touch hers, for instance, in a trunk.

The organized release from the rigid Balinese code occurs on occasions of intense excited group activity. Such appears, for example, in the rehearsals of musicians, actors, and dancers. Then all persons work together without attention to relative rank. In rehearsals the Balinese sits on a level with his social inferiors and accepts their judgment on aesthetic matters if the other's talent is superior to his. Also at communal feasts men accustomed to eating in private enjoy a partial breakdown of taboos. At the celebration of cremation several hundred men together drop their habitual, carefully poised bearing, and convey the body of their friend to

112

his place of cremation. They shout, leap, lift their arms in threatening gestures, and whirl around in a mass, stamping, kicking, trampling with glee. Balinese religion, particularly, provides many occasions for celebration in which people break forth in a riot of release, adorn themselves, and enthusiastically participate in the dancing, music, and drama which the religion prescribes.

In Jane Belo's view, there is no tension; rather, a certain ease is created by the need to maintain balanced equilibrium and a perfect orientation in social and geographical respects. The rules by which the Balinese abide simplify their behavior. The Balinese works in relaxation, and in his pleasure finds intense stimulation. He is able to wait long periods without showing impatience, and he accepts the complete frustration of his plans by denying it happened. "It may be said that the agricultural way of life, requiring suitable physical exertion, and producing in a direct way the food supply, so that there may be no anxiety about it for anyone, contributes to the mental poise of the people; also that the children are surrounded with affection, and very early given a part in the work of the family group, so that they grow up feeling beloved and useful, which gives them as individuals a sense of security."[75]

The very immutability of all laws of conduct relieves the individual of any responsibility except that of obedience. Even though it may seem that the Balinese live in ever present fear of demons and evil spirits, every remedy is known and prescribed.

The Zuni and the Balinese, to be sure, present only two verions of the personality formulas of the cultivators. However, the tendency in both to eliminate certain kinds of aggressive individualism and to place the emphasis upon more genial and accommodating attitudes and to enhance the routines of the cultivator seem to epitomize tendencies everywhere present in the cultivating community. When pastoral nomadism emerged from the context of mixed agriculture, it was accompanied by a shift in personality emphasis toward more aggressive individualized forms reminiscent of the hunting types of pre-cultivating communities once again. However, the pastoral nomad had many traits that separated him from the hunter.

The Urbanite

The peasant community transformed nature into a garden; the city removed man even from this artificially reconstituted environment. The peasant community bound man to the intimacies of the organic cycle of plants and animals; the city community released man into a more purely human environment. The peasant community locked man in kin and clan groups; the city community tore these asunder and relocated the hub of social life in secondary groupings. All such changes had consequences for the personality of man. Life in the city is ordered with respect to artificial rather than organic rhythms, to simplified primary and complicated secondary groupings, to a specialization of people that accompanied the specialization of structure, to rational rather than the conventional or traditional ordering of social relations.

Any characterization of the urbanite is made difficult by the varieties of city in the ancient and contemporary world. The first wave of city formation produced the ancient oriental city in the river valleys of the Near East, Northern India, and China. In time these cities entered a phase of imperialism which transformed their structure. In late antiquity a new wave of city formation got under way in the Mediterranean Sea cities. This civic world, too, terminated in imperialism—first of the Macedonian, later of the Roman empires. These city-based empires also collapsed. In the European middle ages a third major wave of city formation developed. As autonomous cities, those of the Occident were overwhelmed by the nation. Each of these periods of city formation offers communities which contrast with the other. In each period, moreover, there were important internal variations.

Moreover, since cities arise in part by the tearing asunder of previous communities and present milieux in which a wide variety of social types may rub shoulders (soldiers, scribes, priests of various kinds, merchants, politicians, administrators, diplomats, and so on) even in a single city type, some selection is necessary in epitomizing the personality of the urbanite.

Subject to many qualifications, then, the peculiar form of individualization of the full citizen in the classical period of Athens may be taken to illustrate properties which characterize the personality of the urbanite.

The Greek polis of the classical period was dominated by citizen soldiers. Military technology in the Mediterranean Sea city rested on disciplined foot soldiers, hoplites, and sailors. Since the Greek polis was a religious community in which all full citizens participated, no major hiatus existed between priests and lay citizens. In fact many religious offices were filled by lot as were many political offices. The two central occupations of the citizen soldier were war and politics. All full citizens participated equally in the war and in the religious cults of the cities. Military and religious distinctions, thus, could not of themselves settle disputes. Individuals wrestled in the gymnasium to determine comparative military competence; they disputed in the forum to settle religious and political questions. Each individual full citizen was responsible for the whole course of his civic life and inclined to translate all issues into terms that could be settled by his individual physical and mental powers. Whatever problems could not be settled by hand-to-hand encounter could, he assumed, be settled by debate and discussion. This-worldliness, secular mindedness, the demand for clarity, wholeness, and rationality came to characterize behavior in all life spheres: politics, religion, philosophy, art, and literature.

An incisive presentation of the properties of the Greek mind is presented by Kitto.[76] He notes that while the modern mind divides, specializes, and categorizes, the Greek was inclined to see things as an organic whole. The Greek ideal of mind and personality was *arete*, a sort of all-round excellence in moral, intellectual, physical, and practical respects. The Greek hero, such as Odysseus, combined virtues which in our heroic age were distributed between the knight and the churchman.

The most typical of all the Greek citizen's activities was his war game. He was, above all, a soldier. Every city had its gymnasium, where young men of military age met to wrestle naked and practice the skills of hand-to-hand combat. All affairs tended to be transformed into the counterpart of hand-to-hand contests. The *arete* tested by the game was the skill of the whole man, not specialized skill. The great event of the Olympic Games was the pentathalon: comprising a race, a jump, throwing the discus, throwing the javelin, and wrestling.

Closely associated with the emphasis on wholeness of outlook and ability was the Greek belief in reason. The universe was not thought to be capricious, but lawful and capable of explanation. This assumption runs through the whole of Greek philosophy. It also sent the Greek on the road to the development of logic and mathematics—methods of the rational mind.

Correlated with the demand for wholeness and reason was a love of symmetry and form. The whole reach of Greek art and literature reveals this love of symmetry. "The Greek stylistic vice," Kitto observes, "was not incapable shapelessness but bogus formalism."[77]

The traits which Kitto finds in the Greek citizen were also quite self-consciously present in the funeral oration at Athens which Thucydides placed in the mouth of Pericles.

> We do not copy our neighbours, but are an example to them. It is true that we are called a democracy, for the administration is in the hands of the many and not of the few. But while the law secures equal justice to all alike in their private disputes, the claim of excellence is also recognized; and when a citizen is in any way distinguished, he is preferred to the public service, not as a matter of privilege, but as the reward of merit.
>
> We have not forgotten to provide for our weary spirits many relaxations from toil; we have regular games and sacrifices throughout the year; at home the style of our life is refined; and the delight which we daily feel in these things helps to banish melancholy.
>
> Our city is thrown open to the world, and we never expel a foreigner or prevent him from seeing or learning anything of which the secret if revealed to an enemy might profit him. We rely not upon management or trickery, but upon our own hearts and hands. We prefer to meet danger with a light heart but without laborious training, and with a courage which is gained by habit and not enforced by law.
>
> We are lovers of the beautiful, yet with economy, and we cultivate the mind without loss of manliness. Wealth we employ, not for talk and ostentation, but when there is a real use for it.
>
> I say that Athens is the school of Hellas, and that the individual Athenian in his own person seems to have the power of adapting himself to the most varied forms of action with the utmost versatility and grace.[78]

To this day there are persons who believe with Pericles that the Athenian polis evoked the richness of the human personality and provided it with an internal coherence that has never been matched before or since. However this may be, it is most certainly true that in the ancient polis, traits that tend ever to characterize personality in the city were brought to a kind of perfection.

The Knight

The cities of the world have never managed to maintain themselves for long as independent communities. Either they have set themselves on an imperialistic course or have been subject to conquest from the outside. Moreover, the empires which arose and coordinated the ancient cities as administrative units into a comprehensive political structure destroyed the autonomy of the cities, leaving them without a durable internal structure of a compensatory external substitute. In all cases the ancient empires collapsed, to be replaced by subsistence economies and, at times, systems of control of a feudal type. The key role in feudal society was occupied by the knight.

The dominant class, the nobles, of the Western Middle Ages was above all a landed class in that its members derived their revenues primarily from control of the soil. However, where possible they also collected tolls, market fees, and fines on local trade. Some of the seignorial families that rose to dominate Western feudalism were descended from adventurers, from men-at-arms who had received a share of the chief's property and had become his enfeoffed vassals, and from rich peasants who evolved into landlords with a group of tenements.[79]

The noble was not only characterized by the possession of manors (and, of course, treasure in money and jewels), but by his profession as a warrior. He was a self-equipped knight who fought primarily from horseback. Though the knight might dismount during battle, he moved about on horseback. His offensive weapons were the lance, sword, and mace. For defense he wore a helmet and metal garment and carried a round or triangular metal shield. He was accompanied by the squire who looked after the horses and arranged changes of mounts. The squire also carried extra weapons. The knight was, at times, also accompanied by a lightly equipped fighting man (or men) known as the "serjeant." The knight had to be a rich man to supply his equipment and horses. He also had to be a man of leisure to engage in the life-long training in the use of his weapons. During the course of the Middle Ages the cost of equipment rose. In the tenth century, when the stirrup was invented, the short spear of former days was replaced by the heavy lance. Shirts of chain mail also became more usual, replacing the more inflexible forms of armor.

"Pride," Bloch observes, "is one of the essential ingredients of all class-consciousness. That of the 'nobles' of the feudal era was, above all, the pride of the warrior. Moreover, fighting was for them not merely an occasional duty to be performed for the sake of their lord, or king, or family. It represented much more—their whole purpose in life."[80] The place of warfare in the psychology of the knight is revealed in the verve, the accuracy of observation and spontaneity (in contrast to the usual medieval stereotyped conventionality) of a passage on feudal warfare of a twelfth-century troubador, possibly the petty nobleman from Perigord, Bertrand de Born. He dreams of spring with its forests and meadows in new leaf and grass, of tents, of pavilions, of fields of knights on horseback drawn up in battle array, of men at arms, of castles besieged, of stockades overwhelmed.

> Maces, swords, helms of different hues, shields that will be riven and shattered as soon as the fight begins; and many vassals struck down together; and the horses of the dead and the wounded roving at random. And when battle is joined, let all men of good lineage think of naught but the breaking of heads and arms; for it is better to die than to be vanquished and live. I tell you, I find no such savour in food, or in wine, or in sleep, as in hearing the shout "On! On!" from both sides, and the neighing of steeds that have lost their riders, and the cries of "Help! Help!"; in seeing men great and small go down on the grass beyond the fosses; in seeing at last the dead, with the pennoned stumps of lances still in their sides.[81]

Fighting was a source of profit as well as a legal obligation and, at times, a pleasure. It was the nobleman's chief industry. The ransom of prisoners was the general practice. Merchants were routinely robbed on the highways. Peasant villages were pillaged, and sheep, cheese, and chickens were stolen from pens and farmsteads. Heavy wagons followed the armies for the purpose of collecting the spoils of war.

At home the knight defended himself and his possessions behind a series of ditches and stockades against the same sort of pillage he practiced on his own adventures. He also protected his own peasants and the craftsmen who managed and worked his estate. He rarely seems to have bothered with the management of it himself. The knight's amusements included hunting, which was, however, more than mere sport. Kings, princes, and lords monopolized the pursuit of game and reserved areas for hunting. Greyhounds were used in the chase, and various types of hawks and falcons were trained for hunting birds and small game. Among his more serious activities at home was the knight's exercise of jurisdiction over his tenants (which was also a source of fees) and participation in the judicial duties of his class.

The noble's marriage was an ordinary business transaction that often had little to do with his sex life. The castles of the nobility swarmed with bastards. When not attending to various administrative and legal duties or to hunting and hawking, the noble and his cohorts spent their time eating, drinking, and whoring.

From the second half of the eleventh century the texts increasingly mention ceremonies for the introduction to knighthood. An interpenetration was occurring of old Germanic initiation ceremonies and religious ceremonies. The initiation (dubbing) of the knighthood was being supplied with a religious interpretation. During the same period relations between members of the knightly class were being sublimated by a code of honorable conduct between knights. Conduct in the castle was being refined, and the status of the lady was undergoing enhancement. Accompanying the emergence of the code of etiquette of chivalry, the ancient war games going back to pagan times were elaborated into tournaments of considerable pageantry. In all ages imitations of battle (war games) have provided a training ground for the soldier. The feudal age developed its war games into a type of mock battle at which prizes were offered. Participation in tournaments was restricted to mounted combatants equipped with knightly arms. They came to supply the most exciting of all forms of feudal amusement. Tournaments were usually held on the occasion of great courts held by kings and barons. Knightly virtuosos roamed the medieval world from tournament to tournament somewhat in the manner of cowboys of the West who follow the rodeo circuit to engage in the prize competitions. Poor knights interested in wealth and great lords interested in adventure and honors often participated together. Wounds were frequent, and fatalities not unusual. The victor frequently took possession of the equipment, horses, often even of the person of the vanquished, releasing him only for ransom.

At the age of seven or eight the boy of an aristocratic household was sent to the court of a vassal's lord or to the household of some distinguished relative. He was classed as a page and assigned various tasks around the castle from running errands for the ladies to assisting the knights with their horses and gear. At the age of fourteen he became a squire and was attached to an individual knight whom he accompanied and assisted. He carried the knight's extra armor and arms, led his extra horse, laced on his defensive equipment, rescued the knight when he was wounded, and took charge of his prisoners. The squire gradually learned the brutal business of war.

The ideal personality of the knight reflected his training and obligations. From childhood through his long apprenticeship he was continuously in association with warriors and in training for knightly combat. The dimensions of his worth fell on a scale from intrepidity in battle to unquestioning loyalty to his lord. He admired a powerful physique and skill in the use of weapons. His life was spent in association with horses, armor, and in the company of other knights. His deportment in the tournaments and in war contexts with other knights was modified by the code of chivalry, but outside such contexts he was capable of uninhibited brutality. While he dared not incur the slightest suspicion of cowardice or treachery in combat with other knights, while he disdained tricks and would not strike an unarmed foe, while he brooked no insult and did not hesitate to plunge his family into bloody feuds in matters of honor, such "chivalrous" behavior was coexistent with a life resting on war, rapine, the pillage of churches, and the slaughter of peasants. Women were no more than a valuable commodity and were often brutally beaten. In the later Middle Ages some softening of the treatment of women of noble derivation was under way.

The National

In the Western city a new community arose that increasingly eclipsed the countryside. These cities sustained personality types which eclipsed the various rural types. Meanwhile, the nation-state was to complete the decay of the feudal countryside that began with the rise of the city and to reduce the cities to subunits of the emerging national complexes. The contemporary nation, in short, arose at the expense of both the city and the feudal countryside. As national institutions have developed, they have increasingly standardized behavior across the lines of the rural and urban forms. Accompanying such new processes of behavioral standardization a distinctive type, the national, has emerged.

English National Character: Geoffrey Gorer has sought to demonstrate the role of national institutions in the modification of character.[82] Though generalizations about national character are frequently phrased in terms drawn from psychiatry or psychology or psychoanalysis, Gorer hypothesized that "the national character of a society may be modified or transformed over a given period through the selection of the personnel for institutions that are in constant contact with the mass of the population and in a somewhat superordinate position, in a position of some authority."[83] Specifically, Gorer believes that such was the effect of the English metropolitan police.

The English metropolitan police was created by the Metropolitan Police Act of Sir Robert Peel in 1829. The force is directly responsible to the Home Secretary, to the centralized government in contrast to all other police who are controlled by local authorities. At the time of its establishment, the metropolitan police was novel in that it was a force established to prevent crime and violence and to maintain public order rather than to apprehend criminals. It also was given high visibility with a distinctive uniform. It was put on continuous (twenty-four-hour) duty, constituting it as an omnipresent symbol. It was armed only with a truncheon. Every complaint made against the force was publicly investigated. It was never organized in barracks or treated in any way as a paramilitary formation. Recruitment to its ranks was entirely on the basis of merit rather than on previous employment, on patronage, on special skill or special education. Over the years the English metropolitan police has been recruited from all levels of the population—from former butchers, bakers, shoemakers, tailors, laborers, servants, carpenters, bricklayers, turners, blacksmiths, shopkeepers, mechanics, sailors, and so on. Its composition, in fact, reflects the great mass of the population. Increasing industrialization and urbanization have been reflected in the composition of the police which has shown a decline of former agricultural laborers and a rise in the proportion of recruits from urban and industrial trades. The only conditions for selection are by minimum and maximum age limits, no less than a stated height, good character, mental and physical fitness, and sufficient education for police duty.

From the time of its establishment, the emphasis of the British police has been on the preservation of peace and the prevention of crime and violence rather than on the apprehension of criminals. The prevention of aggression and the preservation of peace by a uniformed group of powerful men, demonstrating self-restraint, was a novelty in English experience at the time. Members of the armed forces had proverbially been licentious and lawless or the arrogant liveried servants of the rich and mighty. But this police force was law-abiding and even part of the general public when not in uniform. Its actions soon transformed the image of the wearer of a uniform from that of the symbol of oppressor and exploiter.

Of particular interest has been the capacity of the English Metropolitan police to recruit a stable element from all levels of the population. The basis of its appeal as an occupation has been its steady pay (which is not subject to the caprice of trade and industry), a reasonable pension at a comparatively early age, and lack of special recruitment requirements. The steady rise of its public standing is attributable to the rigid observance in its recruitment policies of a number of guiding principles: selection of the best men available, the preservation of the civilian character of the force, recruitment from the population at large, from a wide variety of occupations, and maintenance of high standards of discipline, integrity, and *esprit de corps.*

In 1951 a sample of 11,000 Englishmen and women from all walks of life filled out a detailed questionnaire on the metropolitan police. A total of 73 percent were overwhelmingly appreciative of the police; a mere 5 percent were genuinely hostile to it. The level of appreciation varied from 80 percent very favorable in the upper middle class to 65 percent very favorable in the lower working class.

Gorer maintains that in the past century the English policeman has not only been an object of respect for his fellow citizens but an actual "model of the ideal male character, self-controlled, possessing more strength than he has ever to call into use except in the gravest emergency, fair and impartial, serving the abstractions of Peace and Justice rather than any personal allegiance of sectional advantage."[84] Gorer believes that as the bulk of the population has come to incorporate the policeman or policewoman into its personal image as an ideal, it has become increasingly self-policing. One respondent stated: "I believe the police stand for all we English are, may be at first appearances slow perhaps, but reliable, stout and kindly. I have the greatest admiration for our police force and I am proud they are renowned abroad."[85]

Japanese National Character: A role comparable to that of the English metropolitan police in forming national character in England is attributed by Haring to police coercion in Japan.[86]

During World War II, in order to plan effective hostilities against the Japanese and to effect a just peace, agencies of the United States government assembled a team of social scientists to sift the evidence and describe Japan's national character. Hundreds of Japanese immigrants, prisoners of war, and Nisei who had attended school in Japan were interviewed, tested, and persuaded to write autobiographies. Americans who had lived in Japan were interviewed. Japanese motion pictures were analyzed to determine their forms of personality appeal. Books about Japan were examined, and translations of Japanese literary works, histories, popular magazines, political pamphlets, and school books were analyzed.

Among the traits of Japanese personal character inferred from these sources were: (1) that psychologically and culturally the Japanese are unusually homogeneous, thinking and acting alike to a much greater extent than Occidentals; (2) that the Japanese conform to numberless exact rules of conduct and are bewildered when required to act on their own without rules; (3) that the major sanctions of conformity to Japanese codes are ridicule and shame (when an individual accepts responsibility for something that has gone wrong, he commits suicide; ceremonial suicide is the sole recourse of an individual who causes his group to "lose face"); (4) that the Japanese are extremely polite (politeness is conceived as adherence to a code that prescribes correct treatment of others in order to maintain one's own "face" and self-esteem); (5) Japanese families and society are rigid hierarchies and individuals must ascertain their precise status in every social situation lest a blunder lead to the treatment of a superior as an inferior or vice versa; (6) veneration of family ancestors and of the emperor flows from the constant awareness of the infinite blessings received from these sources; (7) pleasures of the flesh while not sinful are subordinate to the major goals of life; (8) *makoto* or utter devotion to the codes of conduct is one of the highest of virtues.

Some students have seen this array of character traits as adding up to a compulsive personality which, in turn, is traced to early childhood training in Japan. However, Haring argues that this array of traits can be traced to the influence of a series of dictators who consolidated Japan in their hands in the late sixteenth century and who kept the nation under rigid police discipline for three centuries. The technique employed by the Tokugawa regime for holding the nation in subjection was based on the strict division of the population into social classes and most detailed regulation of the behavior of each. "Houses, dress, food, and etiquette were prescribed for each class by incredibly detailed sumptuary laws."[87] The highest class, the *daimyo*, was compelled to reside at the capital in alternate years, lest they foment rebellion on their fiefs. Loyalty to the overlord was the supreme virtue. In service of this ideal retainers sacrificed wife, children, friends, possessions, and life itself. Omnipresent espionage kept everyone suspicious of his very household. When all classes are subject to such careful control, they will understandably grow restive. Some twelve hundred peasant rebellions occurred during the Tokugawa era. Their leaders were invariably executed, and at times the feudal lords were punished for having permitted the rebellion in the first place.

In contemporary Japan from 1868 to 1945 the ancient discipline was modified and redirected in the interests of imperialistic militarism. Samurai no longer strutted with their two swords, proud of their right to decapitate lesser folk, but in their place an efficient centralized police consolidated the police lore of the West and employed it effectively to implement state plans. Haring reports that in 1925, when he had become a confidant of a high Japanese police officer in Tokyo, on one occasion the official demonstrated the efficiency of the police system by revealing the mass of information that had been accumulated on Haring himself. Every trip, every friend visited, every letter sent or received, was recorded. His dossier even included a detailed account of Haring's activities while in the United States from 1922 to 1924. This accumulation of information did not reflect any suspicion of Haring. All foreigners were kept under the same surveillance as the home population.

Haring is most skeptical of the notion occasionally advanced that pre-war national character in Japan is to be attributed to its child training. "All the features of the alleged 'compulsive personality' of the Japanese are logical fruits of the police state. An explanation centered in diapers is suspect if it neglects three centuries of fear-inspired discipline."[88] And Haring concluded that "in the formation of national character, police coercion shapes and outweighs infant training."

Summary

The great unitary systems of thought, of which positivistic sociology was one, prohibited the study of social persons. However, with the rise of elementaristic sociological theories, around and following the turn of the century, this became untenable. However, by this time the theory of personality had largely been consolidated by the psychological sciences and the sociological theory of personality has only incompletely exploited the field.

The symbolic interactionists have gone farthest, both in developing the theory of social persons and in carrying out empirical studies of the affinities between personality formation and special social conditions. However, despite major beginnings by the symbolic interactionists, this area remains incompletely exploited. The rise of functionalism, its minimization of the comparative significance of the social person in the social order, and its preference for Freudian approaches to personality may in part account for this.

Despite occasional insightful studies of the affinities between particular roles and special social conditions and personality, the systematic study of personality and special social conditions remains to be done. Moreover, in the failure of sociologists to examine the area, other disciplines (psychology, psychiatry, and ethnology) have undertaken the study of the interrelations between community and personality. Evidence has been assembled primarily by these disciplines which strongly suggests that at least with regard to the major historical types of communities (tribes, peasant villages, cities, feudal manors, and nations) such affinities exist.

NOTES

1. Jacob Burckhardt, *The Civilization of the Renaissance in Italy*, trans. S. G. C. Middlemore (New York: Oxford University Press, 1945), p. 81.

2. Ibid., p. 87.

3. Ibid., p. 89.

4. Ibid., p. 93 ff.

5. René Descartes, *On Method*, in *Descartes Selections*, ed. Ralph M. Eaton (New York: Scribner's, 1927), p. 2.

6. Ibid., p. 29.

7. Lord Herbert of Cherbury, *De Veritate* (Bristol: J. W. Arrowsmith, 1937), pp. 291-300.

8. David Hume, *Selections*, ed. Charles W. Hendel, Jr. (New York: Scribner's, 1927), pp. 83-85.

9. Ibid., p. 90.

10. Ibid., pp. 90-91.

11. Ibid., p. 106.

12. Immanuel Kant, *Selections*, ed. Theodore Meyer Greene (New York: Scribner's, 1929), p. 76.

13. Ibid., p. 77.

14. Ibid.

15. Ibid., p. 268.

16. Ibid., p. 270.

17. Ibid., p. 279.

18. Ibid., p. 281.

19. Ibid., p. 309.

20. Ibid., p. 379.

21. Ibid., p. 382.

22. Auguste Comte, *The Positive Philosophy of Auguste Comte*, trans. Harriet Martineau (London: George Bell & Sons, 1896), vol. 2, p. 275.

23. Ibid., pp. 280-81.

24. Ibid., p. 281.

25. Ibid., p. 282.
26. Ibid., p. 284.
27. Ibid., p. 289.
28. Auguste Comte, *System of Positive Polity*, trans. Harriet Martineau (London: Longmans, Green, 1877), vol. 4, pp. 30-31.
29. William Wallace, *Prolegomena to the Study of Hegel's Philosophy* (Oxford: Clarendon Press, 1931), p. 184.
30. Ibid., p. 186.
31. Ibid., p. 188.
32. Ibid., p. 189.
33. Ibid., p. 192.
34. Ibid., p. 194.
35. Ibid.
36. Georg Wilhelm Freidrich Hegel, *The Philosophy of History*, trans. J. Sibree (New York: Wiley, 1944), p. 14.
37. Ibid., p. 25.
38. Ibid., p. 26.
39. Ibid., p. 29.
40. Ibid., p. 31.
41. Arthur Schopenhauer, *The World as Will and Idea*, trans. R. B. Haldane and J. Kemp (Garden City, N.Y.: Doubleday, 1961), p. 126.
42. Ibid., p. 129.
43. Arthur Schopenhauer, *Complete Essays of Schopenhauer*, trans. T. Bailey Saunders (New York: Wiley, 1942), p. 15.
44. Ibid., p. 18.
45. Ibid., p. 32.
46. Ibid., p. 34.
47. *The Journals of Kierkegaard*, trans. Alexander Dru (New York: Harper & Bros., 1959), p. 187.
48. Ibid., p. 219.
49. Eric Russell Bentley, *A Century of Hero Worship* (New York: J. B. Lippincott, 1944), p. 257.
50. *The Philosophy of Nietzsche*, trans. Clifton Fadiman (New York: The Modern Library, n.d.), pp. 951 ff.
51. Georg Simmel, *The Sociology of Georg Simmel*, trans. Kurt H. Wolff (Glencoe, Ill.: The Free Press, 1950), p. 58.
52. Ibid., p. 59.
53. Ibid., p. 32.
54. Ibid., p. 34.
55. Ibid., pp. 36-37.
56. Ibid., p. 37.
57. Ibid., p. 61.
58. William James, *The Principles of Psychology* (New York: Henry Holt, 1890), vol. I, p. 291 ff.

59. Charles Horton Cooley, *Human Nature and the Social Order* (New York: Scribner's, 1922), p. 152.

60. George Herbert Mead, *Mind, Self, and Society* (Chicago: The University of Chicago Press, 1934).

61. William I. Thomas and Florian Znaniecki, *The Polish Peasant in Europe and America* (Boston: Gorham Press, 1919), vol. III, p. 18 ff.

62. Ibid., p. 37.

63. These materials are drawn from Jeanette Mirsky's "The Eskimo of Greenland," in *Cooperation and Competition among Primitive Peoples*, ed. Margaret Mead (Boston: The Beacon Press, 1961), pp. 51-86.

64. Ibid., p. 75.

65. See Frances W. Underwood and Irma Honigmann, "A Comparison of Socialization and Personality in Two Simple Societies," in *Personal Character and Cultural Milieu*, 3rd ed., ed. Douglas G. Haring (Syracuse, N.Y.: Syracuse University Press, 1956), pp. 745-65.

66. Ibid., p. 753.

67. Ibid., p. 752.

68. Abram Kardiner, *The Psychological Frontiers of Society* (New York: Columbia University Press, 1945), p. 47f. Kardiner's empirical material was drawn from information supplied by Ralph Linton.

69. Ibid., p. 87.

70. Ibid., p. 95.

71. Accounts of Zuni appear in Ruth Benedict, *Patterns of Culture* (Boston: Houghton Mifflin, 1961), pp. 57-129, and Irving Goldman, "The Zuni Indians of New Mexico," in *Cooperation and Competition*, ed. Margaret Mead (Boston: Beacon Press, 1961), pp. 313-53.

72. Goldman, in *Cooperation and Competition*, ed. Margaret Mead, p. 320.

73. Ruth Bunzel, "Introduction to Zuni Ceremonialism," *47th Annual Report: Bureau of American Ethnology* (Washington, D.C.: Government Printing Office, 1932), p. 480.

74. Jane Belo, "The Balinese Temper," in *Character and Personality*, vol. 4, *Journal of Personality*, 1935, pp. 120-46. Reprinted in *Personal Character and Cultural Milieu*, ed. Haring, pp. 157-79.

75. Ibid., p. 178.

76. H. D. F. Kitto, *The Greeks* (Harmondsworth, Middlesex: Penguin Books, 1951), p. 169 ff.

77. Ibid., p. 187.

78. Thucydides, *The Peloponnesian War*, in *The Great Historians*, ed. Francis R. B. Godolphin (New York: Random House, 1942), pp. 648-50.

79. This discussion primarily follows Marc Bloch, *Feudal Society*, trans. L. A. Manyon (Chicago: The University of Chicago Press, 1961), p. 288 ff.

80. Ibid., p. 292.

81. Quoted by Bloch, ibid., p. 293.

82. Geoffrey Gorer, "Modification of National Character: the Role of the Police in England," *The Journal of Social Issues*, vol. 11, no. 2 (1955):24-32. Reprinted in *Personal Character and Cultural Milieu*, ed. Haring, pp. 329-39.

83. Ibid., p. 330.

84. Ibid., p. 337.

85. Ibid.

86. Douglas G. Haring, "Comment on Japanese Personal Character: Pre-War," in *Blood on the Rising Sun* (Philadelphia: Macrae Smith Co., 1943), p. 22 ff. Reprinted in *Personal Character and Cultural Milieu,* ed. Haring, pp. 424-45.

87. Ibid., pp. 429-30.

88. Ibid., p. 432.

SELECTED BIBLIOGRAPHY

Bentley, Eric Russel. *A Century of Hero Worship.* New York: J. B. Lippincott, 1944.

Cooley, Charles Horton. *Human Nature and the Social Order.* New York: Scribner's, 1922.

Comte, Auguste. *System of Positive Polity.* Translated by Harriet Martineau. London: Longmans, Green, 1877.

Hegel, Georg Wilhelm. *The Philosophy of History.* Translated by J. Sibree. New York: Wiley, 1944.

James, William. *The Principles of Psychology.* New York: Henry Holt, 1890.

Mead, George Herbert. *Mind, Self, and Society.* Chicago: The University of Chicago Press, 1934.

Nietzsche, Frederich. *The Philosophy of Nietzsche.* Translated by Clifton Fadiman. New York: Modern Library, n.d.

Schopenhauer, Arthur. *Complete Essays of Schopenhauer.* Translated by T. Bailey Saunders. New York: Wiley, 1942.

Simmel, Georg. *The Sociology of Georg Simmel.* Translated by Kurt H. Wolff. Glencoe, Ill.: The Free Press, 1950.

Thomas, W. I., and Znaniecki, Florian. *The Polish Peasant in Europe and America.* Boston: Gorham Press, 1919.

CHAPTER 4

Social Structure

Though social structure (or social organization, or social statics) is one of the oldest areas in sociology, it does not enjoy very precise definition. Writing on "Social Structure" in sociology's sister discipline in anthropology, Claude Levi-Strauss urged that it applied to a wide imprecisely defined group of problems;[1] and Kroeber observed that the term had become fashionable in anthropology and was applied indiscriminately because of its pleasant connotation.

> Of course a typical personality can be viewed as having a structure. But so can a physiology, any organism, all societies and all cultures, crystals, machines—in fact everything which is not wholly amorphous has a structure. So what "structure" adds to the meaning of our phrase seems to be nothing, except to provoke a degree of pleasant puzzlement.[2]

Kroeber's observations apply equally well to the use of "social structure" by sociologists.

The ambiguities in the theory of empirical studies of social structure can be traced in part to three major sources: unresolved theoretical differences between holistic and elementaristic approaches to social life, the rapid growth of specialization between and within the social sciences, and unresolved tensions between popular sociology (which retains the vaguely defined task of supplying a mode of deportment appropriate to contemporary men) and professional sociology dedicated to the task of objective scientific discipline.

Holistic Approaches to Social Structure

Social phenomena, according to Comte, are natural and hence subject to laws which admit of rational investigation. The investigation of social phenomena divides into two basic divisions: the study of statics and the study of dynamics.

> The philosophical principle of the science being that social phenomena are subject to natural laws, admitting of rational prevision, we have to ascertain what is the precise subject, and what the peculiar character of those laws. The distinction between the Statical and Dynamical conditions of the subject must be extended to social science.[3]

In the inorganic sciences Comte argues that the proper approach consists of analysis of the elements constituting the whole. However,

> The reverse method is necessary in the study of Man and of Society; Man and Society as a whole being better known to us, and more accessible subjects of study, than the parts which constitute them.[4]

Not only did Comte believe that one must proceed from the whole to the parts, but one must proceed on the assumption of the primacy of the whole in all matters of consensus. "It is," he argued, "no easy matter to study social phenomena in the only right way—viewing each element in the light of the whole system."[5] We must "insist on the principle which lies at the heart of every scheme of social organization,—the necessary participation of the collective political *régime* in the universal consensus of the social body. The scientific principle of the relation between the political and the social condition is simply this,—that there must always be a spontaneous harmony between the whole and the parts of the social system, the elements of which must inevitably be, sooner or later, combined in a mode entirely conformable to their nature."[6] The essence of social study, Comte urged, consists in the demonstration of the interrelation of different parts of the social system rather than treating them as if they had an independent existence apart from the whole.

Social statics in Comte's view is concerned with three classes of facts: the individual, the family, and society, "the last comprehending, in a scientific sense, the whole of the human species, and chiefly, the whole of the white race."[7] The notion that society originated in utilitarian considerations, as assumed by social contract theorists in the eighteenth century, was rejected by Comte as a metaphysical fantasy. The phrenological theories of Gall were taken as evidence for the origin of society in man's instinctive social tendencies. However, even apart from the reflections of Gall, Comte argues that the preponderance of man's affective over his intellectual faculties and his natural laziness are evidence for the distinctive basis of society. These, he believed, prove that man would have entered into society only if it were in his nature to do so. His perception of the utility of society only came later.

Though social statics opens with an examination of the individual, he is not to be considered a unit of society. "As every system must be composed of elements of the same nature with itself, the scientific spirit forbids us to regard society as composed of individuals. The true social unit is certainly the family."[8] The family rests on the sex impulse which is simultaneously satisfied and disciplined by the family. It is structured by the natural surbordination of women, in whom affective impulses predominate over the intellectual and who, Conte believed, have no talent for rationality and government. From the family there is a somewhat uneven transition to mankind. The "whole human race might be conceived of as the gradual development of a single family, if local diversities did not forbid such a supposition."[9]

Just as the family rests on the natural inequality of men and women, so other institutions rest on the natural inequalities of individuals. "The main cause of the superiority of the social to the individual organism is, according to an established law, the more marked specialty of the various functions fulfilled by organs more and more distinct, but interconnected; so that unity of aim is more and more combined with diversity of means. . . . This reconciliation of the individuality of labour with co-operation of endeavours, which becomes more remarkable as society grows more complex and extended, constitutes the radical character of human operations when we rise from the domestic to the social point of view."[10]

The natural inequalities of individuals inclines some to develop their capacities for moral discrimination and for command. Others are equally disposed toward subordination. "Thus do individual dispositions show themselves to be in harmony with the course of social relations as a whole, in teaching us that political subordination is as inevitable, generally speaking, as it is indispensible. And this completes the elementary delineation of Social Statics."[11]

Herbert Spencer

Herbert Spencer may illustrate the manner in which the holistic position formulated by Comte was expanded. In his *Principles of Sociology* Spencer made quite clear his awareness of the alternative realistic and nominalistic approaches to the nature of society. The key question, he observed, was whether society is to be viewed as an entity.

> It may be said that a society is but a collective name for a number of individuals. Carrying the controversy between nominalism and realism into another sphere, a nominalist might affirm that just as there exist only the members of a species, while the species considered apart from them has no existence, so the units of a society alone exist, while the existence of the society is but verbal.[12]

After the preliminary consideration, Spencer unhesitatingly cast his vote for the realistic position, treating society as an entity, "because, though formed of discrete units, a certain concreteness in the aggregate of them is implied by the general persistence of the arrangements among them throughout the area occupied."[13]

The most convenient way, according to Spencer, to conceive the character of society as an entity is in terms of the organic system. Of the numerous parallels that Spencer draws between society and organism are the increase in structure (with growth) and the differentiation of function which societies and organisms are said to hold in common.

> It is . . . a character of social bodies, as of living bodies, that while they increase in size they increase in structure . . . Progressive

differentiation of structures is accompanied by progressive differentiation of functions.[14]

Moreover, the social, like the individual, organism is said to be held together by three great systems of organs.

> The parts carrying on alimentation in a living body and the parts carrying on productive industries in the body politic, constitute, in either case a sustaining system: sustentation is the office they have in common. The distributing system in the social organism, as in the individual organism, has its development determined by the necessities of transfer among inter-dependent parts. While the alimentary system of animals and the industrial systems of societies are developed into fitness for dealing with the substances, organic and inorganic, used for sustentation, the regulating and expending systems (nerve-motor in the one, and governmental-military in the other) are developed into fitness for dealing with surrounding organisms, individual or social—other animals to be caught or escaped from, hostile societies to be conquered or resisted. In both cases that organization which fits the aggregate for acting as a whole in conflict with other aggregates, indirectly results from the carrying on of conflicts with other aggregates.[15]

The specific organs of society, Spencer urges, are institutions. He classified institutions into domestic, ceremonial, economic, professional, political, and ecclesiastical.

Emile Durkheim

Despite Spencer's self-conscious identification of his approach to society with philosophical realism and his systematic employment of organismic analogies, Durkheim was of the opinion that Spencer was at bottom nominalistic in inclination.

> In spite of the biological analogies upon which he lays stress, Spencer does not see a reality *sui generis* in society, which exists by itself and by virtue of specific and necessary causes, and which, consequently, confound themselves with man's own nature, and to which he is held to adapt himself in order to live, just as to his physical environment—but he sees it as an arrangement instituted by individuals to extend individual life in length and breadth.[16]

Durkheim's approach to social organization is emphatically realistic; society is, he insists, a reality and *sui generis*. There is, to be sure, nothing in social life which is not in the individual consciousness. However, "society does not find the bases on which it rests fully laid out in consciences; it puts them there itself."[17] Durkheim takes it as axiomatic: "If there is one rule of conduct which is incontestable, it is that which orders us to realize in ourselves the essential traits of the collective type."[18] The collective type is described as follows:

> The totality of beliefs and sentiments common to average citizens of the same society forms a determinate system which has its own life; one may call it the *collective* or *common conscience.* No doubt, it has not a specific organ as a substratum; it is, by definition, diffuse in every reach of society. Nevertheless, it has specific characteristics which make it a distinct reality. It is, in effect, independent of the particular conditions in which individuals are placed; they pass on, and it remains.[19]

Law and morality are the totality of ties that bind individuals to society. Society is a necessary precondition of the moral world.[20]

Durkheim's basic theses concerning the evolution of society, on the changing foundations of social solidarity, on the character of the moral and legal ties binding the collective conscience into a unity, are well known. In primitive societies, Durkheim argued, the collective conscience is manifested in a condition of mechanical solidarity. All individuals are more or less alike, being bound together by this very likeness "mechanically" as if by an outside force. Under such circumstances anything that offends the collective conscience is a crime calling forth violent reactions (punishment) to avenge the collective conscience. However, with the growth of material and moral density of the human group (the increase in population and an intensified rate of interaction as persons struggle to survive), a division of labor becomes necessary. The moral obligation of individuals is not to remain like everyone else, but to specialize while becoming interdependent on the basis of interindividual differences. The new type of solidarity is "organic." Violations of the ongoing order now are reacted to, not so much by acts of violence to avenge an outraged collective conscience, as by acts of restitution intended to restore equilibrium between interdependent parts. Hence Durkheim maintained that a shift in the proportionate significance of criminal and civil law can be taken as evidence of evolution from a society based on mechanical to one based on organic solidarity.

Far from treating society as a product of individuality, Durkheim treats individuality as a social product. The changes which accompany the transformation in society from a mechanically to an organically solidary type have a direct effect on the individuals involved. They are made more free of influence of the biological organism and brought under social influence.

> In man . . . and particularly in higher societies, social causes substitute themselves for organic causes. The organism is spiritualized. The individual is transformed in accordance with this change in dependence. Since this activity which calls forth the special action of social causes cannot be fixed in the organism, a new life, also *sui generis*, is superimposed upon that of the body. Freer, more complex, more independent of the organisms which support it, its distinguishing characteristics become ever more apparent as it progresses and becomes solid.[21]

In a society resting on mechanical solidarity, the common life of all the members of the group is identical in each. As societies become large and interaction becomes more intense, a psychic life of a new differentiated sort appears. Individual differences, at first lost in the mass of social likeness, become conspicuous and multiply.

From Comte, Spencer, and Durkheim the realistic approach was transmitted on to contemporary sociology. A single major contemporary theorist may illustrate its current status.

Talcott Parsons

To Talcott Parsons the primary task of sociology consists in the analysis of social systems. A social system is conceived as a plurality of actors interacting with one another in a physical environment in the attempt to maximize their gratifications. Their relations to one another and the situation are implemented by their common culture.[22] To Talcott Parsons analysis properly proceeds from the whole of society conceived as a social system not dependent on some higher one and capable of persisting out of its own resources.[23] All other systems, though constituted in essentially the same manner as a society, are partial systems.

While the micro units of social systems, according to Parsons, are social actions,[24] the macro units are status-role bundles (positions in a structure of relations and what is done in these positions). "It should be made quite clear," Parsons insists, "that statuses and roles, or the status-role bundle, are not in general attributes of the actor, but are *units* of the social system . . . the status-role is analogous to the particle in mechanics."[25] Institutions are complexes of role integrates.[26] In the social system as a whole institutions fall into three general categories: relational (patterning relationships), regulative (ordering the pursuit of interests), and cultural (ordering the expressive symbols and the like).[27]

Between Parsons' formulation in *The Social System* in 1951 and his "Outline of the Social System" ten years later (1961), a considerable formalization of ideas was carried through. In the latter context society is visualized as a giant system composed of four major social subsystems: pattern-maintenance is conceived as the core of the social system with no source other than the social system itself and no destiny apart from it. The other three subsystems are conceived as receiving influences from other systems and making an output of them. Integration receives impulses from and has an output to the organism; goal-attainment receives impulses from and has an output to personality; adaptation has an input from and output to the cultural system.

Society in this analysis is conceived on the model of a giant from the central plant, the executive branch of which is occupied with pattern maintenance. The biological organism, personality, and culture are like three major subbranches.

Elementaristic Approaches to Social Structure

The holists visualized social structure in organismic terms. Institutions were the fundamental organs of society. Individuals were either thrust aside as irrelevant or treated incidentally as raw materials of social systems. The elementarists rejected these estimates of the nature and comparative significance of these phenomena. A few examples may serve to epitomize the contrasts.

Georg Simmel

If we look at human life closely and in detail, Simmel observed, each individual is seen with his peculiarities and uniqueness. If we increase the distance, "society" with its own forms and colors comes into view. Hence Simmel urges that though human existence is real only in individuals, this does not mean that society is not in some sense also real. However, society is never anything other than a way pluralities may act.

> The large systems and the super-individual organizations that customarily come to mind when we think of society, are nothing

but immediate interactions that occur among men constantly, every minute, but that have become crystalized as permanent fields, as autonomous phenomena. As they crystalize, they attain their own existence and their own laws, and may even confront or oppose spontaneous interaction itself. At the same time, society, as its life is constantly being realized, always signifies that individuals are connected by mutual influence and determination. It is, hence, something functional, something individuals do and suffer. To be true to this fundamental character of it, one should properly speak, not of society, but of sociation. Society merely is the name for a number of individuals connected by interaction.[28]

In reducing society to one aspect of how individuals behave, Simmel radically alters the presumed character of the relation of individual to society from that of the holists. One may, to be sure, treat the group "as if it actually did have its own life, and laws, and other characteristics."[29] In the end this autonomy is only what individuals yield to it. A fundamental problem for social science is the difference between the characteristics of the group and those of individual existence, for somehow they seem to be quite distinct, even contrary. Individual actions appear "free"; group actions appear necessary as if determined by natural laws.

It is possible, Simmel believed, to separate in the individual himself the various properties by which he forms groups from those which constitute his private nature. The properties out of which groups are formed can only consist of primitive elements which are shared by all individuals. They lack finesse and intellectuality. The moment traits become refined and differentiated they cease being properties of all and become individualized. Hence, Simmel reverses Durkheim's formula. Durkheim had proposed to derive all forms of higher individuality from the collective; Simmel derives the collective from the lowest common denominators of individuals. All that is singular, refined, and rare sets the individual apart from the mass.

As soon as the individual is considered in his entirety, he appears to possess much higher qualities than those he contributes to the collective unit. This situation has found its classical formulation in Schiller: "Seen singly, everybody is passably intelligent and reasonable; but united into a body, they are blockheads." . . . Solon is supposed to have said that each of his Athenians is a shrewd fox; but that if assembled on the Pnyx, they amount to a herd of sheep. . . . The difference between the individual and collective levels accounts for the fact that the necessity to oblige the masses, or even habitually to expose oneself to them, easily corrupts the character. It pulls the individual away from his individuality and down to a level with all and sundry.[30]

The individual, Simmel insisted, is the anchorage of intelligence. The mass neither lies nor simulates, but at the same time it lacks all consciousness of responsibility. Whoever wishes to affect the mass succeeds by appeal to feelings rather than to theoretical argument, hence, the "level of a society" approximates that of "its lowest components, since it must be possible for all to participate in it with identical valuation and effectiveness."[31]

In accord with his reinterpretation of society as sociation and reversal of the holistic conception of the relation of individual to collective, Simmel swept aside all the usual concepts for dealing with social structure: institutions, organizations, even structure itself. Interaction arises for a variety of specific motives and interests of individuals: erotic, economic, religious, and the like. These form the content of social life. In the course of time various stable relationships or "forms" arise, facilitating the pursuit of interests. Once they prove their efficiency in implementing some shared interests of individuals, social arrangements are capable of being applied to most varied situations. The peculiarity of human social life was located by Simmel in the role of forms and epitomized by him in the phenomena of play.

> This complete turnover, from the determination of the forms by the materials of life to the determination of its materials by forms . . . is perhaps most extensively at work in . . . play.[32]

Actual life is characterized by many recurrent strategies (the hunt, gain by ruse, tests of strength, and so on). When these activities are lifted out of the flux of life to be enjoyed for the activity they organize apart from their serious implications, they acquire a new gaiety and symbolic significance. Play and art represent spheres once part of life which enjoy comparative autonomy. Sociability, Simmel thought, is the most general of all forms of sociation. It is the act of associating lifted out of the flux of life, and enjoyed as an autonomous form for its own sake. Sociability takes most varied forms in tact, in social games, in coquetry, in conversation, in etiquette. Sociability is, so to speak, the play form of sociation. Almost any activity from the whole range of life may appear under its guise to be enjoyed for its own sake apart from serious practical intent.

In place of the analysis of society into institutions, Simmel analyzes sociation into a variety of "forms" of which sociability is one of the most general and comprehensive. He never loses sight of the fact that concrete society, from his perspective, is the behavior of individuals even when he turns attention to the manner in which sociation is affected by various external characteristics such as smallness or largeness of numbers, the quantitative determination of group divisions, the outside regulation of groups, and the like.

Charles Horton Cooley

The approach of Cooley to the problems of self and society bears many parallels to that of Simmel. While Cooley used terminology made current by the holists, he gave its characteristic terms quite different significance. Superficially, it would seem that Cooley presupposed the existence of a group mind. "Mind is an organic whole made up of cooperating individualities, in somewhat the same way that the music of an orchestra is made up of divergent but related sounds."[33] However, it quickly becomes evident that Cooley reduces the self and society to the status of similarly constituted forms of individual behavior.

> Social consciousness, or awareness of society, is inseparable from self-consciousness, because we can hardly think of ourselves excepting with reference to a social group of some sort, or of the group except with reference to ourselves. The two things go together, and what we are really aware of is a more or less complex personal or social whole, of which now the particular, now the general, aspect is emphasized. . . . Self and society are twin-born, we know one as immediately as we know the other, and the notion of a separate and independent ego is an illusion.[34]

If after this one still has any illusion that there was any similarity between Cooley's theories and the concept of super-individual organismic entities, Cooley quickly dispels them. Whether one sees the individual or society, when one examines interhuman action, depends wholly on one's point of view and the direction of his attention. When attention is fixed on the individual, life is seen as a theatre of personal action, the actors of which are private will, responsibility, praise and blame, and the like. However, looked at in its total aspect, life appears under the forms of tendency, evolution, and law. The "larger mind" is what we think and feel and share with others.

> Both consciously and unconsciously the larger mind is continual-
> ly building itself up into wholes—fashions, traditions, institutions,
> tendencies, and the like—which spread and diversify like the
> branches of a tree, and so generate an ever higher and more varied
> structure of differentiated thought and symbol.[35]

In a manner reminiscent of Simmel's concept of play, society to
Cooley is a work of art wholly a manmade contrivance. However,
it is not a product of merely utilitarian purposes, but a total
expression of conscious and unconscious tendencies. "Social organization is nothing less than this variegation of life, taken in the
widest sense."[36] Any distinct and durable detail is a social type.

The context in which society and human nature were originally
simultaneously organized and expressed for Cooley was the primary group characterized by intimate face to face association and
cooperation. Primary groups (typified by the family, play group,
and neighborhood group) are the most fundamental of all forms of
social life and the nursery of human nature.

> Primary groups are primary in the sense that they give the
> individual his earliest and completest experience of social unity,
> and also in the sense that they do not change in the same degree
> as more elaborate relations, but form a comparatively permanent
> source out of which the latter are ever springing.[37]

All higher or more complex forms of society are dependent on
refinements of communication. Among the most significant persis-
tent groups larger than the family, in Cooley's view, are classes.
The two basic principles upon which classes are formed are inher-
itance (which, carried to extremes, leads to caste) and competition (which is the basis of open class systems). Institutions, for
Cooley, are established phases of the public mind.

> An institution is simply a definite and established phase of the
> public mind, not different in its ultimate nature from public
> opinion, though often seeming, on account of its permanence and
> the visible customs and symbols in which it is clothed, to have a
> somewhat distinct and independent existence.[38]

The state and the church with their ancient power, liturgy, build-
ings, and the like are, in the end, only products of human environment, the outcome of an organization of human thought which is
crystalized into enduring sentiments, beliefs, customs, and symbols. Language, government, religion, law, family systems, indus-

try, education, all exist in the individual largely as unconscious habits for realizing his needs. They are largely unconscious because they are common to the group, but the individual is always the cause and effect of the institution. In his conception of institutions as common, largely unconscious aspects of the experience of pluralities, Cooley approximates Simmel's notion of the relation of individual to group.

Max Weber

A quick review of those notions Max Weber advanced for the analysis of problems of social structure is of interest. Weber conceived of the organismic or functionalistic analysis as, at best, a provisional orientation.

> It is the method of the so-called "organic" school of sociology to attempt to understand social interaction by using as a point of departure the "whole" within which the individual acts. His action and behavior are then interpreted somewhat in the way that a physiologist would treat the role of an organ of the body in the "economy" of the organism; that is, from the point of view of the survival of the latter.... For purposes of sociological analysis two things can be said. First, this functional frame of reference is convenient for purposes of practical illustration and for provisional orientation. In these respects it is not only useful but indispensable. But at the same time if its cognitive value is overestimated and its concepts illegitimately "reified," it can be highly dangerous.[39]

For Weber human social events consisted always in the end of interaction which breaks down into specific social acts. Social acts, in turn, are identified by the subjective means attached to them by the actors. While interactions are not determined exclusively by the meanings attached to them by the actors, these meanings are taken by Weber to be the single most important causal component in such determination. However, Weber observes, actions are not always meaningful in the same manner, extent, or degree. Hence Weber suggested a basic typology of actions in terms of the degree to which action is rational (ordered in terms of the technical appropriateness and efficiency of the means to the ends) shading off into unthinking habitual or blindly emotional types. Weber's fascination with rational action seems to flow from his view that this type of action gives the individual maximum control over his fate. At the same time he avoided commitment to the dogma that human nature was rational.

Weber utilized the concept of "social relationship" as a first order of generalization concerning patterns of interaction. In a plurality, the action of any one may rest on the expectation of meaningful action on the part of others. The social relationship consists in the probability that in some meaningfully understandable sense a course of social action is probable. The power to abstract the pattern and react to its possibility is the essence of group life. Among various empirical uniformities in the patterns of actions one may distinguish usages (empirical uniformities), customs (uniformities resting on habit), fashions (usages with respect to some novelty), conventions (usages regarded as part of a legitimate order), and law (usages resting on the force of external sanctions).

Relations may be of a variety of types: conflicting, solidary, open or closed, representative and responsible. They may be formed into systems or orders. An order of social relations is legitimate so far as it is recognized by the actors as binding on themselves. This, however, does not necessarily mean that he in fact conforms to it. A thief, for example, recognizes the validity of the criminal law in that he acts surreptitiously, expecting to be punished if he is apprehended. Legitimate orders of social relations may arise from disinterested motives or from self-interest and may be ascribed by tradition, by affectual attitudes, or self-conscious establishment in a manner recognized as legal.

Weber's concepts of the various types of relations and of legitimate orders. thereof were, in turn, critical to his concept of the corporate group which represents relations ordered in a particular manner. The system of order of corporate groups may be administrative (governing the group as such) or regulative (governing other types). The types of organization (systems of continuous purposive activity) may be voluntary or compulsory. Such orders and organizations define relations of power, imperative control, and discipline. Imperatively coordinated groups are political so far as the order is carried out in a territory by application or the threat of force on the part of the administrative staff. An imperatively coordinated corporate group is hierocratic so far as its order rests on psychic coercion through the distribution and withholding of religious values. In the beginning, for Weber, is the individual and his actions. Relations are the abstract patterns of potentially recurrent action patterns. Groups are merely peculiar systems of relations. A behavioral approach to social structure is never abandoned.

Unresolved Problems Between
Holism-Elementarism

There was some tendency for the holists beginning their analysis with society as a whole to extend their analyses step by step down to various substructures until individual activities eventually began to come into focus. On the other hand, there was an evident tendency on the part of the elementarists beginning their analysis of interaction with the individual and his acts (or some of its components such as attitudes, beliefs, and the like) to bring ever more comprehensive interaction complexes under analysis. One could, thus, anticipate that some place along the respective courses the two approaches to social phenomena would cross.

However, the contrasting theoretical suppositions of the two positions were such that they never quite met—at least not in a theoretical sense. What the holists took as the self-evident starting point—the whole conceived as an effective agent—was to the elementarists a fiction; what the elementarists took as the primary cause of social events (the individual his acts, and its component attitudes and beliefs) was to the holists merely the raw material for the operations of the laws of social life which characterize society. Moreover, the holists were always more at home in the analysis of large-scale units of social life such as cultures, societies, and industrial organizations; the elementarists were generally more at home in the analysis of small-scale structures (Simmel's dyads and triads and Cooley's primary groups) than when analyzing large-scale organizations (Max Weber and some others were exceptions). In the course of the confrontation of the holists and elementarists (1) the extension of holistic suppositions to inter-human complexes less than the whole often brought them under dispute, and (2) increasing uncertainty about the status of the whole as an object of sociological study was manifest.

In the field of economic institutions in the twentieth century, a series of studies have been made which have either proceeded self-consciously out of holistic sociology or which have rested independently on assumptions which permitted their assimilation to the holistic position. These may serve to illustrate the extension to subunits of society of suppositions parallel to those the holists originally applied to the whole.

Before World War I a series of studies gradually took shape under the name of scientific management. Under the leadership of Frederick W. Taylor the studies intended to improve industrial efficiency by the application of scientific modes of study to the interrelation of men and machines.[40] Taylor and others who eventually joined the scientific management movement proposed various time and motion studies of the worker intended to establish the most efficient procedure for accomplishing most tasks; to develop incentive systems to encourage maximum work yields on the assumption that motives were capable of scientific manipulation; to procure the rigid subordination of the worker to the requirements of management, taken as supplying the goals of the organization. The concept of the industrial plant assumed by scientific management envisioned the scientific rationalization of men and machines into a unity of maximum efficiency in which all components were rigidly subordinate to the requirements of the whole.

In the interwar period a new series of studies, sometimes described as the "human relations in industry" movement, took up the problems of scientific management from a new point of view. The primary difference between this movement and that of its predecessors was the broadening of the conception of the plant to include various social relations. The plant was visualized as a social organism, of which the subgroups of cliques maintain themselves in a condition of equilibrium in the whole. These ideas were first worked out in the study of work units in the Hawthorne plant of the Western Electric Company, the largest supply company of Bell Telephone. In a five-year study initiated in 1927, it was discovered that work groups often develop into highly cohesive units in which each man has his place (defined in the habits, ideals, and traditions of the group). The work group typically controls the level of production.[41] While scientific management theorists discovered the tension between the individual and the organization, social relations discovered the tension between the subgroup and the whole.

In the post-World War II period, two schools of students have pushed beyond the lines of the scientific management and human relations theory: the organizational analysts and the small group theorists. The former[42] also have approached the industrial establishment like their predecessors in organismic terms as a social organism in equilibrium but concentrate on organizational objectives and their implementation, decision making, authority, and consent. The small group theorists,[43] also treating the group or organization as an organic structure in a condition of equilibrium, focus attention upon various relations of interdependence and the processual changes that ensue when group equilibrium is destroyed and restored. A series of processes are conceived to emerge in cyclical series until a condition of equilibrium once more is established. These forms of organization theory have been brought under critical review by Sherman Krupp, who observes correctly that they are all versions of the functionalistic approach to organization and share the assumption of a unity of purpose of the whole and a concern with the parts only so far as they relate to this unity. The various approaches to organization theory, he states,

> form a logically connected body of theory with a common emphasis founded in the norm of co-operation and harmony. As a consequence, these theories frame a managerial point of view in the traditions of philosophic conservatism and management engineering. Organization theory forms part of a larger, more general managerial interpretation of society.[44]

As the holists were driven in their analyses down to the smaller units of social life, a crisis was precipitated in their general theory. For the concept of a primacy of the whole and of the significance of the part as a subdivision of it functioning to sustain the whole was apparently contradicted by their findings. Scientific management discovered the individual, not as a cheerful robot happy to serve contemporary industry, but as a potentially intransigent fact tending to become a law unto himself regardless of the plans of management. The whole purpose of scientific management was to transform the individual into a pliable instrument in the fulfillment of industrial aims.

Similarly, the human relations theorists discovered the social subunit of the industrial plant to be not the functioning organ of the whole called forth in the theory, but a small scheme of social life tending toward autonomy within and against the plant as a whole. The organizational analysts, similarly, were oriented to the fact that numerous obstacles appear in the way of the smooth implementation of organizational aims other than presented by the individual or the clique. The small group theorists undertook to study the natural history of a disturbance in situations where group processes tended to break down, only to be restored. However, such processes sometimes tear groups apart. Equilibrium restoration is only one possible group process.

In all instances of the various forms of organization study that have been reviewed, social phenomena had been encountered which violate the holistic theory of social structure. However, the management orientation of these theories led to exclusive preoccupation with the problem of how the condition of the harmonious subordination of the parts to the whole could be brought about. This is a practical rather than a theoretical objective.

The elementarists by and large began their analysis of social structure with the examination of small units. Simmel, for example, paid special attention to the dyad and the contrast between it and various larger units. To Simmel the dyad is not only the most elementary unit of social structure, since further breakdown leaves only isolated individuals, but it has properties unique to it. The differences between the dyad and larger groups arise from the fact that it has only two members. Although to outsiders the dyad functions like an autonomous super-individual unit, to its participants each feels himself confronted only by the other and not by some impersonal collectivity above each.[45] The dyad is inseparable from the immediacy of interaction. This immediacy is the primary basis for its intimacy. This immediacy and intimacy, however, in putting individuals into constant interaction, can place various irrelevancies in the path of stability, hence a constant threat to such dyadic relations as the monogamous marriage. However, so far as the parties to a dyad are inclined to localize the confusions, difficulties, and shortcomings of the relationship in themselves, symbolizing the relationship as if it were interdependent and as representing only the best and purest of each, a dyadic relationship such as a monogamous marriage or friendship may prove to be relatively shock proof.

The introduction of a third party to the relationship fundamentally transforms the pattern of the dyad. Each party now acts as an intermediary to the third. While this opens the possibility that discords between any two parties may be mediated by the third or absorbed into a comprehensive whole, the addition of a third party may threaten rather than strengthen the whole. The possibility is ever present for the alignment of two against the third. While the dyad represents the first synthesis and unification of social action as well as the first separation and antithesis, the third party marks the transition, conciliation, and abandonment of absolute contrasts in patterns of social action. Among typical group formations that appear with third parties are the nonpartisan and mediatory, the *teritius gaudens*, and the process of dividing and conquering.

At a more comprehensive level than such elementary formations, Simmel explored various contrasts between small and large groups and the role of numbers on group formations.

Closely comparable to Simmel's analysis of the more intimate formations of social life was Cooley's examination of primary groups characterized by. "intimate face-to-face association and cooperation."[46] In such groups, Cooley maintained, the social nature and ideals of the individual are integrated. Such complete fusion of individualities may occur in primary groups that the self is virtually inseparable from the common life of the group. However, Cooley warned against the notion that the unity of the group is an undifferential harmony.

> It is always a differentiated and usually competitive unity, admitting of self-assertion and various appropriative passions; but these passions are socialized by sympathy and come . . . under the discipline of a common spirit. The individual will be ambitious, but the chief object of his ambition will be some desired place in the thought of the others, and he will feel allegiance to common standards of service and fair play.[47]

While the elementarists as a whole were most at ease when analyzing small, intimate, and primary groups, they were by no means confined to them. Max Weber's analysis of bureaucracy may illustrate the manner in which the same basic suppositions apparent when small structures were analyzed could be extended to complex social formations.

Modern officialdom, represented by the bureaucratic administration not only of political, but of economic, religious, educational welfare, and scientific structure, may be typified, according to Weber, by a number of properties:[48] the official operates in a fixed sphere defined by rules and regulations; the spheres of the various officials are formed into a graded hierarchy between which there is a chain of command and order of appeal. Management of the office rests on written documents preserved in the files. Officials are qualified for their offices on the basis of expert training; they occupy their positions on a full-time basis as primary lifelong occupations. Knowledge of the rules of the office represents specialized technical training. The official usually qualifies for his office by a prescribed course of training and the passing of a special examination. His office demands his loyalty on an impersonal basis. He enjoys a distinct social esteem guaranteed by the prescribed rules of the rank order. His position is usually held for life. He receives regular pecuniary compensation and old age security benefits provided by a pension. His career, in short, is ordered by the hierarchy in all respects. A bureaucratic administration transforms a plurality of individuals into a complex machine-like structure, the individuals of which can be exchanged like interchangeable parts.

A bureaucracy, Weber observed, can normally develop only on the basis of a money economy and a calculable system of taxation which permits the consolidation of administrative structures in the hands of the state and the payment of officials out of its tax resources. The decisive reason for the development of bureaucratic organization is its technical superiority over other forms. In Weber's image the decisive advantage of the bureaucracy is exactly similar to that of the machine over nonmechanical operations.

> Precision, speed, unambiguity, knowledge of the files, continuity, discretion, unity, strict subordination, reduction of friction and of material and personal costs—these are raised to the optimum point in the strictly bureaucratic administration, and especially in its monocratic form.[49]

Bureaucratization of organization went hand in hand with the development of rational interpretations of law on the basis of formal procedure. Bureaucratic structure accompanied concentration of the material means of management in political structure, capitalistic enterprises, military organizations, university instruction, and scientific research. Bureaucratic organizations have usually come into power by leveling economic and social differences. Moreover, once developed, the bureaucratic structures are virtually indestructible, even from the standpoint of those they serve. Moreover, every bureaucracy tends to increase the superiority of the professionally informed by keeping their knowledge and intentions secret.

As illustrated by Weber's analysis of bureaucracy, the elementarists were able to undertake the analysis of large structures from a behavioral rather than a functionalistic standpoint. Although various of the holists and elementarists have come to examine approximately the same subject matter, their respective analyses never quite meet on the same point. It is notable that the types of variables all important to the holists—organicity, cohesiveness, equilibrium, reciprocal interaction, and the like—play almost no role in the analyses of the elementarists. The elementaristic analysis of social structure, on the other hand, never loses sight of the individual in his immediate and long-range (career) interests. The interaction of individuals in groups is constantly seen in terms of the ever-changing conflict and compromise of diverse interests. At best the analyses of the holists with the constant preoccupation with the point of view of management tends to be seen by the elementarists as isolating only one—and not necessarily the most significant—segment of collective formation. In the words of Krupp, who writes from an elementaristic perspective:

> The danger of the functionalist approach is that it may conceal harmony-laden teleologies. Thus, an interpretation of the business firm through the language of "group cooperation" may be analogous to a description of a jungle using a theory of a farm.[50]

The Ambiguous Status of the Whole

While one consequence of the conflict of holistic and elementaristic approaches to social structure has been to leave a number of unresolved problems in the alternative treatment of groups and organizations, another has been to assign the whole an increasingly ambiguous status. The early sociologists, illustrated by Comte, had treated the whole as consisting of mankind in its entirety living and dead. Their followers found it necessary to define the whole in less comprehensive terms: making the "wholes" studied by sociologists more or less coextensive with communities or societies. However, most elementarists were insistent that these "wholes" were only fictitious entities, at best possessing heuristic utility for provisional orientation to the subject matter of social science.

Repeatedly from the time of Spencer the attempt to answer the criticism of the elementarists led holists to set up criteria for the whole. For Spencer, society was not simply an aggregate of individuals but an aggregate occupying a specific territory whose behavior constituted an organismlike entity, the organs of which were institutions organized into a number of general systems such as the sustaining, distributing, and regulating systems. Somewhat unsystematically the practice developed of designating various older, simpler, local territorially based systems of activities as communities and various complex, contemporary, more recent systems of activities as societies. There was widespread agreement among holists applying the concept of evolution to human affairs that the primary direction of change had been from societies or communities (of the former) to societies or communities of the latter type: Comte's theological and positivistic society; Spencer's militaristic-theological and industrial-peaceable society; Tönnies' *Gemeinschaft* and *Gesellschaft;* Durkheim's mechanical society and organic society; Redfield's folk and secular society.

The development of contemporary communication and transportation facilities has tended to emancipate human social life from its older types of special anchorage. Hence, so far as the territorial location has been retained as a criteria of the community or society, it has been the source of much confusion. The actual interactive-adjustments in interhuman behavior no longer bear the unambiguous relation to a specific territory. It is very possible that this emancipation from specific territorial location has been one of the major unconscious motives in the tendency of contemporary holists (particularly the functionalists) to abandon the older concepts of community and society for the more abstract concept of social system. Then at times, as in the case of Parsons, society is redefined as a total social system.

Moreover, a new source of confusion has appeared when holistic assumptions were applied to interhuman complexes less comprehensive than the society, community, or total social system without specifying which whole is taken as basic. If society is basic, then all subunits are not. If such subunits are differentiations within society, there is no fundamental reason why they should be identical to society or to one another. The organ of an organism is not itself an organism; nor is there any reason to conceive one organ is necessarily similar to another—the heart, for example, need not resemble the lungs or the blood. Hence when holistic suppositions were applied to groups and organizations without accommodation to the original theory that only the whole is autonomous and self-sufficient, the whole itself was cast into an ambiguous position. This is one of the primary problems in Parsons' formulation, when he sought.

> to define an organization by locating it systematically in the structure of the society in relation to other categories of social structure. It seemed appropriate to define an organization as a social system which is organized for the attainment of a particular type of goal; the attainment of that goal is at the same time the performance of a type of function on behalf of a more inclusive system, the society. It proved possible to bring to bear a general classification of the functional imperatives of social systems and with this to identify the principal mechanisms necessary to bring about the attainment of the goal or the organization purpose. The classification used has proved its applicability both for the level of the total society and for that of the small group. The present

application to an intermediate level further increases confidence in its generality.[51]

Hence, despite the concern with problems such as the prerequisites of social systems and boundary maintenance, the status of the more comprehensive interactive units has tended to become obscure. Meanwhile, the concern of the elementarists to avoid the reifications of the holists has generally steered them away from problems represented by society, the community, or the total social systems.

Consequences of Specialization for the Theory of Social Structure

At the time sociology arose the differentiation and specialization of the social sciences still lay in the future. Sociology was envisioned by its founders as the general science of man's social life. The early sociologists, thus, could follow any lead their analyses suggested without any feeling that they were trespassing on alien territories. In time the development of demography, social geography, and ethnology would change all this somewhat, for students would frequently drop analyses which seemed to be proper to other specialists.

At the first stage of its development, the sociological term "structure" could be retained in the specific sense or including a variety of individuals with their demographic potential, a range of environmental factors, a stock of cultural forms in terms of which people relate to one another and to their environment. The analysis of social structure under such circumstances had a definite significance. However, the development of demography, geography, and ethnology in the special sciences tended to take these subject matters out of the sphere of sociology, leaving to it only the analyses of interaction. Had the term "structure" been abandoned with the loss of these subject matters as primary sociological material, much confusion could have been avoided. However, it has been retained and applied to interaction. Some of the consequences of this practice were identified by John Rex in his analysis of Radcliffe-Brown's functionalism.

To Radcliffe-Brown functionalism consisted in the application of ideas and methods developed with respect to the organic to the social sciences. Radcliffe-Brown had argued:

To turn from organic life to social life, if we examine such a community as an African or Australian tribe, we can recognize the existence of a social structure. Individual human beings, the essential units in this instance, are connected by a definite set of social relations into an integrated whole. The continuity of the social structure, like that of an organic structure, is not destroyed by changes in the units. Individuals may leave the society, by death or otherwise; others may enter it. The continuity of structure is maintained by the process of social life, which consists of the activities and interactions of the individual human beings and of the organized groups into which they are united. The social life of the community is here defined as the *functioning* of the social structure. The *function* of any recurrent activity, such as the punishment of a crime, or a funeral ceremony, is the part it plays in the social life as a whole and therefore the contribution it makes to the maintenance of the structural continuity.[52]

Rex observes of Radcliffe-Brown's argument that a series of analogies were drawn between the biological and social organisms. The units of the biological organism are cells, structure is the relation between cells, activities are observed behaviors, functions are their role in maintaining the structure; the units of the social organism are individual human beings, structure is the relation between them; activities are observed behavior of human beings and groups, and functions are the role of these activities in maintaining the social structure. The term "structure," Rex urges

is of crucial importance, because according to Radcliffe-Brown's version of functionalism any activity is regarded as explained when it is shown that it has the effect of maintaining the social structure.[53]

However, Rex points out that Radcliffe-Brown's organic analogy quickly got him into trouble, for he was forced to admit that in contrast to the animal organism where structure can at least to some extent actually be observed apart from its functioning, in human society so-called social structure can be observed only in its function. Rex observes:

The spatial arrangement of human beings has no equivalent significance for the sociologist to that which the spatial arrangement of cells has for the biologist. It can be observed, of course, but the sociologist is not especially interested in it. It is not what he means by the social structure. . . . Radcliffe-Brown speaks of the social structure being capable of being observed only "in its functioning". . . . Racliffe-Brown has contradicted his own definitions in using this phraseology. For according to his own definition it is activities rather than structures which function.[54]

If one retains the original conception of social phenomena held by sociologists before demography and geography became special sciences, a meaning of social structure parallel to that used by students of the biological organism could be retained in a qualified sense. Radcliffe-Brown, however, does not reason from this early position.

Pointing up still further the discrepancies that emerge between theory and fact when the organic model is clamped on social phenomena, Rex observes that when people do things entailing cooperation with others, they do not necessarily have the effect of maintaining a social structure if their action is thought of as a stabilized interaction pattern. If one says that social activity is explained when its effect of maintaining a structure has been established, this would have the consequence of eliminating from consideration all sorts of significant social materials.

> The primary activities of human beings, although they may be socially oriented, may not have any role to play in the maintenance of the social structure.[55]

The specialization of the social sciences, on the one hand, and the reifications of holistic analyses on the other have compounded the ambiguities surrounding the concept of social structure. Various demographic, geographic, environmental, and ethnographic conditions of social life remain unanalyzed in many sociological accounts (since they are conceived to be the proper materials of other social sciences) or remain only incompletely analyzed when sociologists conduct their studies of interaction. Meanwhile, the patterns of interaction are reified and a peculiar kind of explanation by reduplication substitutes for "structural analysis." One consequence of this, as Rex indicates, is to set aside many sorts of primary social activities which people in fact considered to be most vital.

The Conflict of Popular
and Professional Sociology

Finally, the problems of the student of social structure which arise from the conflict of holism and elementarism and specialization have been further complicated by the conflict between popular and professional sociology. Popular sociology has typically been addressed to large-scale and general human concerns and oriented to the demand for ethical interpretation and ideological direction. Professional sociology has been addressed to the problem of attaining precision and oriented to the demand for scientific objectivity. The student of social structure has, as a result, too often found himself trapped between precise trivialities and vague ideological generalities.

Toward Theoretical Reconstruction

While there are a variety of lines along which the theoretical reconstruction of the theory of social structure can fruitfully proceed, at least three stand out: a fuller understanding of the role of reification in social fact and social theory; a restoration of the study of the raw materials and conditions of social life to its status as a necessary preliminary phase of analysis of interaction; a review and extension of the theory of communities.

Reification in Social Fact and Social Theory

A major point of contention between the elementarists and the holists centers on the status of collectivities, from groups to communities: the former typically have insisted that collectivities in the end are nothing but activities of individuals, the latter that they are something more, not reducible to individuals. An unusually clear statement of the contrasts between the holistic (sometimes called universalistic) position and the elementaristic (individualistic) is presented by Felix Kaufmann.

> It has been hotly debated whether social collectivities are real objects existing independently of the persons who form them or whether they are merely mental constructs. . . . The issue does not concern matters of fact but relations of meaning. If we understand by "independent existence of a social collectivity" only that we may have the same collectivity even if none of the persons who once formed it still belongs to it, then we must ascribe independent existence to social collectivities. . . . If, however, "independent existence of a social collectivity" is taken to mean that the term "social collectivity" is irreducible to terms denoting human relationships, then we must deny that social collectivities have "independent existence."
> Universalists, beginning with the logical priority of society over

the individual, draw the methodological conclusion that we must not try to derive social phenomena from principles concerning the behavior of fictive "isolated" individuals. They insist that society is not a "sum of individuals" but a "whole" and that we can understand the behavior of people in society only if we take into account their social function. They make frequent use of the analogy—which does not extend very far—between organism and society. This argument is correct in pointing out that in order to find adequate schemes of interpretation for social actions we must in most cases refer to given *ends* to which the behavior in question is supposed to be conducive.

Corresponding to these ends is the "public" interest, and this may conflict with other "private" interests of the persons bound together by social relationships. If, however, society is hypostatized into a "person of higher order"—as it is by universalists and organicists—then *a priori* reasoning is often thought to be capable of achieving "the" just reconciliation between the public interest and the often conflicting private interests of the members of society. And so ultimate justification of political doctrines is sought in the "nature of society."[56]

Kaufmann also clarified the ideological underpinnings of the respective positions.

The proponents of these doctrines argue that the value of a person is determined by his social function and by what he does in the performance of this function. Furthermore, these functions and accomplishments of people, together with their value, are conceived as determined by their knowledge, ability, character, or wealth. This view is frequently associated with the political demand that the rights of each person be "proportional to his value," a demand directed against the democratic principle of the equality of rights of all members of society.

On the other hand, the individualistic conception of society is likely to lead its proponents to a favorable attitude toward democracy.[57]

Perhaps the simplest way of clarifying the problems flowing from the reification of collectivities is to draw a clear distinction between reification for pragmatic social purposes and reification at the level of theory. As a matter of practical social fact men conceptualize collectivities apart from the individuals that compose them. They treat them as if they were a special class of individuals with properties, aims, and needs of their own. The capacity of men to treat their collectivities as individuals provides them with new powers over their collective life. The collective, however, has no life and existence other than the set of notions associated with this very reification. The nature of the collective is exhaustively contained in the informal or formal rules in terms of which its fictitious individuality is defined.

> We speak of actions of a social collectivity if persons act who are selected in accordance with certain rules referred to in the scheme of interpretation, and if, moreover, these persons act in accordance with certain other rules contained in this scheme. Such persons are called "organs" of the social collectivity. If the organs *qua* organs are acted upon, we say that the social collectivity is acted upon. Analysis of the concept of "legal person" (such as a joint-stock company) will aid in clarifying this point. A legal person is "represented" by its organs, but it remains the same even if all its organs change. Such a company may be sued and ordered to pay a debt regardless of changes in the personnel of its executives or stockholders. What actually occurs in such cases is that steps are taken against *individuals* who are selected in terms of legal rules as organs of the corporation.[58]

In practical social life such reification and the various attendant notions of the objectives, needs, and rules of the collective which specify its character provide a degree of autonomy to various objectives that a plurality of individuals share. Over and against these are various needs and interests of the same individuals which are experienced as uniquely their own and conceived to some extent in opposition to those assigned to the collective. It is important not to lose sight of the fact that significant social objectives are achieved by the pragmatic reifications of everyday social life.

However, the moment the reifications of everyday life are taken as scientific truths, a number of theoretical and practical anomalies appear. In everyday life the reification of the collective provides a degree of autonomy to various shared objectives of the individual members of pluralities without which such shared objectives might be swept away by the power and variety of special individual interests. Despite the fact that these general or collective or official interests may in fact be of minor importance to most individuals of the collectivity, their preservation may be essential to providing a framework within which a rich diversity of special interests is realized. Hence to the individuals of the collectivity the official interests of the collectivity may in fact be secondary, instrumental, or facilitating rather than primary. In accepting the reification of the collectivity as a starting point of scientific analysis, what is secondary in social fact is assigned priority in theory. Moreover, one is entrapped in other absurdities, such as attempting to derive the variety of interests defined as unique or individual from the general interest. Moreover, it is easy to lose sight of the fact that the general interest is by no means a fixed formula but is everywhere subject to continuous negotiation and change.

A precondition for the clarification of problems of social structure is the clear separation of the consequences of the reification of social structures as pragmatic operation for special purposes in empirical social life from the consequences of reification when taken as a theoretical orientation to social phenomena.

The Study of Raw Materials and Conditions

It is hardly necessary to say much about the value of the restoration of the study of the various demographic, geographic, environmental, and cultural resources and conditions available to a plurality at the time it undertakes its various interpersonal adventures. In various ways many social scientists do undertake such analyses, but usually in a rather inconsistent manner.

Much of social ecology in fact consisted in an inventory of various demographic and environmental factors. Occasionally, though this was not usual, ecologists also made an inventory of the cultural resources of pluralities.

However, social ecology has gone out of fashion. Though there were a number of reasons, the most important was the notion promulgated by many ecologists that their studies were self-sufficient to account for social phenomena when in fact they were only a useful first step. When it was eventually made clear that ecological analysis was not sufficient to account for social phenomena, the intemperate claims made in the name of ecological analysis took their revenge in the rather complete decline in the popularity of ecological analysis.

There is much to be said for the transformation of the study of social structure (though it is unlikely that this will occur) into a much expanded form of ecological analysis. Then much of what currently is included in the study of social structure could be reconceptualized as the study of social process—a much more accurate description avoiding the dangers of reification.

The Revision and Extension of Community Theory

The theory of community must be freed from the reifications of holism and the inclination to shun the analysis of complex social formations by the elementarists. The theory of community is concerned with the more comprehensive movements toward stability in interhuman action. Neither holists nor elementarists deny that such movements toward stability occur, or that they take place over and beyond the process of group formation representing, in part, a modification of groups.

Groups are formed to stablize various shared (collective) and private objectives. However, the same plurality may form many groups. Any given set of individuals may participate in a variety of groups in part with each other and in part with others outside the set. The problem inevitably arises both for individuals and for pluralities as to the proportionate amount of energy that will go into various of the groups in which they participate. Moreover, it is inevitable that some of the devices effective in one group will diffuse into another. Forces are always at work toward making the various groups in which pluralities of men are distributed consistent with one another.

While the process of stabilization of collective life in groups and the achievement of some sort of consistency between them are more or less directly apparent, the limiting conditions within which such processes operate are not always so clearly perceived. There is an initial plausibility in the notion that the more harmonious a related set of groups, the better for the participants. It is on this point that the holistic and elementaristic theories are in sharp conflict, for the holists take this notion as their first premise in the analysis of social systems. To the holists the entire meaning of the part (group) lies in service to the unity of the whole; the elementarists, however, place the emphasis in their analysis of social interaction on the efficiency of actions and groups in solving the specific problems of collective life.

Often obscured in holistic approaches to the community is the fact that the adjustment of the requirements of different human groups to one another does not necessarily make each of them more effective in the area of its primary operation. One can, in fact, insist upon such complete harmony in the whole as to make the operation of some of the original groups virtually impossible. If, however, these are vital to the collectivity, the whole may be threatened if one impairs them too severely. On the other hand, if no other consideration is allowed in the formation of collective life, then the efficiency of the working groups, some of the requirements of a rich, full collective life, are almost certain to be set aside. Hence, the formation of a communal system achieves some sort of completeness within two major limiting conditions:

sufficient unity to permit a plurality to confront all the issues of the climatic and life cycle, but sufficient flexibility not to impair the effectiveness of the basic groups. In any given situation there is often a considerable range of discretion between these two limits. The community formula may, in fact, alternate between trends toward centralization and particularistic autonomy of the basic groups.

The important role played by territoriality in the theory of community in the past rests upon the fact that every collectivity must ultimately survive in nature. There is always in the end a direct or indirect independence of the natural world. Prior to the development of scientific technologies this dependence anchored pluralities relatively close to some area of the earth's surface. However, contemporary technologies draw the resources of the natural world from much more comprehensive areas, cutting the tie between community formation and limited territorial areas.

NOTES

1. Claude Levi-Strauss, "Social Structure," in A. L. Kroeber, *Anthropology Today* (Chicago: The University of Chicago Press, 1953), p. 524.

2. A. L. Kroeber, *Anthropology* (New York: Harcourt Brace, 1958), p. 325. Quoted by Levi-Strauss, ibid., p. 524.

3. August Comte, *Positive Philosophy*, trans. Harriet Martineau (London: George Bell & Sons, 1896), vol. 2, p. 218.

4. Ibid., p. 226.

5. Ibid., p. 225.

6. Ibid., pp. 221-22.

7. Ibid., p. 275.

8. Ibid., pp. 280-81.

9. Ibid., p. 281.

10. Ibid., p. 289.

11. Ibid., p. 298.

12. Herbert Spencer, *The Principles of Sociology* (New York: D. Appleton, 1888), vol. 1, p. 435.

13. Ibid., p. 436.

14. Ibid., p. 437-38.

15. Ibid., pp. 486, 506, 507, 508.

16. Emile Durkheim, *The Division of Labor in Society*, trans. George Simpson (Glencoe, Ill.: The Free Press, 1947), pp. 342-43.

17. Ibid., p. 350.

18. Ibid., p. 396.

19. Ibid., pp. 79-80.

20. Ibid., pp. 398-399.

21. Ibid., p. 346.

22. Talcott Parsons, *The Social System* (Glencoe, Ill.: The Free Press, 1951), p. 5ff.

23. Ibid., p. 19. Also, Talcott Parsons, "An Outline of the Social System" in *Theories of Society,* ed. Talcott Parsons, Edward Shils, Kaspar D. Naegele, and Jesse R. Pitts (New York: The Free Press of Glencoe, 1961), vol. 1, p. 44.

24. Parsons, *The Social System,* p. 24.

25. Ibid., p. 25.

26. Ibid., p. 39.

27. Ibid., pp. 51-52.

28. Georg Simmel, *The Sociology of Georg Simmel,* trans. Kurt H. Wolff (Glencoe, Ill.: The Free Press, 1950), pp. 9-10.

29. Ibid., p. 26.

30. Ibid., pp. 32-33.

31. Ibid., p. 37.

32. Ibid., p. 42.

33. Charles H. Cooley, *Social Organization* (New York: Scribner's, 1909), p. 3.

34. Ibid., p. 5.

35. Ibid., p. 21.

36. Ibid., pp. 21-22.

37. Ibid., pp. 26-27.

38. Ibid., p. 313.

39. Max Weber, *The Theory of Social and Economic Organization,* trans. A. M. Henderson and Talcott Parsons (New York: Oxford University Press, 1947), pp. 102-3.

40. Frederick W. Taylor, *A Piece Rate System* (London: Routledge, 1919); *The Principles and Methods of Scientific Management* (New York: Harper & Bros., 1912); *Shop Management* (New York: Harper & Bros., 1911).

41. Representative studies include: Thomas N. Whitehead, *The Industrial Worker* (Cambridge: Harvard University Press, 1938); Fritz J. Roethlisberger and William J. Dickson, *Management and the Worker* (Cambridge: Harvard University Press, 1939); Elton Mayo, *The Human Problems of an Industrial Civilization* (Boston: Harvard Graduate School of Business Administration, 1946).

42. Illustrated by Chester I. Bernard, *The Functions of the Executive* (Cambridge: Harvard University Press, 1959) and *Organization and Management* (Cambridge: Harvard University Press, 1952); Herbert A. Simon, *Administrative Behavior* (New York: Macmillan, 1958); James G. March and Herbert Simon, *Organizations* (New York: Wiley, 1958).

43. Illustrated by Robert F. Bales, *Interaction Process Analysis* (Cambridge: Addison-Wesley, 1950), and George C. Homans, *The Human Group* (New York: Harcourt Brace, 1950).

44. Sherman Krupp, *Pattern in Organization Analysis* (Philadelphia: Chilton Company, 1961).

45. Simmel, *The Sociology of Georg Simmel*, p. 123.

46. Cooley, *Social Organization*, p. 23.

47. Ibid., pp. 23-24.

48. Max Weber, *From Max Weber*, trans. H. H. Gerth and C. Wright Mills (New York: Oxford University Press, 1946), p. 196ff.

49. Ibid., p. 214.

50. Krupp, *Pattern in Organization Analysis*, pp. ix-x.

51. Talcott Parsons, *Structure and Process in Modern Societies* (Glencoe, Ill.: The Free Press, 1960), pp. 56-57.

52. Alfred R. Radcliffe-Brown, *Structure and Function in Primitive Society* (Glencoe, Ill.: The Free Press, 1952), p. 180.

53. John Rex, *Key Problems of Sociological Theory* (London: Routledge and Kegan Paul, 1961), pp. 63-64.

54. Ibid., p. 64.

55. Ibid., p. 65.

56. Felix Kaufmann, *Methodology of the Social Sciences* (New York: Oxford University Press, 1944), pp. 163-64.

57. Ibid., p. 164.

58. Ibid., pp. 162-63.

SELECTED BIBLIOGRAPHY

Bales, Robert F. *Interaction Process Analysis.* Cambridge: Addison-Wesley, 1950.

Barnard, Chester I. *The Functions of the Executive.* Cambridge: Harvard University Press, 1959.

_____. *Organization and Management.* Cambridge: Harvard University Press, 1952.

Comte, Auguste. *Positive Philosophy.* Translated by Harriet Martineau. London: George Beel & Sons, 1896.

Cooley, Charles H. *Social Organization.* New York: Scribner's, 1909.

Durkheim, Emile. *The Division of Labor in Society.* Translated by George Simpson. Glencoe, Ill.: The Free Press, 1947.

Homans, George C. *The Human Group.* New York: Harcourt Brace, 1950.

Krupp, Sherman. *Pattern in Organization Analysis.* Philadelphia: Chilton Company, 1961.

March, James G., and Simon, Herbert. *Organizations.* New York: Wiley, 1958.

Martindale, Don A. *Institutions, Organizations, and Mass Society.* Boston: Houghton Mifflin, 1966.

Mayo, Elton. *The Human Problems of an Industrial Civilization.* Boston: Harvard Graduate School of Business Administration, 1946.

Parsons, Talcott. *The Social System.* Glencoe, Ill.: The Free Press, 1951.

Roethlisberger, Fritz J. and Dickson, William J. *Management and the Worker.* Cambridge: Harvard University Press, 1939.

Simmel, Georg. *The Sociology of Georg Simmel.* Translated by Kurt H. Wolff. Glencoe, Ill.: The Free Press, 1950.

Simon, Herbert A. *Administrative Behavior.* New York: Macmillan, 1958.

Spencer, Herbert. *The Principles of Sociology.* New York: D. Appleton, 1899.

Weber, Max. *The Theory of Social and Economic Organization.* Translated by A. M. Henderson and Talcott Parsons. New York: Oxford University Press, 1947.

CHAPTER 5

Social Change

Many of the problems that haunt the area of social change are a heritage from the theory which first dominated early sociology. The theory of Comte and his immediate successors was a secularized, inverted version of the medieval Christian philosophy of history. It is of some interest to trace major points of similarity and difference as a key to some current confusions.

The Medieval Christian
Philosophy of History

The medieval Christian philosophy of history was brought to its early synthesis by St. Augustine (Aurelius Augustinus, 354–430 A.D.), Bishop of Hippo in proconsular Africa, who had successively subscribed to Manichaenism and Neo-Platonism before his conversion to Catholicism. When he eventually succeeded to the position of Bishop of Hippo and found himself answerable for the discontent directed at the official church as an organ of the Roman Empire during its declining days, it was from the standpoint of a familiarity with the major intellectual trends of the period.

It was no discovery of St. Augustine that the once presumably imperishable Roman Empire was in a state of decay. The Roman emperors and administrators and her educated strata had long been aware of it. However, expedients to stay the process were of no avail. The international commercial economy of Rome rested eventually on the productive labor of slavery. The institution of slavery, in turn, depended on a source of cheap slaves and was cross-tied with Roman military activity. However, the stage had long been passed in Roman military history where the costs of the operations of the imperial armies were worth the risk of counter-attacks by barbaric tribes on the frontiers. The military balance was being tipped in favor of the latter. The wars of the empire eventually lost the character of slave raids and turned into wars of defense. Eventually this inclined the emperors to establish peaceful relations with the barbaric tribes, but this also cut off at its primary source the supply of slaves needed by the economy.

Another major trend was associated with the reduction of the city from the status of an autonomous community to an administrative organ of the imperial government. The urbanite lost much of his former capacity to determine his own fate which he retained so long as he was a civilian soldier. Moreover, tendencies in the ancient economy toward the formation of large-scale slave plantations and large-scale, slave-operated industrial establishments could no longer be held in check by politically and militarily competent free citizens, for whom such trends were comparable to current influence of giant corporations on the competitive situation of small businesses. Under conditions of competition with the large slave holders, small slave owners and independent peasants and craftsmen continually lost ground and were reduced to the ranks of a growing urban proletariat living on doles.

The conjoint effects of such processes forced up the prices of items in the international commercial traffic to a point where they became prohibitive. When the Roman emperors attempted to meet the problem by arbitrary maximum price legislation, the producers for international trade found themselves in a cost-price squeeze and went out of business rather than face disaster. Meanwhile, many urban services which had formerly been a source of profit and prestige assumed the character of thankless burdens inclining the imperial government to so-to-speak legislation of servitude (transforming them often as a punishment for minor offenses into hereditary obligations) to secure their performance.

Such details, however, belong to the history of the ancient world and are mentioned here only in passing to emphasize the fact that ever present in the declining days of Rome was the realization on the part of thoughtful men that things were going badly and all usual expedients seemed only to make matters worse.

While for several centuries the institutions of the Empire were decaying, the Christian Church was displaying an unusual vitality. It gradually distinguished itself among the hundreds of competing sects that sprouted from the ruins of urban decay. It rose from the status of a chiliastic sect to an expanding denomination that had begun to recruit members high in the social scale. The poor but free artisan who had originally formed its congregational core was beginning to recede into the background as the sect propagandized the middle classes. Periodically Roman administrators responded to the growth of Christianity with alarm and undertook sporadic persecutions against its members; these were of no avail.

Eventually Constantine (288–337 A.D.), who had been converted in 312 A.D., decided that Christianity was itself what the Empire most needed. After 313 A.D., he conferred a series of privileges and immunities on the Catholic Church and its clergy but delayed, perhaps for motives of political expedience, his transformation of it into the official religion of the Empire. Upon completion of the conquest of the Empire, Constantine took this final step. In 325 A.D., he convened the Council of Nicaea to consolidate the doctrine of the church.

With the conversion of Christianity into the official faith of the Empire, the religion acquired a structure parallel to that of the imperial government with bishops, metropolitans, popes, and councils. It also underwent a vast expansion. However, as an organ of the Empire it also became a focal point for discontent and unrest, as the process of the decay of imperial institutions continued.

The tremendous advantages that accrued to Christianity by being made into the official religion of the Empire might easily have been canceled by the close identification with it. When Rome was sacked by the Goths under Alaric in 410 A.D., many persons attributed the disaster to Christianity. The pillage of Rome after more than one thousand years of greatness, in fact, shook pagan and Christian alike. To many it looked like the first phase of the destruction of the world. Thus, nearly one hundred years after Christianity had been transformed into the official religion of the Empire, Augustine set upon the task of separating the fates of the Empire and the Church once more, addressing himself directly to the problem that troubled many sensitive Christians—how were they to interpret the sack of Rome?

Augstine re-drew the lines of distinction between the spirit and the flesh, observing that the saints lost nothing in losing their temporal goods.

> They ... who lost their worldly all in the sack of Rome, if they owned their possessions as they had been taught by the apostle, who himself was poor without, but rich within ... could say in the words of Job, heavily tried, but not overcome: "Naked came I out of my mother's womb, and naked shall I return thither; the Lord gave, and the Lord hath taken away as it pleased the Lord, so has it come to pass; blessed be the name of the Lord."[1]

In accord with ancient Judeo-Christian traditions, St. Augustine assumes that the world is God's creation and its history represents the play of human aspiration and its consequence around God's designs for man. "There are," Augustine insists, "no more than two kinds of human society which we may justly call two cities, according to the language of our Scriptures. The one consists of those who wish to live after the flesh, the other of those who wish to live after the spirit."[2] The two cities, "have been formed by two loves: the earthly by the love of self, even to the contempt of God; the heavenly by the love of God, even to the contempt of self. The former, in a word, glories in itself, the latter in the Lord."[3]

The division of aspiration that led to the formation of two societies was anticipated by the rivalry of the angels in Heaven that eventuated in the banishment of Satan. It was anticipated from the onset of human history in the temptation of Eve and of man's original sin. The formation of the two cities soon followed upon the events of Eden.

> Of these two first parents of the human race ... Cain was the first-born, and he belonged to the city of men; after him was born Abel, who belonged to the city of God.[4]

The founder of the early city was a fractricide who out of envy slew his brother, a citizen of the eternal city and a sojourner on earth. The crime of Cain, in Augustine's view, is archetypal with a corresponding crime (the murder of Remus by his brother Romulus) appearing at the time of the founding of Rome. The presence of this archetypal crime at the base of the earthly city is a major component in Augustine's account of the inevitable decay of the earthly city, in contrast to the progressiveness of the heavenly city.

> The quarrel . . . between Romulus and Remus shows how the earthly city is divided against itself; that which fell out between Cain and Abel illustrated the hatred that subsists between the two cities, that of God and that of men. The wicked war with the wicked; the good also war with the wicked.[5]

Thus Augustine's formulations take two major secular trends of late imperial times—the decay of secular institutions and the progressiveness of Christian institutions as the fulfillment of God's intentions for man. All that has happened or will happen until Judgment Day is an inevitable product of these forces.

This formulation endured as the uncontested philosophy of the medieval church for a thousand years. It had been based so solidly on secular social trends that until the rise of late medieval urban life, nothing seemed to contradict it. However, in the cities and the national states the secular trends reversed. The Renaissance historians began to question the suppositions of the medieval philosophy of history. The eighteenth-century philosophy of history developed by the enlightenment philosophers moved farther along the lines laid down by the Renaissance historians. Their ideas, in turn, supplied the foundation for sociology's first doctrine of social change. A few deatils of this transformation may clarify the major ingredients of the eventual sociological synthesis.

The Breakup of the Medieval Philosophy of History

So powerfully ensconced in Western thought was the Augustinian philosophy of history that even long after secular trends no longer sustained its plausibility and men began to turn to the classics of antiquity, becoming acquainted with alternative approaches to history, the intellectuals long hesitated to challenge it. Hence Thomas Aquinas, for example, in response to the rise of the city and the thought of antiquity, undertook a new synthesis of thought and modified the Augustinian position in other respects but left the philosophy of history virtually intact. However, short of the direct challenge to the Augustinian position, the Renaissance historians began to reconceptualize the materials of social history.

Renaissance and Baroque Reformulations

In response to the new secular trends and authorities other than the Bible and the church fathers, Renaissance thinkers quietly erased the lines between the sacred and the profane. At the same time they hesitated to challenge the traditional Christian formula directly. This may have been a major factor in the preoccupation with method typified by Jean Bodin (1530–1596).

Bodin initially embarked upon a priestly career but shifted to the law. Eventually he pursued a career in civil service. In his *Method for the Comprehension of History* (1566),[6] Bodin, like Augustine, assumed that human history was an orderly whole. In fact, to discover the universal law constitutes the major reason for studying history.

> In history the best part of universal law lies hidden; and what is of great weight and importance for the best appraisal of legislation—the customs of the peoples, and the beginnings, growth, conditions, changes, and decline of all states are obtained from it.[7]

What was the universal law of history Bodin never indicated, but it is noteworthy that he did not identify it with some sort of Divine Plan of God for man but shifted the problem to secular contexts.

The influence of the ancients, whom Bodin is more fond of quoting than the Bible and Church Fathers, is evident throughout the *Method*. He seems to have been convinced, perhaps under their influence, that there is a relation between climate and history.[8] Bodin was convinced that human society was originally much simpler than it has become and has developed out of domestic institutions in a manner that suggests possible influence of Thucydides and Aristotle.[9] His conception of cycles suggests the influence of Polybius.[10] His notion that social changes may be calculated from Pythagorean numbers was influenced by Plato.[11] And finally, he directly attacks the conception of a golden age and of four monarchies appearing in the Book of Daniel,[12] indicating his inclination to question religious sources.

In all these respects, while treating history as an orderly whole with laws of its own, Bodin had begun to shift attention away from the characteristic notions of the theologians.

The Baroque writer, Giambattista Vico (1668–1744), who became Professor of Rhetoric at Naples, revived Augustine's conception of divine progress as the clue to man's history. However, Vico worked out his solution in ways that go considerably beyond Augustine and that anticipate features of the early sociological theory of change. Vico's *New Science* (the title was taken from Francis Bacon) was a study of classical philology set down in axioms, postulates, and correlaries (probably under Descartes' influence). Its intention was to use language, custom, and law (under the influence of Bodin and the great seventeenth-century jurists, Grotius and Pufendorf) to demonstrate the existence of a divine purpose operating through history.

Common sense, Vico argues, is judgment without reflection, shared by an entire class, people, nation, or even the entire human race. Uniform ideas originating among peoples unknown to one another must have a common basis of truth.

> This axiom is a great principle which establishes the common sense of the human race as the criterion taught to the nations by Divine Providence to define what is certain in the natural law of nations.[13]

Society, Vico believed, began with religion.[14] Segments of mankind are nations. Every nation in its rise, development, maturity, decline and fall[15] traverses three general stages: an age of gods, an age of heroes, and an age of men. As illustrated by the case of Egypt, institutions such as language assume a form in harmony with the properties of the age. The Egyptian language evolved through a hieroglyphic or sacred form, a symbolic or heroic form to the epistolary or vulgar language of men employing conventional signs for the communication of everyday needs.[16] Through the cyclical movement of nations Divine Providence provides a unifying theme, and while the same ages appear the result is not so much a mere repetition as an upbuilding spiral.

While Vico preserved the medieval holism and concept of Divine Providence as the unifying element of history, he was quite evidently attempting to press matters that were being explored from a purely secular point of view (law, language, myth, religion) into a religious formula. In the very act of accepting elements from the medieval world they were being transformed.

The eighteenth-century rationalists broke away from the medieval philosophy of history in two fundamental respects. They abandoned the notion of history and mankind as representing an organic whole. History was merely the record of man's doings. The order displayed by history was a product of human nature which is everywhere the same. The variations in human behavior from place to place and time to time is explained by geographic and sociocultural circumstances and man's capacity to learn from past experience. Various ways in which these rationalistic notions were expressed may be illustrated by Turgot, Condorcet, and Kant, all of whom supplied ideas which were influential on other formulations.

Jacque Turgot (1727–1781), in an address delivered at the Sorbonne at the age of twenty-four (in 1750), "On the Successive Advances of the Human Mind," argued that human behavior arises in response to climatic, biological, and psychological factors. Human capacities such as reason and the passions and social circumstances such as liberty conjointly give rise to new events. Writing was a particularly important invention, permitting men to accumulate information, putting at the disposal of each succeeding age all that had gone before. Hence, from the time of its origin man has accumulated knowledge and has shown continuous progress. The rate of progress accelerated with each advance. The way men have accounted for the world has led through three stages: initially phenomena were attributed to invisible beings, not dissimilar from men; in time, recognizing the absurdity of this, men began to explain phenomena in terms of abstract principles or essences or faculties; finally they learned to formulate hypotheses mathematically and to verify them on the basis of the reciprocal mechanical action of bodies.

One of the most influential formulations of the rationalistic view of history was made by Condorcet (1743–1794) while in hiding from the Jacobins during the French Revolution, which, though a nobleman, he had supported. Condorcet's *Outline of an Historical Picture of the Progress of the Human Mind* rests on the assumption that man's intelligence has undergone continuous progress from the first vague observations of primitive wise men to the giants of contemporary science. He divided intellectual history into ten periods: (1) that of primitive hunters; (2) that of shepherds; (3) that of tillers; (4) the ancient Greek period; (5) the period from the conquests of Alexander the Great to the Decline of Rome; (6) the period of the medieval world to the Crusades; (7) the late Middle Ages until the invention of printing; (8) the period from the invention of printing to the attacks on authority by Luther, Descartes, and Bacon; (9) the period from Descartes to the French Revolution. The tenth period, the future, was to enjoy the final triumph over nature by science.

At the close of the rationalistic period, Kant (1724–1804) also turned his attention to the problem of history in *The Ideal of a Universal History from a Cosmopolitical Point of View* (1784). In accord with the rationalistic suppositions the past history of mankind to Kant was primarily a record of human error and folly. However, if one focused attention, not simply on the detailed actions of any individual or group or nation, but on human history as a whole, a kind of pattern and order became discernible as man's capacity for reason unfolded through the vicissitudes of time. Among the propositions that Kant advances for the interpretation of human history are: that all capacities natural to a creature are destined to unfold themselves completely in time; that man's only unique faculty (setting him apart from the animals) is his Reason; that by his Reason man produces out of himself all that goes beyond his animal nature; the mechanism for the development of man's capacities is mutual antagonism in a social state, so far as such competition becomes at last an order among men regulated by law; the most important practical problem facing man is the establishment of a civil society administering right according to law; this problem is the most difficult and last to be solved by men; it requires the regulation of the external relations of states conformably to law; the history of the human race as a whole may be viewed as the realization of this plan; the attempt philosophically to work out the universal history of the world in terms of the plan of nature in its movement toward a perfect civil union is itself a part of the plan of nature.

Hume, Voltaire, and a number of other rationalistic thinkers held views essentially similar to those of Fontanelle, Turgot, and Condorcet, but these are sufficient to epitomize rationalistic analysis. The rationalists abandoned the holism of the medieval theologians. History was conceived as a field for the strategy of rationally endowed individuals in their war against the blind forces of nature.

Nineteenth-Century
Philosophies of History

In the Renaissance and Baroque periods the notion was retained that history had an order as a whole. However, typical medieval concepts of that order were set aside. Without fanfare Bodin erased the traditional line between the sacred and profane, placing emphasis on the latter. Vico's very insistence on the integral place of religion in human history acknowledged the fact that this was being called into question. Vico tried to restore religion to the historical picture in a manner quite different from that of the medieval theologians. In the eighteenth and nineteenth centuries the rationalists largely abandoned the notion of an order in history which, in their view, consisted of man's follies, errors, and false starts. Man's achievements were, to be sure, progressive, but this consisted as much as anything else in his emancipation from the errors of the past—his freedom, so to speak, from historical determination.

The nineteenth century picked up the problem of history at the point where it had been left by Bodin and Vico. In contrast to the rationalists, history was conceived as an orderly whole once more. However, the conceptions of rationality and progress developed by the thinkers of the Enlightenment were lifted from the context of individual experience and assigned to the collective. The effect of this was to complete the inversion of the medieval philosophy of history. The two primary versions of the nineteenth-century formula appear in German lands in the development of thought in Hegel to Marx and elsewhere in the West in the sociological theories of progress and evolutionism.

The foundation of the dominant Germanic concept of change was laid by Johan Gottfried Herder (1744–1803) in his *Ideas for the Philosophy of History of Mankind* (1784). Herder believed that man was the highest of all created species. Man, he believed, can only be understood in terms of his social environment. Man and society develop together, reaching their climax in humanity. Society and culture are organic developments. The nation is the unit in which mankind is embodied at a given time and place.

Georg Wilhelm Friedrich Hegel (1770–1831) brought to logical synthesis suggestions that were somewhat inconsistently presented in Herder's work. Like St. Augustine, Hegel viewed human history as religiously significant, but in quite a different sense from his medieval counterparts. To Augustine human history was God's testing ground for man to ascertain whether he was worthy of being taken up permanently into the divine fellowship. Thus God in some sense stands apart and above the world. To Hegel God does not stand apart from his creation but is identical with Spirit, Mind, or Reason as they are manifest in history. God, Spirit, and

Reason, properly understood, are one in the same thing. They are manifested in individuals but cannot be reduced to properties of the individual. Rather, the individual serves as a "vehicle" of the Spirit.

The essence of Spirit is freedom, evident as a capacity for self-movement in extreme contrast to material nature whose existence is gravity, the property of being moved only from without and not by its own power. The drama of Spirit is its gradual emancipation from physical nature.

The creation of the world was conceived by Hegel in unique terms. In the beginning was God as pure idea, an infinite goodness, infinite perfection, and infinite power. But the Idea was purely formal and, hence, sublimely empty. Infinite goodness, perfection, and power are not infinite at all as long as they are without substance—they are mere empty formulas. Thought is thus compelled to call up the idea of physical thing, standing over and against pure spontaniety—brute mass is moved only from without. However, the problem for thought has now become complex, for it possesses two ideas which contradict and threaten to cancel one another. Only some idea which will bring such contradictory ideas into a higher synthesis can prevent such a result. So it is that the contradictory ideas of Spirit and Nature (God and the World) call into being a third—Man. Man belongs to nature, but in Man, Idea or Spirit is present as a potentiality struggling for expression. The problem of History centers on Man in whose development the Spirit rises to a condition of full self-consciousness.

The ordinary person following Hegel for the first time through such turgid reflections often experiences the bafflement of entering some fantastic world in which the lines between ideas and the things they refer to have been erased. It is understandable that the subjective life of Hegel may well have presented a seething shapeless chaos of notions, that the idea of God should have dawned upon Hegel's self-awareness like a light shining on the face of the waters, that he then may have stuggled with its possible relation to other ideas, but on what basis does he assign his own mental groping to the processes of nature and of the history of mankind?

In the end Hegel seems always to be a mystic and pantheist. He experiences himself as an aspect and vehicle of the Spirit. From this standpoint the processes in his own mind are not merely "about" Spirit; they "are" the Spirit itself. Hence, when Hegel struggled with the chaos in his own mind, he interpreted this struggle as the Spirit itself groping for self-expression.

Nevertheless, the true agents of history are not individual persons, but nations (an idea taken over from Herder) in whose development and contests the spirit is brought to an ever higher plane of self-realization. Ordinary individuals moved by their passions, to be sure, are the ultimate vehicles or instruments of the spirit. However, so long as one's perspective is confined to them, history seems to be a blind, cruel business. To Hegel, history was the slaughter bench of human happiness. However, if one shifts perspective to the nation one sees the quite different picture of a rising spiral of spiritual development.

Some individuals at a given time and place, though moved by personal ambitions, tear apart their existing social orders and precipitate the movement of the spirit to a higher plane. These are the heroes of history who serve purposes of objective development quite outside their private intentions. When the heroes of history have accomplished their mission, they are cast aside by the course of events.

In the general movement of the spirit toward self-realization, Hegel maintains one can discern three broad stages: in the ancient Orient only one person, the monarch, was free; in the world of classical Greece some persons were free; in the world of the German nation all were free. Freedom, to Hegel, means voluntary conformance with social necessity.

Because of his love of theological terminology, Hegel's fundamental difference from Augustine is easy to miss. Augustine's God stood apart from his creation, though, to be sure, he was vitally interested in it. For Hegel the spiritual element of history *is* God. Augustine drew a distinction between the sacred and profane, the counterpart of which is not to be found in Hegel, for distinction between spirit and nonspirit cuts across Augustine's distinctions. Against Augustine's concept of the decay and final judgment of the earthly city is Hegel's concept of the progress toward self-realization of the spirit.

The same basic set of ideas as found in Hegel's work received a redefinition in the formulations of Karl Marx (1818–1883). As a student, Marx was strongly influenced by the "left Hegelians." The orientations toward social reform which he shared with this group turned Marx toward a career in journalism rather than toward teaching. For fifteen months, until it was suppressed, he edited the radical middle-class newspaper, the *Rheinische Zeitung.* During this period he began to reconsider his adherence to Hegelianism.

In 1844 Marx took up the study of economics in Paris. When expelled for revolutionary activity, he continued his studies in Brussels. In 1848 he returned to Germany to participate in revolutionary upheavals. When the 1848 revolution collapsed, Marx took up his researches in London (1849), continuing a life of scholarly work under conditions of extreme poverty until his death.

Like Hegel, Marx conceived the development of civilization as a continuous process. However, Marx was more inclined to emphasize the role of objective rather than subjective forces in this development. The mainspring of civilization, Marx believed, was the mode of productions (the processes by which men solve the problems of their material life). The mode of production represents the conjoint operation of three sorts of factors: man, nature, and technique.

The fundamental law of development in all spheres of reality (in nature, in society, and in thought) is the dialectic. Change is always basically a form of growth and occurs through a continuous process of casting up of contradictions and surmounting them. The transformation from one productive system to another is the critical form of the dialectic of human history. Any mode of production tends to bring into being other forms of production. Moreover, as a mode of production declines so, too, does the social order that rests on it. As new forces of production take shape, they require a social order appropriate to them. However, a new social order cannot appear until all the material conditions for its existence have matured in the womb of the old society.

To the present, Marx believed, mankind has evolved four basically distinct productive regimes: the asiatic, the ancient, the feudal, and the capitalistic. Asiatic communities (which Marx thought were illustrated in the present by some Slavic and Russian communities and by some communities of India) were characterized by communal property and directly associated labor. A change in family organization, the rise of the patrilinial lineage, and the appearance of private property brought about the disintegration of such primitive communism. The discovery of iron was a major component in the technology of the new productive order that arose to replace primitive communism. The major innovation in the ancient economy with respect to the human factor in the mode of production was the use of slave labor.

The critical feature in the transition from the ancient to the feudal mode of production was found in the differentiation of free from slave labor and the necessity for a new social order. Under feudalism peasant agriculture and independent handicraft industry formed the basis for the mode of production. Against these were formed various modes of industrial and commercial production which were components in bringing the feudal economy to an end. Marx envisioned the future differentiation of socialistic modes of production from those of capitalism which would in turn require a new social order in place of a capitalistic society.

To Marx, much in the manner of Hegel, man makes history, but the impetus of historical development is borne not by individuals but by classes. Marx's attitude toward great men was also quite parallel to Hegel's: the individual is significant only so far as he acts in class formations. The heroes of history are those who play a critical role in bringing new modes of production into being and to full development. History at bottom is the history of class struggles as the social order appropriate to new modes of production are brought into being against the entrenched forces of tradition.

Institutions other than those involved in the mode of production (such as the state or the law) and ideas are a mere superstructure resting on economic relations and expressing their character in ideal and social form. Marx assumed that history formed a meaningful whole in a manner quite comparable to Hegel.

The foundation of the second major nineteenth-century approach to change was laid by Saint-Simon (1760–1825). The scion of a French noble family at a time when the stratum to which he belonged was breaking up, Saint-Simon illustrated one possible fate when he evolved into a soldier of fortune. He fought in the American Revolution and adventured in Mexico and Spain. When the French Revolution came, he identified for a time with it until attracted by opportunities for profit in speculations in expropriated noble and church lands. After breaking with his business partner, Saint-Simon turned his attention to the exploitation of the new trends in thought, becoming, as it were, an ideological soldier of fortune.

Saint-Simon appropriated the conceptions of progress and faith in science which were a nineteenth-century heritage from the Enlightenment and the Revolution. However, he abandoned the individual as the vehicle of progress for a faith in the new society. Moreover, while he thought that traditional forms of religion were retrogressive and no longer appropriate to the new world, Saint-Simon was convinced that religion was essential for the maintenance of social unity. The reconstruction of society, he thought, required the substitution of the cult of science for traditional Christianity. As early as 1803 Saint-Simon envisioned an international scientific cult coordinated by a hierarchy of scientist-priests, the *élite* of a reorganized European community. He periodically directed his reflections to the notion of a synthesis of the sciences on the basis of a generalization of Newton's laws. In all these respects Saint-Simon anticipated the first synthesis of sociology.

August Comte (1789–1857) assimilated most of Saint-Simon's notions during the period in which he had served as his friend and secretary (1818–1824). After breaking with Saint-Simon, Comte spent the rest of his life in the systematic development of his own and Saint-Simon's insights—a kind of enterprise Saint-Simon found impossible.

Comte took over, as indeed Saint-Simon had, Condorcet's notion that the key to historical change is the progressive development of knowledge. With Saint-Simon and against the rationalists, he accepted the notion that religion plays an indispensable role in human affairs. Any given religious system corresponds to a stage in the development of science and society. Religion, in fact, is merely the inadequate form that science takes in its primitive condition. Science is the perfection of religion.

With Saint-Simon and in contrast to the rationalists, mankind in all its past and future developments was conceived to be an organic whole. It is also organic in its interconnections at any given time: the religious, political, and economic institutions of a society are organs whose interrelations form a unity.

Like Saint-Simon, Comte sought a "law" of social development. Saint-Simon had believed that epochs of organization and construction and epochs of criticism and revolution succeed one another alternately. Since the medieval period had been one of organization, it was necessarily followed by a revolutionary period. Inevitably, thus, the new epoch had to be one of organization once more. In a similar manner, Comte believed that there is an inevitable succession of social stages. He followed Turgot's sequence. The essence of history is opinion. Each branch of knowledge evolves through three stages: theological, metaphysical, and positive. In the first the mind invents, in the second it abstracts, in the third it submits ideas to the test of positive fact.

However, Comte believed the various divisions of human activity are not necessarily at the same stage. Man's knowledge of the physical world, for example, is already in the positive stage. In other spheres this is not the case. If one wishes perspective on the whole society, it is best to estimate it from the status of social and moral ideas, since these are the sciences of highest rank. In this area of man's life, as in all others, the movement of history follows from man's tendency to improve his condition. In the long run, thus, political, moral, and intellectual progress are related. Though variations in his development may be produced by race, climate, or deliberate political action, the significant changes come from within the historical process itself.

The theological stage in human history ended around 1400, from which time Comte dates the period of revolution, the metaphysical period. This period, in turn, Comte thought was nearing its close in the early nineteenth century. The general periods of humanity can be further subdivided. The theological period, for example, had three substages: fetishism, polytheism, and monotheism. Within each of these subdivisions a typical synthesis of institutions was to be found. The polytheistic period, for example, was typified by slavery and a confusion of the spheres of spiritual and temporal power. In the monotheistic period spiritual and temporal powers were separated; the spiritual power was then responsible for education, the temporal power was responsible for action. This separation, however, led to numerous conflicts. The social decay associated with these conflicts marked the onset of the metaphysical period which terminated in revolution and disorder.

The destructive phase of the revolutionary period was opened by Hobbes, Spinoza, and particularly Helvetius with his notion that all human intellects are equal. This notion spawned the dogmas of popular sovereignty and social equality, which in turn justified the right of private judgment. To Comte this was all sheer anarchism. Popular sovereignty, Comte thought, is fatal to orderly institutional life by making superior persons dependent on masses of inferiors. Equality is a vicious principle for, Comte maintained, men are not in fact equal to one another. When men act as if they are equal, revolution is inevitable. Revolution, however, was quite necessary to reveal the decay of society under the suppositions of the metaphysical age.

The characteristic feature of the positivistic period will consist of the reorganization of society by means of a scientific sociology which will assume charge of spiritual life. One of sociology's first duties will be to devise a new code of ethics.

Herbert Spencer (1820–1903) accomplished a transformation in Comte's ideas parallel to that worked out by Marx and Engels in

Hegel's—placing them on a somewhat more materialistic foundation. The task of science, Spencer maintained, is the interpretation of all phenomena in terms of matter, motion, and force. As in the case of the movement from Hegel to Marx, this would seem to terminate in an unqualified materialism.

> The interpretation of all phenomena in terms of Matter, Motion, and Force, is nothing more than the reduction of our complex symbols of thought, to the simplest symbols; and when the equation has been brought to its lowest terms the symbols remain symbols still.[17]

Neither a materialistic nor a spiritualistic interpretation of the universe is adequate, according to Spencer. Spirit and matter are equally plausible and reasonable interpretations of "the Unknown Reality which underlies both."[18]

Spencer's Unknown Reality, moreover, operates in a manner not unlike the medieval conception of God or Comte's concept of humanity providing unity in certain fundamental principles. Among the primary truths of the universe, Spencer maintained, are: "the indestructibility of Matter," the "Continuity of Motion," and "the Persistence of Force."[19] The last is ultimate, the others derived. These operate in such manner as to make the law of evolution the key to changes in all orders of existence. Evolution involves the integration of matter and the concomitant dissipation of motion, operating not only in the whole, but in the parts into which every whole divides.

> By the aggregate Solar System, as well as by each planet and satellite, progressive concentration has been, and still is being, exemplified. In each organism that general incorporation of dispersed materials which causes growth, is accompanied by local incorporations, forming what we call organs. Every society while it displays the aggregative process by its increasing mass of population, displays it also by the rise of dense masses in special parts of its area. . . . From this primary re-distribution we were led on to consider the secondary re-distributions, by inquiring how there came to be a formation of parts during the formation of a whole. It turned out that there is habitually a passage from homogeneity to heterogeneity, along with the passage from diffusion to concentration. While the matter composing the Solar System has been assuming a denser form, it has changed from unity to variety of distribution. Solidification of the Earth has been accompanied by a progress from comparative uniformity to extreme multiformity. In the course of its advance from a germ to a mass of

relatively great bulk, every plant and animal also advances from simplicity to complexity. The increase of a society in numbers and consolidation has for its concomitant an increased heterogeneity both of its political and its industrial organization. And the like holds of all superorganic products—Language, Science, Art, and Literature.[20]

Long before Spencer formally came to incorporate his thinking in an evolutionary framework in his *Social Statics* (1851), he took over Comte's doctrine of progress as the central clue to the problems of evil, happiness, and the relation of man to society. "All evil," according to Spencer, "results from the non-adaptation of constitution to conditions."[21] Evil conceived as nonadaptation perpetually tends to disappear. "In virtue of an essential principle of life, this non-adaptation of an organism to its conditions is ever being rectified; and modification of one or both, continues until the adaptation is complete."[22] Happiness is the reverse of a condition of "evil"; it is the natural fulfillment by an organism of its nature. For man happiness is achieved in and is limited by society. "Hence, to compass greatest happiness, the human constitution must be such that each man may fulfill his own nature, not only without diminishing other men's spheres of activity, but without inflicting unhappiness on other men in any direct or indirect way."[23] The development of civilization consists of "progress towards that constitution of man and society required for the complete manifestation of every one's individuality."[24] This automatically implies the fullest happiness of each and the greatest happiness of all.

The "highest individual" will be conjoined with "greatest mutual dependence,"[25] and "the ultimate man will be one whose private requirements coincide with public ones . . . indeed, human progress is toward greater mutual dependence, as well as toward greater individuation."[26]

Progress conceived by Spencer in *Social Statics* as a necessity of the very nature of man and the constitution of society was generalized in his later work in a manner which made it identical with the doctrine of evolution. It also was extended to the entire universe. In this form of the progress-evolution doctrine, the universe itself is conceived as a gigantic design to force man toward a condition of perfect happiness. On the way toward perfection and in accord with the principle that nothing happens without a reason, all crimes, follies, and catastrophes are visualized as either essential conditions of evolution concealing a higher good or as temporary deviations and minor missteps in the march toward perfection.

Ironically, Spencer was convinced that the most serious of all man's missteps consists in his very attempts to improve his condition. Attempts at social amelioration always bring multiple evils in their wake.

The Sociological Inversion of Medieval Theology

In many essential respects Comte and other early sociologists, like their German counterparts, inverted the Augustinian philosophy of history. In place of the decay of the secular world, they substituted the concept of its progress. In place of the primacy of theological knowledge they substituted the primacy of philosophy or of positivistic science. In place of the notion that the design of historical events consists of the unfolding of the Divine Plan of a deity standing apart from his creation, they substituted the historical self-realization of man.

However, in a number of respects the theory of change of the early sociologists was similar to the medieval Christian formulas it contravened: it presumed that human history is a single meaningful whole. This was as true for the social evolutionism of John Stuart Mill and Herbert Spencer as for the progress doctrine of Comte. Like its medieval predecessor, this doctrine was an ideology, or philosophy of history, an evaluative interpretation of the total meaning of human history and of man's place in the cosmos. Like its medieval predecessor, its plausibility and presumed empirical character was derived from the long range secular trends (in this case the rise of contemporary urban and national communities and the successive extensions of scientific modes of thought to new fields of human endeavor) which had been reset at the core of a series of evaluations.

It could well have been the proud boast of Comte and Spencer that they found the doctrine of St. Augustine standing on its head and set it on its feet.

The Offspring of Progress Doctrines:
Holism and Meaningfulness

The notions which first dominate a sphere of human endeavor enjoy considerable advantage over alternatives, for they operate like an established system of highways, pulling the traffic in their course. Despite the frequent disasters suffered one after another by versions of Progress-Evolutionism, sociology's search for a theory of change has been dominated by the insistence upon (1) holism and (2) meaningfulness as criteria of adequacy.

Progress theorists from Comte to Durkheim and evolution theorists from Spencer and Mill to William Graham Sumner tried to explain the course of human history as a whole. But this is to assume that human history *is* a whole with a comprehensive course. And while these thinkers admitted some influence of extra-social factors (such as demographic pressure and environmental possibilities), on the course of history they insisted that only imminent factors and processes account in any decisive sense for the course of human history. In contrast to the medieval doctrine which visualized man's salvation as a product of supernatural intervention, the delivery of man was now located in his collective formations.

Two major branches of conflict theory arose to challenge the first school of sociological theory. However, both branches of conflict theory (the right wing represented by Bagehot, Ratzenhofer, and Small and the left represented by Marx, Engels, and other of the scientific socialists) also sought to account for the course of human social history as a whole on the basis of imminent processes (successive resolutions of group conflicts or the dialectical overcoming of class conflicts). Early conflict theory was, by and large, a special form of Progress Doctrine.

When imminent evolutionism and progress theories went into eclipse, the search for meaningful, holistic explanations of human history was taken up by the cultural organicists who developed a series of cyclical theories, the most famous of which were by Spengler, Toynbee, and Sorokin. Cultures and civilizations were conceived as wholes which undergo organismic, cyclical processes. Once again the impetus for change was located in imminent factors: Destiny Ideas which set in motion a cycle of development in the peasantry to perish in the city; the successful responses to challenges first of the environment but later to society which harden into increasingly inflexible institutional form; ideate or

182

sensate definitions of reality or truth subject to strains of consistency which incline them to such extremes as to bring their eventual exhaustion and collapse.

The persistence into the present of demands that a theory of social change be measured by the standards of holism and meaningfulness are evident in the theory of change at present tentatively embraced by some sociological functionalists. Once again the attempt is being made to chart the course of social history as a whole on a meaningful basis. The resultant theory of change inclines toward a new form of imminent evolutionism.

The Influence of Holistic
Suppositions on Elementarism

The forms of sociological theory which were quickly reviewed were holistic. They analyzed social and cultural phenomena from the standpoint of the whole as society, humanity, civilization, the historical epoch, or the total social system. The traditional bias toward holism in the area of social change found a responsive echo in these schools of theory. This is not the case, however, for elementaristic sociological theories including formalism, pluralistic behaviorism, and social action theory. Elementaristic sociological theories analyze social phenomena from the standpoint of some presumed basic unit, element, or atom such as social form, social relation, innovative and imitative action, or meaningful action. Complex social arrangements are not conceived by the elementarists as possessing new or emergent properties unresolvable into their components. The characteristic criticism by holistic theorists is that the elementarists are reductionistic. The characteristic criticism by elementarists is that the holists have been victimized by their reifications into the pursuit of chimeras.

Since the area of social change was established by holistic social theorists, it has inevitably been strongly influenced by the climate of opinion they created. When elementaristic social theorists ventured into the area they were either repelled by the twin demands for holism and meaningfulness which dominated the area or they have been unconsciously drawn toward them—to their embarrassment. These two possibilities may be illustrated by formalistic and by pluralistic behaviorist orientations to social and cultural change.

Sociological formalists, illustrated by Georg Simmel, rejected the notion that society was some sort of entity per se. This, Simmel maintained, is pure reification. All that ever exists is a process in which manifold interpersonal arrangements enter in endlessly varied combinations. The task of sociology is to isolate the arrangements or forms in abstraction from the contexts in which they are embedded.

In this formulation of the task of sociology, the traditional field of social change was brushed aside by Simmel as outside the proper sphere of the discipline. If society is in fact only a name, a convenient fiction for social processes, it makes no sense whatsoever to look for laws of evolution or progress in it in terms of criteria of meaningfulness. The field of social change as traditionally conceived was, thus, complicitly treated as the pursuit of rainbows or mirages.

Simmel was aware of the fact that the application of his formalism had significant implications for the theories of change current at the time. He observed:

> Perhaps, in fact, sociological analyses of this sort are apt quite generally to point the way toward a conception of history which is more profound than historical materialism, and which may even supersede it. Historical changes, at their properly effective level, are possibly changes in sociological forms. It is perhaps the way in which individuals and groups behave toward one another; in which the individual behaves toward his group; in which value accents, accumulations, prerogatives, and similar phenomena shift among the elements of society—perhaps it is *these* things which make for truly epochal events.[27]

However, these suggestions of a major new attack on social change were left undeveloped.

Pluralistic behaviorism stemming from the writings of Tarde in France and Ross and Giddings in America, manifest in such persons as F. Stuart Chapin, William Fielding Ogburn, and such contemporaries as H. G. Barnett and Richard T. LaPiere, was also elementaristic, taking the components of social life to be innovative and imitative (repetitive) acts based on the beliefs and desires of individuals. All complex social phenomena were visualized as special arrangements of innovative and repetitive acts with no mysterious emergent properties.

Tarde was keenly aware of the extent to which this approach conflicted with typical nineteenth-century notions of social change. He called attention to the fact that his position ran counter to all concepts of unilinear evolution.

This leads me to examine [a] leading objection which may be raised against me. As a matter of fact, I have gained little in proving that all civilizations, even the most divergent, are rays from a single primordial center, if there are reasons for thinking that, after a certain point, the distance between them begins to diminish rather than increase, and that, whatever may have been the point of departure, the evolution of languages, myths, crafts, laws, sciences, and arts has been drawing nearer and nearer to a beaten track, so that their goal must always have been the same, predetermined and inevitable.

It is for us to ascertain if this hypothesis be true. It is not true. Let me first point out the extravagant consequence that it involves. It implies that, given sufficient time, the scientific spirit must lead, no matter what its path of speculation may be, to the infinitesimal calculus in mathematics, to the law of gravitation in astronomy, to the union of forces in physics, to atomism in chemistry, and in biology to natural selection or to some other ulterior form of evolution. . . . Now, unless I am much mistaken, one might as well say that from its very beginnings and throughout all its metamorphoses, life tended to give birth to certain predetermined forms of existence and that the duck-bill, for example, or the lizard or ophrys or cactus or man himself was a necessary occurrence. Would it not be more plausible to admit that the ever fresh problem of life was of itself undetermined and susceptible of multiple solutions?[28]

From Tarde's standpoint the ultimate origins of patterns of social action can only be found in inventions. The origin of inventions, in turn, he reasoned, is influenced by the inherent difficulty of combining the ideas whose constitution constitutes the invention, the grades of mental ability in society, and the presence of social conditions favorable to the achievements of ability. The essential social process consists in imitation. Imitation obeys the general law of spreading from an initial center in geometrical progression with respect to the number of persons affected. Moreover, rays of imitations are refracted by the mediums through which they pass. Among the social influences which affect the patterns of imitation are various logical influences (the consistency or inconsistency of the inventions with things already socially accepted) and extralogical factors such as the tendency of imitation to proceed from the inside to the outside, to the socially inferior from the socially superior. Moreover, ages of custom tend to alternate with periods in which fashion dominates, during which people are attracted by the novel and the foreign rather than the traditional. Giddings, who followed Tarde's lead, argued that "consciousness of kind" is one of the powerful factors in drawing similarly inclined persons into a complex. This was an attempt to spell out the character of the social medium favorable to social life. Ross, Ogburn, and Chapin attempted to spell out in greater detail those properties of the social medium which speed or retard the adoption of innovating acts. Among these properties of the social medium are such things as tradition, vested interests, special interests, and rational expediencies. Ogburn visualized them as resistance to change.

> Perhaps the most numerously observed cases of cultural inertia are due to difficulties of diffusion of culture. A comprehensive and far-reaching study would reveal a great variety of difficulties of a purely cultural sort, which might or might not be classified into a few general types. . . . Particularly in modern times can the processes of change be seen frequently and in great detail. In modern society, divided into classes, those classes deriving differential benefits from existing conditions tend to resist any change that will lessen those benefits. Difficulties of changing the social conditions are also found to have a prominent psychological aspect as well as a cultural side. Some of the more conspicuous psychological resistances to change are seen in the phenomena of habit, the social pressure for conformity, and the process of forgetting the unpleasant which results in a distorted view and admiration of the past.[29]

Barnett and LaPiere, as major contemporary pluralistic behaviorists, have passed analyses along similar lines, suggesting that a variety of roles may intersect in the process of innovation; they isolate advocates and adopters from innovators.[30]

One of the most revealing developments in the theories of pluralistic behaviorists, illustrating, incidentally, one of their own arguments—that the social medium may determine the progress of an innovation—was the way some of them were pressed by the general sociological milieu on a course toward a holistic and meaningful interpretation of history not required by their theoretical assumptions. Such was the culture-lag theory primarily identified with the name of William Ogburn. A distinction was drawn between material and nonmaterial culture. Material culture then was interpreted in the progress-evolution tradition. All those situations which did not fit the progress formula were then reconceptualized as arising because of a lag of development between material and nonmaterial culture.

> Where one part of culture changes first, through some discovery or invention, and occasions change in some part of culture depen-

dent upon it, there frequently is a delay in the changes occasioned in the dependent part of culture. . . .

A large part of our environment consists of the material conditions of life and a large part of our social heritage is our material culture. These material things consist of houses, factories, machines, raw materials, manufactured products, foodstuffs and other material objects. . . . But a good many of the ways of using the material objects of culture involve rather larger usages and adjustments, such as customs, beliefs, philosophies, laws, governments. . . . The cultural adjustments to material conditions . . . include a larger body of processes than the mores; certainly they include the folk ways and social institutions. These ways of adjustment may be called . . . the adaptive culture. The adaptive culture is therefore that portion of the nonmaterial culture which is adjusted or adapted to the material conditions.

When the material conditions change, changes are occasioned in the adaptive culture. But these changes in the adaptive culture do not syncronize exactly with the change in the material culture. There is a lag which may last for varying lengths of time, sometimes, indeed, for many years.[31]

Almost from the day of its appearance the culture-lag theory was subject to criticism. The most important of the criticisms were (1) that the whole notion of "lag" had built-in value suppositions of an extrascientific character, for what is called a "lag" depends on one's values, (2) no unambiguous distinction can be drawn in all cases between material and nonmaterial culture, leaving a large margin of uncertainty subject to arbitrary construction, and (3) actual social development has frequently reversed the direction of development. There have been significant cases of rapid change in the nonmaterial culture (so far as this can be unambiguously identified) without corresponding changes in material culture.

However, despite such major criticism for two decades, the culture lag hypothesis dominated the approach to social change. The fact that it arose at all and persisted so long despite criticisms of such moment is a tribute to the force of the unconscious suppositions that dominated the area. The pluralistic behavioral position, of course, does not stand or fall with the culture-lag theory. The wrirings of Barnett and LaPiere may in part be interpreted as new attacks on the problems of social change from a pluralistic, behavioral point of view without recourse to the hypothesis.

There was nothing about the pluralistic behavioral position in itself which compelled it to seek an overall or single design in human history. Tarde, as noted above, immediately called this idea into question. Human social events could be analyzed into innovative and repetitive activities whether or not there is a master plan for the human race. There is not, moreover, anything necessarily wrong with attempting to break down the forms of culture as in the distinction between material and nonmaterial culture. However, when advocates of the position tried simultaneously to salvage the doctrine of progress as the master plan for mankind and to utilize the concept of nonmaterial culture to account for defects in it, they were lured beyond their depth by the holistic and meaningful presuppositions traditional to the area.

Two possible responses, thus, to the climate of opinion traditional to the area of social change were abandonment of the area (illustrated by formalism) or yielding to its despite the conflicts it created in one's theory (as illustrated by pluralistic behaviorism's concept of cultural lag). There was a third possibility. One could investigate particular sequences of change without formally designating them as studies of social change. Many social action theorists took this course. Such were: Robert MacIver's studies of the transformations of political institutions, John R. Commons' studies of the intersection between legal institutions and the institutions of capitalism, Max Weber's studies of the interrelation between religious ethics and economic conduct, the influence of secular trends toward rationalization of institutions and the development of Western musical forms, the role of charisma and its routinization in institutional change. There are many others. However, as long as social change was conceptualized as designating a single master plan for the human race, such studies of particular changes have ambiguous standing.

Prospects

The fact that so many specific investigations have been made of many phases of social life without their being acknowledged to be studies of social change is the strongest possible testimony of the persistence of a climate of opinion which depresses the area away from scientific responsibility and toward an ideology or a philosophy of history. The scientific prospects for the area are inseparable from the readiness of contemporary students to win this area at long last for science. This requires abandonment of the suppositions that have traditionally dominated the area.

There is no scientific evidence to suggest that man's history is a single unit in which everything is related to everything else. Nor is there any scientific evidence that human history is developing toward some destiny which provides significance or meaning to all that has happened or will happen. These are articles of faith, not scientific hypotheses. From a scientific standpoint human history as a whole is without meaning.

When holism and meaningfulness are abandoned as criteria of an adequate theory of social change, important theoretical and practical consequences ensue. There is no longer a problem of social change; there are *many problems*. Theoretically the most reasonable way to attack the problems of social change is by examining, one at a time, the specific types of social arrangements. Many studies not usually viewed as studies of change can, at last, be seen as the significant contributions to the area. Moreover, there is considerable advantage in isolating and examining separately the problems (1) of civilization, (2) of communities, and (3) of groups and institutions. The many studies already made of these phenomena contain theoretical suggestions as well as important bodies of empirical material.

Civilizations may be conceived as high cultural syntheses. Culture, the forms learned by man as a member of society, is analytically distinct from the interpersonal practices out of which culture arises. While there is no such thing as a society without culture, and while a culture which is not embedded in practice is a mere set of possibilities, all persons in varying degrees discriminate between forms and practices. Complex societies develop specialists (sages, wise men, intellectuals, journalists, artists, poets, musicians) in various categories of cultural forms. The ideal may emerge of bringing about a synthesis of the culture. In any case, the rise of civilizations is not altogether an unconscious process. Moreover, civilizational syntheses achieved in connection with particular institutions and communities are in part separable from them. In the ancient world the high culture synthesis achieved in connection with the city-state was used as an instrument of imperial policy under changed social circumstances by Alexander the Great and the Roman emperors.

Once the problems of civilization are isolated, and acknowledgement made of the fact that generalizations about civilization do not necessarily hold for other social formations, the work of many sociologists appears in new perspective. Much of the work of Max and Alfred Weber has relevance for the study of civilization. Some of the criticism that has been directed at Sorokin's work becomes irrelevant, when it is perceived that he was seeking to isolate the

189

problems of civilization. Many of Sorokin's works were attempts to isolate the bases of style formation in high cultural syntheses. The sociology of art, of knowledge, and of science may be seen as limited studies in the sociology of culture and the studies of the sociology of the intellectual and of the scientist are concerned with special types of cultural specialists. These are all subdivisions of the theory of civilization.

Communities, in contrast to civilizations, are systems of social activities comprehensive enough to bring a plurality of people through the cycle of a normal year and the cycle of a normal lifetime. Many types of communities have been isolated and studied extensively by social scientists: a wide variety of tribal communities, a multiplicity of peasant villages, feudal communities, city communities, guest or ethnic communities, and nations. A vast literature rich with theoretical suggestions and empirical material is available for the student who wishes to concentrate on this significant branch of social change.

Also separable both from the problems of civilization and community formation is the establishment and transformation of particular groups and institutions. The problems of some particular area of group and institutional life, such as the family, are not necessarily identical with those of the entire community. Such problems have proved to be so various that a whole series of sociological specialties has arisen for the examination of particular institutions: the sociology of the family, industrial sociology, political sociology, the sociology of education, and so on. Virtual libraries of literature have been produced on the changes in particular institutions. One of the special tasks for the student of social change is to exploit this rich literature for the general information it can supply on the formation and destruction of groups and institutions.

The prospects for a scientific study of social change seem, thus, in part to depend on separating out and attacking separately the formation and destruction of civilizations, communities, and groups and institutions. But the question may be raised as to whether there is anything left of the field *as a whole*, for the suggestions just made seem to have substituted three fields where there is originally only one. However, civilizations, communities, and groups and institutions are not completely separable either in fact or in theory. It will never be possible to account for changes in one without considering the bearing of others. Perhaps the one thing that will remain distinctive of the field of social change as a whole will consist in the specialized study of its interrelations.

NOTES

1. St. Augustine, *The City of God*, trans. Marcus Dods (New York: Hafner Publishing Company, 1949), vol. I, p. 15.

2. Ibid., vol. I, p. 2.

3. Ibid., vol. II, p. 47.

4. Ibid., vol. II, p. 50.

5. Ibid., p. 55.

6. Jean Bodin, *Method for the Easy Comprehension of History*, trans. Beatrice Reynolds (New York: Columbia University Press, 1945).

7. Ibid., p. 8.

8. Ibid., pp. 85 ff. Herodotus, for example, held such notions.

9. Ibid., p. 153; pp. 212 ff.

10. Ibid., pp. 215 ff.

11. Ibid., pp. 228 ff.

12. Ibid., pp. 291 ff.

13. Giambattista Vico, *The New Science of Giambattista Vico*, trans. Thomas Goddard Bergin and Max Harold Fisch (Ithaca, N.Y.: Cornell University Press, 1948), paragraph II, 145.

14. Ibid., III, 176.

15. Ibid., III, 245.

16. Ibid., III, 173.

17. Herbert Spencer, *First Principles* (Edinburgh: Williams & Norgate, 1884), p. 558.

18. Ibid.

19. Ibid., p. 530.

20. Ibid., pp. 543-44.

21. Herbert Spencer, *Social Statics* (New York: D. Appleton & Co., 1908), p. 28.

22. Ibid.

23. Ibid., p. 34.

24. Ibid., p. 253.

25. Ibid., p. 260.

26. Ibid., p. 26.

27. Georg Simmel, *The Sociology of George Simmel*, trans. Kurt H. Wolff (Glencoe, Ill.: The Free Press, 1950), p. 16.

28. Gabriel Tarde, *The Laws of Imitation*, trans. Elsie Clews Parsons (New York: Henry Holt, 1903), pp. 51-52.

29. William Fielding Ogburn, *Social Change* (New York: Viking Press, 1927), pp. 194-95.

30. H. G. Barnett, *Innovation: The Basis of Cultural Change* (New York: McGraw-Hill, 1953), and Richard T. LaPiere, *Social Change* (New York: McGraw-Hill, 1965).

31. Ogburn, *Social Change*, pp. 201-3.

SELECTED BIBLIOGRAPHY

Augustine. *The City of God.* Translated by Marcus Dods. New York: Hafner, 1949.

Barnett, H. G. *Innovation: The Basis of Cultural Change.* New York: McGraw-Hill, 1953.

Bodin, Jean. *Method for the Comprehension of History.* Translated by Beatrice Reynolds. New York: Columbia University Press, 1945.

Comte, Auguste. *The Positive Philosophy of Auguste Comte.* Translated by Harriet Martineau. London: George Bell & Sons, 1896.

Hegel, Georg Wilhelm Friedrich. *The Philosophy of History.* Translated by J. Sibree. New York: Wiley, 1944.

LaPiere, Richard T. *Social Change.* New York: McGraw-Hill, 1965.

Martindale, Don. *Social Life and Cultural Change.* Princeton, N.J.: D. Van Nostrand, 1962.

Marx, Karl, and Engels, Friedrich. *Basic Writings on Politics and Philosophy.* Edited by Lewis S. Feuer. New York: Anchor Books, 1959.

Ogburn, William Fielding. *Social Change.* New York: Viking Press, 1927.

Simmel, Georg. *The Sociology of Georg Simmel.* Translated by Kurt H. Wolff. Glencoe, Ill.: The Free Press, 1950.

Sorokin, Pitirim. *Social and Cultural Dynamics.* New York: American Book Co., 1937–41.

Spengler, Oswald. *The Decline of the West.* Translated by Charles Francis Atkinson. New York: Alfred A. Knopf. 1929.

Tarde, Gabriel. *The Laws of Imitation.* Translated by Elsie Clews Parsons. New York: Henry Holt, 1903.

Vico, Giambattista. *The New Science of Giambattista Vico.* Translated by Thomas Goddard Bergin and Max Harold Fisch. Ithaca, N.Y.: Cornell University Press, 1948.

PART III

The Types of Sociological Theory

Sooner or later the student of theory must confront the problem posed by the similarities and differences between social scientists in their approach to the subject matter of their disciplines. These differences exist in almost every degree of intensity and extent. Furthermore, social scientists view themselves as essentially similar or different from one another. The determination of some order or pattern in this maze of similarity and difference is the central task of typology.

Typologies may be set up from a variety of perspectives, such as from the standpoint of the self-identification of the theorists studied, from the standpoint of the origin (conceptual or practical) of his point of view, from the standpoint of his objectives, and so on. Once granted the basis for a typology, the task is to discern patterns of "essential" similarity despite variations and differences of detail.

In *The Nature and Types of Sociological Theory*, for example, where the primary problem was to trace the historical emergence of the major patterns of contemporary sociological theory, a combined analytical-historical perspective was assumed in typing the various current forms of sociological theory. Inasmuch as some explanations of human social life which were still popular in the first quarter of the twentieth century had lost their attractiveness to the modern mind, they were quietly dropped. For this reason various geographic, climatic environmental, biologistic, and racial explanations of social life were eliminated from the account.

The question as to what was to be considered to be an "essential" similarity of perspective, a shared set of similarities sufficient to warrant placing thinkers in the same school regardless of differences of detail, was answered in terms of the assumptions about the nature of social life and about how it was best studied (methodology). In these terms differences in terminology, scope, and application were set aside, and thinkers were organized into "schools," even if they did not perceive themselves in identical terms.

Finally, in order of consideration a historical perspective was assumed. Schools of thought were taken up in the rough order that they made their appearance. Their backgrounds in Western, particularly philosophical, thought was traced and the development of a school from the time of its origin to its most recent manifestations was traced. The resultant treatment was a compromise between a strictly analytical and a strictly historical review of the types of sociological theory. In the process some minor movements were set aside. Five major types of sociological theory were isolated and analyzed: Positivistic Organicism, Conflict Theory, Formalism, Social Behaviorism, and Functionalism.

In the present section, following as it does the review of various ontological, epistemological, and ethical problems which continue to plague sociological theory, a more purely analytical approach is made to the types of sociological theory, locating, beside the types noted above, a number of minor types which may grow more significant in time.

CHAPTER 6

Humanism, Scientism, and the Types of Sociological Theory

In the curriculum of the modern university the courses fall into three clear divisions: the humanities, the sciences, and the social sciences. Even persons who have not attended closely to the development of Western intellectuality are well aware of the fact that the humanities are the oldest and the social sciences are the youngest of the trilogy. Moreover, one can quickly assure himself that the social sciences are insurgent between the humanities and science, borrowing from and somewhat in tension with each. Many a hardheaded physical scientist of the old school will explain, if pressed, that the social sciences "are not even sciences." And many a traditional humanist is so sure that social concerns belong properly in the humanities as to find the very idea of a social science "revolting." The social scientists, for their part, often smugly experience themselves as the true synthesizers of the thought and experience of modern man, as the bearers of the discipline which fused the humanistic and scientific poles of western thought. Auguste Comte thought sociology was the queen of the sciences, and the late C. Wright Mills observed:

It is *not* true, as Ernest Jones asserted, that "Man's chief enemy and danger is his own unruly nature and the dark forces pent up within him." On the contrary: "Man's chief danger" today lies in the unruly forces of contemporary society itself, with its alienating methods of production, its enveloping techniques of political domination, its international anarchy—in a word, its pervasive transformations of the very "nature" of man and the conditions and aims of his life.

It is now the social scientist's foremost political and intellectual task—for here the two coincide—to make clear the elements of contemporary uneasiness and indifference. It is the central demand made upon him by other cultural workmen—by physical scientists and artists, by the intellectual community in general. It is because of this task and these demands, I believe, that the social sciences are becoming the common denominator of our cultural period, and the sociological imagination our most needed quality of mind.[1]

In this forthright statement sociology is the true synthesis of the intellectual currents of the West, and only in the hands of sociologists may its affairs be trusted. "To be aware of the idea of social structure and to use it with sensibility is to be capable of tracing . . . linkages among a great variety of *milieux*. To be able to do that is to possess the sociological imagination."[2]

The rise of sociology as a discipline which sought to substantiate claims such as those of C. Wright Mills to be the representative outlook of contemporary man is intimately bound up with its relation to the intellectual currents and the substantive issues of Western man. The two main streams of Western thought are humanism and science which summarize the alternative ways by which Western man solves the problems of his social and natural world. The two most comprehensive substantive problems which Western man must solve are those of the individual and those of the collective (society). No orientations to the problems of existence are more fundamental than those which take the individual as primary (individualism) and those which take the collective as primary (collectivism). It is not misleading to take these two methodological orientations (the humanistic and the scientific) and substantive theoretical alternatives (individualism and collectivism) as the primary compass points of Western thought (see table 4).

If we pass quickly in review the main methodological orientations of Western thought and the major substantive theoretical alternatives, it is possible to employ the resultant sketch to map the evolution of sociology. The primary forces playing upon sociology arise out of the experience of Western man.

196

Table 4

Main Compass Points of Western Thought

P e r s		Substantive	Alternatives
		Individualism	Collectivism
p e c t	Humanistic	Humanistic Individualism	Humanistic Collectivism
i v e s	Scientific	Scientific Individualism	Scientific Collectivism

Humanism as the Pioneering Outlook of Western Man

The distinctive communities of the Middle Ages were agrarian and religious in character: peasant villages, feudal manors, and monasteries.[3] Though they have roots in the Middle Ages, the first of the distinctive communities of the contemporary world were cities.[4] Humanism, the pioneering outlook of Western man, was born in the city. Early civic humanism can be most simply defined as a secularized, man-centered outlook and methodology developed for the needs of civic man in contrast to the God-centered outlook and salvation technology of the members of typical medieval communities.

The most highly valued types of men of the Middle Ages were chivalrous knights and ascetic monks. The most meaningful life was one devoted to God's work, whether this consisted of vigils, fasting, ascetic privations, prayer, or engaging in military activities in the name of the faith. The most sanctified of all modes of deportment were those of the monastic recluse. The technology of the religiously significant life centered in withdrawal from sensual pleasure, fasting, privations, and prayer—especially in contemplation of the holy.

In the rising cities the modes of deportment associated with chivalrous adventurers or contemplative ascetics were retrograde. In the streets of the city knights and monks rubbed shoulders with new commercial and industrial types: plutocrats rich from international trade and able by their new wealth to deck themselves out with fineries from afar in a manner that outshone the poor knight and poorer monk. Moreover, in the streets there appeared a variety of others: traders from afar speaking strange tongues, craftsmen, former serfs enjoying the freedom of the city. While knight and monk lost comparative status with the rise of the new commercial types, they lost it also with the rise of the new freemen from the base of society. In those cities a new thriving secularity was evident. The silent watches and vigils of the knightly novitiate or the silence of the monastic chamber had no place here. The religious structures serving the city were propelled to a new grandeur. In the cities the magnificent Gothic cathedrals were being subscribed and constructed. The humble monasteries were withdrawing to a vine-veiled countryside as the tides of life surged away from them.

The overpowering sense of the evil of the secular world which had sent Christianity into the monastery in the days of the decay of the Roman cities was replaced by a new optimistic sense of abundant life. In the cities Western man even began to re-tool his religion to correspond to the new secular optimism that fired his aspirations. In the cities men were individualized, cast upon their own resources, and compelled to employ their own talents to construct the institutions they needed.

> In the Middle Ages both sides of human consciousness—that which was turned within and that which was turned without—lay dreaming or half awake beneath a common veil. The veil was woven of faith, illusion, and childish prepossession, through which the world and history were soon clad in strange hues. Man was conscious of himself only as a member of a race, people, party, family, or corporation—only through some general category. In Italy this veil first melted into air; an *objective* treatment and consideration of the State and of all the things of this world became possible. The *subjective* side at the same time asserted itself with corresponding emphasis; man became a spiritual individual, and recognized himself as such. In the same way the Greek had once distinguished himself from the barbarism, and the Arab had felt himself an individual at a time when other Asiatics knew themselves only as members of a race.[5]

Already in the twelfth century, in response to the need for guidance in their new civic communities, the humanists had begun to examine the classics of antiquity. It was not the slightest intention of the persons engaged in this enterprise to deify the past. Quite the contrary. They recognized in the literature produced in the ancient polis the writings of people with an experience in many points similar to their own. In the course of their interest in the exploitation of classical sources, they pioneered an elaborate array of new skills: they acquired the classical languages and began to insist on the study of the classical texts in the original; they developed philological techniques; and they began to elaborate the standards of historical criticism in a manner not seen since the days of the classical Greeks.

The humanists belonged to the civic types responsible for developing the institutions of the city: corresponding secretaries, the tutors in important political and merchant families, advisers of princes, and at times, even the princes and popes themselves, rich merchants with strong voices in the councils of the cities, and professors in the newly forming universities.[6] While a single coherent philosophy cannot be assigned to the humanists as a whole, they were characterized by their optimistic theory of human nature, the employment of scholarship as a device for the solution of contemporary problems, the evaluation of classical learning as a source of guidance in social and intellectual affairs, and the development of alternatives to medieval theological explanations of the world.[7]

By the twelfth century the traditional powers of the medieval world had become fully aware of the new spirit that was breaking away from its control. At the University of Paris in 1210, 1215, and again in 1231, professors and students were excommunicated for having disobeyed orders of the Church by reading Aristotle. In the cities the new social and intellectual ferment so completely eluded traditional structures as to lead to the formation of a wide variety of voluntary associations. Some of the new formations were eventually taken over by the Church and made into new official monastic movements like the "Four Orders," the Dominicans, Franciscans, Carmelites, and Austin Friars.[8] But other semireligious social movements such as the Beguines and the Beghars of the Low Countries, the Humiliati of Italy, and the Poor Men of Leon were not blessed with the approval of the Church.

Representatives of the new mendicant orders pressed their way into the newly forming universities and took up the battle against the new intellectual ferment. It was quickly perceived that one could not destroy the new intellectual currents. The task was to turn them to the religious advantage of the Church. If masters and students were going to read Aristotle at the risk of excommunication, the task was to take over Aristotle and purge the texts. The reconciliation of Aristotle with Christian theology was urged by great Franciscan scholars such as Robert Grosseteste, and by even more prominent Dominicans such as Albert the Great (1200–1280) and Thomas Aquinas (1225–1274). In the thirteenth century the Benedictine orders won the day and clamped an official scholasticism down on the universities.

With this development, the humanists were forced to minor positions in the universities and to purely private circles, where at times, like Ficino, they established private academies, and at times promoted the cause of Platonism against official scholasticism and Aristotelianism which was becoming dominant in the universities.[9] By the fifteenth century in private circles of the Italian cities, the tide had turned. Humanism broke through the spell of official scholasticism and achieved a kind of classic fullness.

The Emergence of
Western Science

In the same civic world where humanism had formed, Western science emerged. Humanism arose in circles of cultivated social and political strata; science arose in the circles of artists and craftsmen. Humanism pioneered a new mode of deportment in the social and political world, while science pioneered a new method of procedure toward the world of physical things.

The peculiarities of science are found in its fusion of a rational conception of knowledge with a systematic experimentalism toward the world of facts. From the ancient world the West inherited the rational proof and the dream of systematically transforming all thought into a comprehensive rational unity.[10] Social developments in the ancient polis had cast its citizen-intellectuals on their own conceptual resources without the opportunity for recourse to institutional devices to settle differences of opinion. Under these circumstances, the philosophers of ancient Greece began to analyze the thought process in the attempt to establish rules which would automatically guarantee the truth without the need to appeal to any agency outside the thought process itself. The unique place of Socrates among the Greek philosophers was bound up with the self-consciousness he brought to this search for an autonomous thought process. The great monuments to the search for the rational proof were Euclidian geometry and Aristotelian logic.

However, the rational proof and the dream of the rational

integration of all knowledge born in Greek philosophy was restricted from any extensive application to the world of fact by the social situation of the ancient philosopher. The ancient philosopher was a citizen-soldier[11] in a society where the status of work was determined by slavery. Wherever slavery appears the conduct of practical activities tends to be technologically unprogressive. While the ancient world supplied the rational proof to science, it could not supply the progressive technology which science also needed.

Contrary to those historians of science who see no contribution at all to science from the Middle Ages and the Renaissance, they supplied it with the technology that science required. The decline of slavery in the Middle Ages freed technology from its bondage to that unprogressive system. The new progressiveness has been skillfully phrased recently by Lynn White, Jr. The heavy wheeled plow which was invented and developed to cultivate the heavy soils of northern Europe in turn sustained developments critical to the emergence of the modern world.

> The increased returns from the labour of the northern peasant raised his standard of living and consequently his ability to buy manufactured goods. It provided surplus food which, from the tenth century on, permitted rapid urbanization. In the new cities there arose a class of skilled artisans and merchants, the burghers who speedily got control of their communities and created a novel and characteristic way of life.... In this new environment germinated the dominant feature of the modern world: power technology.[12]

It was of crucial importance for the rise of science that when the medieval cities arose, they grew out of and continued to evolve on the basis of the free technologies of the medieval world.

> The later Middle Ages; that is, roughly from A.D. 1000 to the close of the fifteenth century, is the period of decisive development in the history of the effort to use the forces of nature mechanically for human purposes. What had been, up to that time, an empirical grouping, was converted with increasing rapidity into a conscious and widespread programme designed to harness and direct the energies observable around us. The labour-saving power technology which has been one of the distinctive characteristics of the Occident in modern times depends not only upon a medieval mutation of men's attitudes towards the exploitation of nature but also, to a great extent, upon specific medieval achievements.[13]

Under a slave economy, the capitalist owns both slaves, as a kind of human cattle, and the tools with which they work. It is usually to the advantage of the slave to work as little as possible to keep the level of demands on himself reduced. He has no incentive either to preserve the tools with which he works or to improve them. He is far more inclined to express his resentment for his condition by sabotage of his tools. However, men working for themselves and in possession of their own equipment experience their tools as a virtual extension of their personalities. Moreover, any improvement they make in their tools or in the use of nonhuman forms of energy eases the burden of their labors and increases the supply of the material things which enhance their styles of life. The conditions of a free economy, thus, may promote an attitude of systematic instrumentalism toward tools and the material conditions and things of life. Pragmatic instrumentalism has appeared frequently among preliterate peoples. The technology of the Eskimo, for example, is dominated by a hard-headed pragmatic instrumentalism.

> The physical environment of the Eskimo is so forbidding and its peculiarities so extreme that a human group, finding itself in this environment, would perish unless it achieved a very special adjustment to environmental conditions. This is precisely what has happened in the case of the Eskimo. By means of a large number of special devices they have managed to make the inhospitable Arctic their home, and so well have they solved this difficult problem that occasional visitors from the outside world, such as white traders or ardent anthropologists, have been known to accept the Eskimo mode of life rather than, in usual fashion, impose theirs upon the Eskimo.[14]

A study of Eskimo technology shows that there were times in the past when the Eskimo's fascination with tools and implements led to surprisingly delicate elaborations which adapted them to tasks of a refinement that could not possibly have had survival value and which, if retained, could have operated against survival. Such periods of empirical tool and implement refinement are invariably followed by a reaction in the direction of practical efficiency once again. In the end pragmatic instrumentalism always dominated the Eskimo's orientation to nature.

However, pragmatic instrumentalism in man's orientation to his tools and to nature is not, per se, science. Science presupposes a rational ideal of knowledge conjoined to a method of establishing "truths" in the world of fact comparable to the role played by logic and mathematics in establishing truths in the world of ideas. The rational proof in the world of ideas was recovered from antiquity by the humanists. The breakthrough from the pragmatic instrumentalism of the medieval rural and urban worlds to the rational ideal of knowledge was the work of the Renaissance craftsman-artist.

When the artist is a slave, as he often was in antiquity, he can hardly be expected to pioneer a new orientation in thought binding on his times. The free artist of the Western city, on the other hand, operating with a free technology, was in quite a different position. The artist worked in a world of material things and tools. His competence was related, in the first instance, to his knowledge of and control over them. When in addition the artist was expected to create new patterns with his materials and tools, he had only one recourse. It was necessary to experiment. The Renaissance artist over and over again had recourse to experimentalism to explore the possibilities of materials. He often found himself in the position where he had to invent new instruments for his researches. Systematic experimentalism was being transformed into a general procedure as fundamental for the investigation and establishment of "truths" in the empirical world as logic and mathematics were in the world of thought.

In the medieval and Renaissance cities, where systematic experimentalism was emerging as a basic method for the investigation of nature, the humanists had recovered the rational proof from antiquity. In the instant these two configurations (rational proof and empirical experimentalism) were linked, science was born. Their conjoint operation in the minds of the Renaissance artists is evident in the notebooks of Leonardo da Vinci. Da Vinci went to considerable lengths to recover mathematical treatises from antiquity. In the world of thought, he argued, mathematics provides certainty.

> He who blames the supreme certainty of mathematics feeds on confusion, and will never impose silence upon the contradictions of the sophistical sciences, which occasion perpetual clamour.[15]

To anyone who wished to understand the world, he advised: "O students, study mathematics and do not build without foundations."[16] However, at the same time Da Vinci recognized that empirical knowledge has a nonmathematical origin in the world of fact. "All our knowledge originates in our sensibilities."[17] However, the world of fact, knowledge of which is gained by experience, also has an order. By means of experiment, experience can be made to yield up its certainties.

> Experience is never at fault; it is only your judgment that is in error in promising itself such results from experience as are not caused by our experiments.[18]

When one undertook to experiment with nature, he was convinced that it was advisable to proceed by the most direct and least complicated route possible. "When you wish to produce a result by means of an instrument, do not allow yourself to complicate it by introducing many subsidiary parts, but follow the briefest way possible." And once one has ascertained natural causes, the need for further experiment ceases. "There is no result in nature without a cause; understand the cause and you will have no need of the experiment."[19] In short, nature presents a lawful world.

Contrasts between
Humanism and Science

Humanism arose in educated and politically responsible circles of the medieval and Renaissance cities; science arose in artistic and industrial circles. Humanism arose as a new secular orientation toward social and intellectual affairs; science arose as a new orientation toward instruments, material things, and the physical world.

The methodological differences between humanism and science are of considerable interest, since they supplied the major discipline of the university. Humanism developed a series of techniques for exploring ancient literature and contemporary experience for guidance in current affairs. It elaborated the techniques of philological criticism and historical research. Science, on the other hand, developed systematic experimentalism into a general procedure for the investigation of nature.

The sharpest differences, however, appear in the objectives of humanism and science. Humanism was a man-centered (secular), normative orientation intended to justify as well as implement the new kinds of individuality and community represented by the citizen and the medieval city. Humanism was inspired by an optimistic view in contrast to the pessimistic medieval view of human nature. Humanism saw the fullness of man's powers in terms of his achievements in secular contexts. Science, on the other hand, arose as a non-normative method for investigating nature. Its objectives were not to establish a particular state of natural or social affairs but to acquire the most exact knowledge of nature possible and to increase to the maximum man's ability to control the material world.[20]

The elements of the fundamental polarity in Western thought, humanism and science, arose in the city, the first distinctive community of Western men. However, the initial polarity was between humanism and theology with science as a subtheme of both. In the sixteenth century the new community represented by the nation-state[21] had begun to replace the city as the primary community of Western man. Humanism gravitated to the new national communities, where it became foundational to seventeenth- and eighteenth-century rationalism.[22] At this time the old tensions between humanism and theology began to break down. Theology was beginning to cast its lot with the humanities. Science began to display its unparalleled powers to increase man's objective knowledge of nature. It was found to be invaluable in the new military and economic contexts associated with the rise of the nation. With this development the basic polarity of Western thought achieved its classic form.

Individualism and Collectivism
in Western Thought

There are no more basic problems to men attempting to account for themselves and for their social world than the comparative significance to be assigned to the individual and to the collective. In the medieval monastic communities there was even a hermitic (individualistic) and cenobitic (communal) theory of monastic life. The major contrast between the forms of Eastern and Western monasticism was in the hermitic character of the former—a property which transposed Eastern monastic establishments into laissez-faire communities of competitive religious virtuosos. In Western monasticism, stemming from St. Benedict, on the other hand, cenobitic patterns prevailed and individual ascetic virtuosity was always subordinated to the collective requirements of the monastery as a whole under the abbot. Eastern monasticism, in short, rested on the theory and practice of ascetic individualism; Western monasticism rested on the theory and practice of collective asceticism.

The individualistic or collectivisitic orientations emerge in every community. When these perspectives are raised to the level of systematic philosophies of the importance of the individual and of the group, they formulate a very fundamental ideological contrast. Individualism is an ideology which maintains that the person is the highest of all values and the vindication of a society is to be found in its assistance in the maximum unfolding of the individual's potential. Collectivism is an ideology which maintains that the highest of all values is the society (and the peace and harmony it guarantees). From the standpoint of collectivism, while individuals are important, they are second to the community, for without the community the individual is insignificant. Individualism on the other hand leads naturally to the assumption that society and institutions are instrumental—institutions are made for people, not people for institutions. Collectivism leads naturally to the position that peace is the highest of all values, without which only chaos ensues. Hence, collectivism maintains that people must order their behavior to the priority of the community.

As shown by the hermitic and cenobitic theories of monasticism, there is an individualism and collectivism in the monastic community as well as in any other type of community, be it a rural community, a city, or a nation-state. As these ideologies developed in Western thought, the individualistic position has been most closely linked with liberalism; the collectivistic position has been most closely linked with conservatism. However, the terms "liberalism" and "conservatism" are not consistently linked with individualism and collectivism, hence this terminology is avoided in the present instance.

While individualism and collectivism represent alternate categories of life in every community, and while they are never completely absent as alternative perspectives, they are very often present in quite different proportions. Without attempting to account for minor cycles in the alteration of individualism and collectivism in the course of the development of a community, it can be noted that individualism tends to be strong in the periods of the formation of a community. Collectivism, on the other hand, tends to dominate the period of a community's maturity. The reasons for this are not difficult to discover.

At the time people are in the process of creating a new community, they are forced to solve problems which are quite new. This is what it means to create a new community. Since there are no established patterns to go on, individuals must be free to create new ones. At such times the average age of the community's leaders tends to be lowered. The outstanding individual is followed because of his creativity and without regard for external qualifications (such as derivation from an old or an outstanding family). It is the time of the charismatic leader. Every community tends to remember from its formative period an array of charismatic leaders whom it may apotheosize later as cultural heroes.

On the other hand, once the new community has been formed and its institutions stabilized, there is a tendency to discourage individualism which can, at this time, appear only as a disruptive principle. The age of a community's leaders is often raised, for people prefer the stable older men and not the young hotheads. Anti-individualistic, collectivistic ideologies enjoy greater popularity during the maturity of a community.

The rhythm of an early individualism followed by a mature collectivism is discernible first in the Western city and later in the nation-state. In the formative period of the Western city (in the eleventh and twelfth centuries), a new spirit of individualism was apparent in the works of the first wave of humanistic intellectuals. In the songs of the jongleurs a new impudent note of social criticism was manifest. In the same period the universities were beginning to take shape out of voluntary associations (guilds) of scholars and teachers. Famous teachers wandered from place to place with remarkable independence and were often followed by their students. By the end of the twelfth century most of the institutions of the city had been established, and the process of perfecting them into an urban synthesis was under way. At this very time, the counterattack on the individualism which had been released in the city was launched by the mendicant friars, particularly the Dominicans and Franciscans. The counterattack was successful. The method of Abelard, who had been a spokesman for the newly powerful secular clergy, a method of dissolving all issues into a conflict between equally impressive authorities and freeing thought for a new formulation, was transformed into the procedure of scholasticism for disposing of the objections of the opposition. Aristotle, for the reading of whose works scholars and masters at Paris had once been excommunicated, was fused with medieval theology and lifted into the position of a dogmatic authority.

Without tracing the cycles more closely, in the early city the humanistic individualism of the eleventh and twelfth centuries was followed by the scholastic collectivism of the thirteenth and fourteenth. Unfortunately, the analysis of the individualistic and collectivistic aspects of the civic humanism of the fifteenth- and sixteenth-century city has never been carried out.

Again in the formative period of the nation-state, the time when it was fusing into an integrated community (in the seventeenth and eighteenth centuries), the wave of philosophy from Descartes to Kant reflects a powerful upsurge of individualism. Even Descartes' formula, which is frequently taken as the starting point of modern philosophy, *cogito ergo sum*, expressed the assumption that the one indubitable reality is the individual. The indisputable reality (unquestioned assumption) of the collectivistic medieval world was *God is*, but in Descartes' world one starts with the individual. All other realities, including God, were to be established by a chain of logical reasoning beginning with the first reality of individual thought.

However, once the revolutions of the nineteenth century had brought the modern nation-state into existence, collectivistic philosophies (Hegelianism, Absolute Idealism) became popular. Within the nation-state the individualistic ideologies of the seventeenth and eighteenth centuries were thrust into the background by the comparative dominance of collectivistic ideologies in the nineteenth and twentieth centuries.

Some Important Subdistinctions in the Modern Individualistic and Collectivistic Ideologies

Recent individualism and collectivism have been subdivided in further ways. Individualism has been in two major forms, depending on whether the forms of rationalism were or were not made central. One may agree that the individual is the most significant of all realities without considering men to be primarily distinguished by their reason or rationality. It is possible to distinguish rationalistic and nonrationalistic forms of individualism even at an early period. In the cities, for example, a form of theological collectivism, scholasticism, attempted to press the forms of ancient rationalism to the support of scholasticism. In reaction to this attempt, many humanists fused their humanistic individualism with a nonrational (mystical or emotional) conception of the individual. On the other hand, eighteenth- and nineteenth-century rationalists detached rationalism from scholastic contexts and found the essence of the individual in his rational faculties. On the other hand, various forms of nineteenth-century romantic individualism found the essence of the individual to be in his feelings and his emotional life, not in his rationality. Western individualism has alternated between rational and nonrational forms.

Collectivism, too, has significant subforms. Collectivism is identified by its establishment of the primacy of the community over the individual. However, the collective has different implications, depending on whether it is under the control of the upper or lower classes. In the nineteenth century a basic division appeared in the contrast between Hegelianism and Marxism. The Hegelians were spokesmen for middle- and upper-class collectivism; Marxism, together with other forms of so-called scientific socialism, was spokesman for a collectivism in the name of the lower classes.

It is possible to diagram some of the major positions in recent Western thought in terms of their humanistic and scientific components and their positions with respect to one or another of the individualistic or collectivistic ideologies, as shown in table 5.

Early Sociology:
Science or Scientism

From the time of Francis Bacon there were sporadic suggestions for the application of science to social phenomena. However, a

Table 5

Some Major Intellectual Positions
in Terms of Their Humanistic-Scientific
and Individualistic-Collectivistic Components

Methodological Perspective		Substantive Issues			
		Individualism		Collectivism	
		Ration-alistic	Nonration-alistic	Left Wing	Right Wing
	Humanism	17th & 18th Century Rationalism	Phenomen-ology Existentialism	Radical Roman-ticism	Neo-Thomism
	Science	Laissez-faire Neo-Kantianism Utilitarianism	—	Marxism Scientific Socialism	Hegelianism Absolute Idealism

209

number of factors in Western thought and social experience prevented this for a time. In the first place, sometimes a possible line
of intellectual development is frustrated by the prior occupancy of
the field. The scientific analysis of social phenomena was prevented in the city from the twelfth to the sixteenth century by the
fact that the interpretation of social phenomena was virtually
monopolized by the theologians (the Roman Catholics in Southern Europe and, somewhat later, the Protestant theologians in
Northern Europe) and the humanists. Comparable to the division
of the sphere of thought between the humanists and the scholastics in the early period (twelfth and thirteenth centuries) was the
division of the sphere of social thought between the northern
humanists and such Protestant leaders as Luther and Calvin in the
later period (fifteenth and sixteenth centuries).

Meanwhile, also operating against the application of science to
social affairs was the adaptation of science to the study of physical
things. Science had developed as a form of nonevaluative instrumental knowledge. Human social experience, on the other hand,
was traditionally a sphere for evaluation, To extend science to
social phenomena meant, literally, that one had to treat men "like
things." This was a notion for which humanists and theologians
(both Roman Catholics and Protestants) had an almost instinctive
repugnance. Hence, one could expect a science of social phenomena to be seriously proposed only if science had proved beyond
any question its value for the study of the physical world, while
the humanistic and theological interpretations of the social affairs
had been brought into serious question. Both of these contingencies came to pass.

The religious wars of the sixteenth century shook European
man to the foundations of his being and left him for a time
determined to avoid all forms of religious excess. Meanwhile, the
primary arena of social development was shifting to the nation-
states. The religious wars powerfully promoted their formation. In
the newly forming nations, a reconstituted humanism was taking
shape in which rationalism (which had been torn loose from its
anchorage in scholasticism) was conjoined to humanistic values.
However, enlightenment thought gradually evolved the social criticism and provided the rationalizations for the revolutions which
rocked eighteenth-century society.

The French Revolution terminated in the terror and then in the
dictatorship of Napoleon. The whole of European society was
shaken, first by her example, and then by the force of French
arms. When the storm of revolution had passed, responsible groups

in European society were sick to death of revolution and everything it signified. Above all, there was a profound repugnance on
the part of many people for those ideas which had justified
revolution and provided its program.

However, the reaction to the excesses of revolution occurred in
a world which revolution had brought into being. Medieval institutions had been swept away. The new mass societies of the contemporary world had made their appearance. In the nations of Western Europe and in the United States, the middle classes had been
thrust into central position. A continuation of the revolutionary
ferment which had brought the middle classes to power, however,
were setting in action the laboring classes of the rising nation-
states. Once the friend of the middle classes, revolution had
become their enemy, for if revolution had given birth to middle-
class democracy, it also had spawned socialism.

The Western world was at last ripe for an attempt to employ
science for the analysis of social phenomena. The theological
interpretation of social events and the humanistic program for
them had both been cast into disrepute. However, if science was to
take over the ancient role of theology and humanism, it would be
expected to do more than analyze in a spirit of complete neutrality. Nevertheless, in the instant that science undertakes the task of
justifying one social arrangement rather than another, it ceases
simply to be science. Whenever science becomes normative and
assumes tasks that exceed empirical explanation, it is, perhaps,
best described as *scientism.* Sociology arose under conditions
which virtually guaranteed that it would be a form of scientism.

However, the fact that sociology arose under conditions which
tended to subordinate it to ideological requirements of special
social groups does not eliminate the possibility of a scientific
sociology. Whenever it abandons normative objectives and devotes
itself purely to the task of investigating and explaining social
phenomena, sociology is on the road to science. It was a foregone
conclusion that whatever ideological elements were present in
early sociology would eventually come into conflict with scientific
requirements.

From Positivistic Organicism
to Functionalism

The three persons conventionally viewed as the founders of sociology—Comte in France, Spencer in England, and Ward in the

United States—were spokesmen for nineteenth-century middle-class groups in their respective nations. France in the early nineteenth century was fresh from the throes of revolution. The nation had glided into the hands of the new middle classes. But as an earthquake that sends out minor tremors after the main shock waves, the revolutionary ferment continued. Comte turned his face against scientific socialism with which he had flirted as a young man (as a disciple of Saint-Simon). In England the country had slipped into the hands of the middle classes by more peaceable means. Spencer opposed the forces of radical democracy and socialism which represented English parallels of the French scientific socialists. In America the Revolution also had placed the nation in the hands of the middle classes. Coming from the middle-class strata of the American Midwest, Ward was spokesman for those groups pressing the federal government for assistance in opening the West. Inasmuch as Spencer was opposed to government interference in social affairs, while Ward urged it, the mistake has occasionally been made of supposing that they were intrinsically opposed. Quite to the contrary, in Spencer's nineteenth-century England, social reform meant a movement in the direction of radical democracy and socialism, but in the American Midwest the efforts to secure government assistance meant the promotion of the interests of the same groups which Spencer wished to protect with his policies. When it was suggested that Ward's program was identical with socialism, Ward was—quite correctly—thoroughly shocked. Comte, Ward, and Spencer were all spokesmen for the middle classes in their respective countries, and their differences were related to the peculiar problems of their respective countries.

In any case Comte, Spencer, and Ward subscribed to an organismic theory of society and attempted to found it on a scientific methodology. They were quite aware that they were recombining the traditions of Western thought in an essentially new manner. They conceived sociology as the great intellectual synthesis of the West. They proposed to take materials from the humanistic discipline, above all the discipline which had come more than any other to combine humanistic perspectives—from history. At the same time they all proposed to analyze historical (and ethnographic) materials by means of the methods of the physical sciences.

The more fully Comte developed his system, the clearer it became that a specific normative intent lay at the foundation of his thought. He proposed to establish a new religion of humanity in a society under the guidance of sociologist-priests. The secular affairs of society were to be placed in the hands of businessmen who would possess so much power that they would no longer be greedy. Women would be returned to the home. Some twenty thousand sociologist-priests, Comte thought, would be required for the administration of social affairs in Europe alone. He generously suggested his own services as chief high priest with his head-quarters in Paris. Historically, Comte's idea was most clearly approximated by the Indian caste system, whose stability he praised. He evidently conceived of sociologists as the Brahmins of his sociocracy.

Not all adherents of the positivistic organismic position ex-pressed its normative presuppositions with so much clarity. How-ever, a strong normative orientation remains characteristic of a large number of positivistic organicists even into the period of its decay. According to Lundberg, science operates as a kind of mental hygiene: "The mere possession of scientific knowledge and scientific habits of thought regarding the natural universe relieves us of a world of fears, rages, and unpleasant dissipations of energy."[23] The lines between normative theory and empirical theory are erased in the instant one speaks of "scientific solutions of social problems." This Lundberg does in a forthright manner.

> It is not true . . . that scientific solutions of social problems face a peculiar situation in that large numbers of people do not want such solutions and would be under no compulsion to accept them. Scientific solutions, in the long run, carry with them their own compulsions for acceptance. This demonstrated superiority of scientific methods has been, in the last analysis, the major reason why they have triumphed. Also, once scientific criteria are accepted in a community as the final arbiters, no one challenges their decisiveness.[24]

This formulation by Lundberg rests on scientism in relatively pure form. His position stands on the notion of the self-evident superiority of the value of the community over individuals.

> There can be no doubt at all that the authority of a properly *constituted state* is preferable to what seems to be the alternative, namely, private and self-constituted legislatures, police, and courts, as they occur today among all kinds of organizations, seeking to impose their private wishes upon the larger public. [25]

213

Lundberg's sociologist is not far removed from Comte's sociologist-priest.

> When people are in trouble, they will look for a savior. . . . They
> are likely to surround themselves with seers, poets, playrights,
> and others alleged to possess . . . powers of "seeing." The idea is a
> sound one. The only reform needed is a substitution of scientists
> for these soothsayers and soothseers.[26]

Toward the end of the nineteenth century competitors to positivistic organicism began to appear on the scene. Nevertheless, this first school of sociological theory retained much of its original prestige and only began to disintegrate into its component parts (positivism and organicism) in the interwar period.[27] It is quite possible that the worldwide depression of the 1930s which shook people's confidence in the self-evident superiority of the collective played a role in the decline of positivistic organicism. However, after World War II the functionalistic schools of sociological theory rapidly took shape, combining an organismic theory of society with a revised positivism of method, once again making it the true heir of positivistic organicism.[28]

Beyond any question the dean of contemporary functionalism is Talcott Parsons. Hence, if there are still elements of scientism in functionalism, his work offers the most authentic of all sources for their study. In 1961 Talcott Parsons, Edward Shils, Kaspar D. Naegele, and Jesse R. Pitts joined their talents to bring out the most ambitious selection of readings in sociological theory ever attempted. The result appeared in two huge volumes together with long introductions by the editors. In all, several hundred fragments of early sociological writings were cut and pasted into a framework provided primarily by Parsons' functionalistic theory.

Rarely has a monument of such proportions been erected to a scholar while still alive, for the huge two-volume assemblage of elements from early sociology is organized into the form of an anticipation of Parsons. Moreover, his theories are stated to be the great climatic synthesis of sociology. The reason why 1935 is the break-off point for the assemblage of readings in sociological theory seems to be explained by the conviction of the editors that since 1935 Parsons' functionalism is the only theory that counts. In Shils' apotheosis of the dean of functionalism, these points are explicitly stated.

> *The Structure of Social Action* was the turning point. It was this
> work that brought the greatest of the partial traditions into a

214

measure of unity. It precipitated the sociological outlook that had been implicit in the most interesting of the empirical inquiries; it made explicit the affinities and complementarity of the sociological traditions that had arisen out of utilitarianism, idealism, and positivism. It redirected sociology into its classical path, and in doing so, it began the slow process of bringing into the open the latent dispositions that had underlain the growth of sociological curiosity. Abstract and complicated though its argument was, *The Structure of Social Action* laid out the main lines of the concrete sociological outlook that has come forward in academic study and in the public appreciation of sociology since its appearance.[29]

Shils too frequently and too emphatically emphasizes the fact that functionalistic sociology intentionally eliminates the lines between normative and empirical explanation to permit the possibility that this is unintentional.

Sociology has come into its present estate because its own development bears a rough correspondence to the development of the consciousness of mankind in its moral progress.[30]

A few pages later Shils formulates the relation between the sociologist and his objects of study as priest-like:

Sociology is not . . . a purely cognitive undertaking. It is also a moral relationship between the human beings studied and the student of the human being.[31]

And finally, Shils blurs the lines between sociology and the reality it studies:

Sociological theory is not just a theory like any other theory; it is a social relationship between the theorist and the subject matter of his theory. It is a relationship formed by the sense of affinity.
   The sociological theory that grows from the theory of action is simply a more forward part of a widespread consensual collectivity.[32]

In a word, morally and ethically sociology is itself the best that contemporary society has to offer.

Once this extraordinary position has been put forward, Shils henceforth speaks of the sociological position that he shares with Parsons as *consensual* sociology. He describes its operation as follows:

> The content of a human life flows outward into other minds and
> lives through the medium of sociology. The "larger mind" is
> extended and deepened through the program of the sociology
> that moves in the direction of the theory of action. . . . The
> consensual impetus to sociological inquiry is . . . something new
> in the world, and a positive addition to the moral progress of the
> race.[33]

All sociology which does not accept the "consensual" position
is described by Shils as oppositional sociology. Those who accept
oppositional sociology, he argues, are often "former or quasi-
Marxists who, without giving their allegiance to Marxism, wish
nonetheless to retain its original disposition."[34] Such sociology,
he insists, has an "alienated outlook" and the analyses of its
members have "an overtone to the effect that those in authority
have acted wrongly, out of incompetence, blindness, or disregard
of the good. . . . The result is an outlook that radically distrusts
the inherited order of society."[35] Having hung the stigma of
"Marxists" on all who disagree with functionalism, Shils sum-
marizes his view that "consensual sociology is alone capable of
satisfying the requirements of an adequate theory and a proper
relationship to policy."[36]

The Scientific Impulse
in Sociology

In its first school of sociological theory, positivistic organicism
attempted to synthesize a scientific method for the study of social
phenomena with a collectivistic theory of society. The humanistic
individualism of the Enlightenment had lost prestige by its association with the revolutions which ushered in the mass democracies.
Besides, the rationalistic impulse of the Enlightenment had been
borne in large measure by the advisers to and critics of the
enlightened despots, who proposed to reform the monarchies, not
replace them with democracies. In the nineteenth-century world,
the point of gravity had shifted to the middle classes which had
never been the primary bearers of the humanistic outlook. Moreover, the intellectual program of the middle classes in the postrev-
olutionary period was the reverse of its program in the prerevolutionary world. It now had the task of conserving and justifying a
social and political order that had been taken over into its own
hands. In the prerevolutionary period, its objective was to elimi-

nate the remnants of medievalism and other obstacles standing in its path.

At the time of its origin, thus, positivistic organicism was structurally parallel to Hegelianism. As a matter of fact, when Hegel's work was called to Comte's attention, Comte saw the essential similarity between their positions. To Comte, Hegel's absolute idealism was merely a more metaphysical form of his own position.[37] In his youth Comte had dallied with the brilliant scientific socialism of Saint-Simon but soon reacted powerfully against it, though he did not hesitate to appropriate large blocks of Saint-Simon's ideas. There is little question that in Comte's own mind sociology was a conservative answer to scientific socialism, as it still is for Shils and Parsons.

Positivistic organicism numbers powerful figures among its adherents, including Comte, Spencer, Ward in the early period, Tönnies, Pareto, and Durkheim later, and Sorokin, Lundberg, and Redfield in the modern period. When contemporary functionalism, thus, conceives of itself as the legitimate heir of the whole of sociology, it must be admitted that it is at least the heir of the single most pervasive of the early positions. And when contemporary functionalists automatically identify anyone who disagrees with them as "Marxists," they are repeating a drama as old as Comte's denunciation of Saint-Simon and the reaction of some Hegelians to the Marxists.

However, there was no reason why the scientific impulse in sociology should be exhausted by the combination of positivism and right-wing collectivism in the manner of positivistic organicism and functionalism. From an analytic point of view, the most obvious second school of scientific sociology to develop should have been a form of positivistic, left-wing collectivism. In view of Comte's self-conscious opposition to Saint-Simon and the scientific socialists, this would seem doubly probable. When Marxian sociology eventually developed, this possibility was finally realized. However, it was a late rather than an early development.

The slowness of a positivistic form of left-wing collectivism to develop must be sought in social conditions. Schools of thought do not develop among the sociological theorists simply because in the panorama of intellectual positions they are abstractly possible. Positivistic organicism had developed because it was needed by the middle classes in whose hands the modern nation-state had formed. Left-wing collectivism, on the other hand, was in a position appropriate to the needs of the modern proletariat. In the nineteenth century at the time sociology arose, it was practically impossible for a sociology representing a positivistic form of left-wing collectivism to make its way alongside positivistic organicism and be heard in the same forums. While the middle classes were sponsoring the development of the social sciences in the colleges and universities, the lower classes were in no position to place their versions of social science in competitive position with them. Only in the twentieth century has a sociological counterpart of scientific socialism made its appearance. Moreover, it is more frequent in Europe than in America.

It was quite possible, however, that various forms of sociological theory representing combinations of positivism and individualism should appear. As noted earlier, in any given community a differentiation appears between the collectivists and the individualists. Once the nation-state had begun to assume its modern form and find its point of gravity in the middle classes, a new differentiation could be expected among the middle classes between collectivists and individualists. Two schools of sociological theory combining scientific positivism and individualism and positivism and modified collectivism eventually made their appearance: conflict theory and neo-Kantian formalism.

Conflict theory developed first. A number of persons in different countries such as Bagehot in England, Gumplowicz and Ratzenhofer in Austria, and Small in America were thoroughly convinced that a science of social phenomena was not only possible but necessary. If anything, they found themselves opposed to the positivistic organicists on the grounds that they were too lax in their positivism. However, they found themselves far more dissatisfied with the organismic theory of society. This theory, they believed, obscured the fluid dynamism that everywhere came into view whenever one actually looked at social life. To the conflict theorists, society is not an organism; it is a process. Its events consist of endlessly varied encounters between people not so much as individuals as in groups. Each combination is in hot struggle to advance its own peculiar interests.[38]

Moreover, conflict theory was no return to the optimistic individualism of the Enlightenment. It had no faith in human reason and had serious doubts about the doctrine of progress sponsored by positivistic organicism. Peace was a kind of treaty marking an interval between the wars and contests of groups. Most individuals, according to its view of things, are weak and sheeplike. It is only in groups that the fundamental combativeness of the individual is able to manifest itself in full force. *Conflict theory, thus, was a positivistic form of modified collectivism.*

Although there was a sharp impact of realism about conflict theory, it presented some anomalies. It was a form of collectivism hardly calculated to appeal to the ordinary individual, who was conceived of as sheeplike but inwardly aggressive. Society was visualized as a series of major and minor arenas of conflict. Most persons find both pictures rather unappealing. The case was different with sociological formalism.

In the course of the continuing differentiation of individualistic perspectives within the nation-state, it was perhaps a foregone conclusion that the pessimistic formulas of the conflict theorists would not satisfy the demand. Toward the end of the nineteenth century a neo-Kantian revival took place not only in Western philosophy but in a number of other humanistic disciplines. It carried with it strong impulses toward rationalism and optimism. Sociological formalism reflected this movement in sociology. The movement in sociology sustained an optimistic outlook toward the individual, which was far more attractive to most people than was conflict theory. The rationality of the individual had not received equivalent emphasis since the eighteenth century. At the same time, this rationalistic revival occurred in a framework of science rather than of humanism.

Social life was conceived by the neo-Kantian formalists as distinguishable into form and content. Sociology was visualized as a discipline like geometry and concerned with the forms of social life in separation from their content. Such forms, moreover, were conceived as in some respect directly accessible to man's reason. Sociological formalism seemed to offer the prospect of integrating the whole of social life in terms of forms of varying degrees of comprehensiveness. For a time, it appeared that formalism would sweep the entire field.

The Humanistic Counterattack
on Sociology

As has been observed, from the time of Comte to the contemporary functionalists, there have been strong normative elements in sociology which in any strict construction have no scientific standing. The humanists who were skilled in analyzing value suppositions at an early date brought the value premises of the new science of society under critical review. In 1887 Isabel Hapgood brought out a volume of Tolstoy's essays, which were at the time circulating in Russia in manuscript form. In one of them Tolstoy analyzed the evaluative elements of the sociology of Comte and Spencer.

> The justification of all persons who have freed themselves from toil is now founded on experimental, positive science. The scientific theory is as follows:
> "For the study of the laws of life of human societies, there exists but one indubitable method,—the positive, experimental, critical method.
> "Only sociology, founded on biology, founded on all the positive sciences, can give us the laws of humanity. Humanity, or human communities, are the organisms already prepared, or still in process of formation, and which are subservient to all the laws of the evolution of organisms.
> "One of the chief of these laws is the variation of destination among the portions of the organs. Some people command, others obey. If some live in superabundance, and others in want, this arises not from the Will of God, not because the empire is a form of manifestation of personality, because in societies, as in organisms, division of labor becomes indispensable for life as a whole. Some people perform the muscular labor in societies; others, the mental labor."[39]

Tolstoy formulated the central argument of the positivistic organicists as follows:

> The theory is as follows: All mankind is an undying organism; men are the particles of that organism, and each one of them has his own special task for the service of others. In the same manner, the cells united in an organism share among them the labor of the fight for existence of the whole organism; they magnify the power of one capacity, and weaken another, and unite in one organ, in order the better to supply the requirements of the whole organism. And exactly in the same manner as with gregarious animals,—ants or bees,—the separate individuals divide the labor among them. The queen lays the egg; the drone fructifies it; the bee works his whole life long. And precisely this thing takes place in mankind and in human societies. And therefore, in order to find the law of life for man, it is necessary to study the laws of life and the development of organisms.[40]

It is on this new doctrine, Tolstoy observes, "that the justification for men's idleness and cruelty is now founded."[41]

From this view of science, it appears that all previous knowledge was deceitful, and that the whole story of humanity, in the sense of self-knowledge, has been divided into three, actually into two, periods: the theological and metaphysical period, extending from the beginning of the world to Comte, and the present period—that of the only true science, positive science,—beginning with Comte.[42]

This whole edifice, Tolstoy argues, rests on an error—that of conceiving humanity as an organism. "In humanity itself all actual signs of organism—the center of feeling or consciousness—are lacking."[43]

Comte's work, Tolstoy observes, had two parts: his positive philosophy and his positive politics. Both had evaluative aspects. However,

Only the first part was adopted by the learned world,—that part which justified, on new premises, the existent evil of human societies; but the second part, treating of the moral obligations of altruism, arising from the recognition of mankind as an organism, was regarded as not only of no importance, but as trivial and unscientific.[44]

Tolstoy's argument was sound. There were evaluative elements in both aspects of Comte's sociology.

Some fifteen years, at least, after Tolstoy wrote these lines, he summed up his estimate of the sociology deriving from Comte and Spencer in an essay on "The Restoration of Hell." In it Beelzebub, the chief of the devils, received reports on the state of the contemporary world from various of his cohorts. To distract men from spiritual things, one reports:

I have devised for them . . . sociology, which consists in studying how former people lived badly. So instead of trying to live better themselves according to the teaching of Jesus, they think they need only study the lives of former people, and that from that they will be able to deduce general laws of life, and that to live well they need only conform their life to the laws they thus devise. . . .

And as soon as those who are considered the promoters of science become persuaded of their infallibility, they naturally proclaim as indubitable things that are not only unnecessary but often absurd, and having proclaimed them they cannot repudiate them.[45]

Tolstoy's comments on Comte's and Spencer's positivistic organicism may illustrate how devastating the humanistic critique of the ideological elements of early sociology could become. However, it was perhaps to be expected that the humanities should also mount a methodological counterattack on sociology. After all, Comte had proposed taking over bodily the materials of history. However, Comte brushed aside the assumptions on which the study of history had traditionally rested; that it was manifestation of men's ideas, thoughts, and feelings of the human spirit. In accord with his positivism, history was reduced by Comte to the overt happenings in human behavior. The existence of the human spirit behind them was denied.[46] Sociology analyzed such occurrences with the methods of natural science and the notions of succession, coexistence, and cause, thereby establishing the general laws of social evolution.[47] Comte's arguments were reinforced by John Stuart Mill, who also hoped to improve the state of the social sciences by application of the methods of natural sciences. Mill thought it possible to deduce the successive states of consciousness from the physiological functions of the brain. This was the first step, Mill believed, in establishing the natural laws of activity of human pluralities.[48]

Comte, Mill, Henry Thomas Buckle, and others not only developed a collectivistic view of society and man which was radically in opposition to the traditional humanistic and individualistic conception of society and man but which brushed aside the methods by which the humanists had studied man and society. Sociology might claim to be the queen of the sciences, but history was the queen of the humanities. If a counterattack on sociology were to proceed out of the humanities, it was most plausibly to be expected from history. When this counterattack came, as it did, it could be expected to be from a historicism different from its eighteenth-century rationalistic forms, for the rationalistic humanism of the eighteenth century had seriously suffered from its identification with revolution. Moreover, the rationalistic impulse in Western thought was being preempted by science. Rationalism, thus, was twice damaged in the view of many humanists: first by its identification with the cause of revolution, then by its role in the social sciences, where it seemed to many persons to be bringing about a wholesale destruction of spiritual values.

A major attempt to combat positivism by means of a reconstructed historicism was made by Johann Droysen, who in 1852 developed a course at the University of Berlin on the "Methodology and Encyclopedia of the Historical Sciences," which sought to study history on historical foundations. Droysen[49] drew a sharp distinction between the methodology of the natural and historical sciences and argued that the spheres of history and science are quite distinct: history deals with the sphere of moral judgment which eludes statistical and causal study. However, statistical and causal methods are appropriate to the study of things.

The scholar who more than any other came to synthesize the counterattack by a reconstituted historicism was Wilhelm Dilthey. Without tracing the steps by which he arrived at his final position, it may be noted that Dilthey took history, not sociology, to be the most fundamental of all disciplines. In Dilthey's opinion, positivism was not new. Comte's positivism was merely the culmination in modern times of the materialistic explanation of events running through d'Alembert and Hobbes to Comte.[50] The peculiarities of the materialistic philosophy of history are its attempts to explain mental and spiritual events in terms of categories originally developed to explain things.

However, if we cut beneath such gross materialism as that of Comte and Mill, which would explain spiritual events by categories appropriate to things, we must still recognize that their materialism is an outlook (*Weltenschauung*), a form of analysis, and an activity of mind. History is more fundamental than sociology or any science, because its subject matter is not one or another of the products of mind (of which positivism is only one), but because *its subject matter is life itself*. Yet this does not mean that rationalism or idealism is more fundamental than positivism. They, too, are world views, the ultimate source of which is life.

> The ultimate root of any world view is life itself. Life is present all over the globe in innumerable particular lives, and is lived and re-lived by every individual. Being but an instant of time present, it eludes strict observation. But in retrospect and in its objective manifestations Life is better capable of being fully grasped and meaningfully interpreted than life according to our personal knowledge, and in its countless forms today, and thus it reveals everywhere the same identical traits and common features.[51]

History, to Dilthey, was the most fundamental of all disciplines, because its subject matter is the mind. History is meaningful, because it is the product of the forms of the mind. The ultimate category of mind is meaning, and history is the study of the manner in which the mind objectifies itself according to its own principles.

Thus it may be seen that Dilthey shares with the eighteenth-century rationalists the conception (humanistic) of a universal human nature manifesting itself according to its own principles. However, since Dilthey has treated rationalism as merely one of the products of the human mind, and reason as only one of its capacities, he was not in the position to derive the forms of human life as manifest in history from man's reason or from the categories of the mind in the manner of Kant or any other of the rationalists. Rather, Dilthey followed a suggestion contained in Schopenhauer and in his one-time associates at Basel, Burckhardt and Nietzsche. Poetry may be more revealing than logic as a source of insight into the forms which come to serve as the receptacles for systems of ideas in which human life ultimately objectifies itself.

> In the Basel *Introduction* (1867) Dilthey declared that poets had taught him to understand the world. The systems of Schelling, Hegel, and Schleiermacher were but logical and metaphysical translations of a *Lebens-und-Weltansicht* of a Lessing, a Schiller, and a Herder. The poet is the interpreter of a state of mind, which permeates a generation and crystalizes it into a system. A system lives or dies, not according to reasons or logic, but by virtue of the duration of that state of mind which has originated it.[52]

If history is to yield its richness for the study of man, some method other than that of the physical sciences (which would treat man other than things) is essential. Moreover, such analysis cannot proceed simply on the basis of logical forms which are appropriate to only one of the basic aspects of life (its cognitive aspect). In addition, life has affective (emotional) and conative (moral) dimensions. Depending on which one of these basic properties of experience is uppermost, the mind objectifies itself in different ways. These objectifications, in turn, become the vehicles of world views which define immediate experience and give them form. There are three fundamental world outlooks: objective idealism, the idealism of liberty, and naturalistic realism. The third of these is contained in the view of Comte and Spencer. "The Naturalistic concept of 'type' not only renders historiography schematic, but reduces it to sociology."[53]

Dilthey's methodological attack on sociology led him to offer typology as the peculiar method of the spiritual (historical) sciences.

The Humanistic Impulse
in Sociology

In sketching some of the forms of the humanistic counterattack on sociology, it was not intended to set up a particular sequence of influences. An essay is not the vehicle for such an enterprise. Tolstoy's and Dilthey's reactions to sociology were selected, not because they brought about changes in sociology, but because they typify some of the forms of the humanistic reaction to sociology's value commitments and positivistic method. Tolstoy's critique of sociological collectivism and the philistine support of the *status quo* by the positivistic organicists may dramatize the fact that so far as sociologists remained sensitive to the humanistic critique of their theories, they would find reason for a shift to more individualistic orientations. On the other hand, Dilthey's vigorous criticism of the positivistic analysis of social phenomena and his development of typology as an alternative method for the analysis of sociohistorical events could well force some sociologists to re-examine their methods.

As time has gone by a number of forms of humanistic individualism and collectivism have appeared. These, however, have developed in very different degrees and at different times. Forms of humanistic individualism have developed first and most completely; forms of humanistic collectivism have developed only recently and rather sporadically.

It could, perhaps, be assumed—if abstract possibilities were the primary consideration—that humanistic collectivism would have developed in sociology before humanistic individualism. After all, the oldest school of sociological theory was positivistic organicism. The organicism of the early sociologists so strongly sustained the need of the new middle classes to justify the *status quo* (which had recently come into their hands) that a nonpositivistic organicism would seem to have been a logical product the moment the application of physical science methods to social events was questioned. However, until such time as sociology was firmly established, the reaction to the physical science bias of early sociology tended rather to take the form of rejection of sociology altogether rather than of the establishment of a new school of sociology. It was only after sociology became indubitably established and had made its way into the universities as one of the basic academic disciplines that it became desirable formally to establish a kind of right-wing humanistic collectivism which still described itself as a sociological theory. When, eventually, the attempt was made in Roman Catholic circles to establish sociology on the basis of Neo-Thomism, this possibility was realized. Perhaps the mainstream of what is, at times, called Roman Catholic sociology fits this category.

The conditions for the development of a humanistic form of left-wing collectivism which still described itself as a form of sociology are even more difficult to realize. For this to occur, the given individual would have to reject both right-wing collectivism (positivistic organicism, functionalism, and Roman Catholic sociology) and science; otherwise the thinker would fall into the camp of Marxism or of other scientific socialists.

This seems to be the precise description of the form of sociological theory which was being embraced by C. Wright Mills at the time of his death. In his impressive major works, *Character and Social Structure* (with Hans Gerth), *White Collar*, and *The Power Elite*, Mills conducted his theorizing within the framework of social behaviorism.[54] However, in his later works Mills increasingly subscribed to a collectivistic position which was combined with a forthright anti-empiricism. In an essay for Llewelyn Gross' *Symposium*, Mills stated:

> Now I do not like to do empirical work if I can possibly avoid it. . . . Besides, and more seriously, in the social sciences there is so much to do by way of initial "structuring" . . . that "empirical research" is bound to be thin and uninteresting.
>
> In our situation, empirical work as such is for beginning students and for those who aren't able to handle the complexities of big problems; it is also for highly formal men who do not care what they study so long as it appears to be orderly. All these types have a right to do as they please or as they must; they have no right to impose in the name of science such narrow limits on others. Anyway, you ought not to let them bother you.[55]

Later in the same year, Mills generalized his opposition to physical science.

> The cultural meaning of physical science—the major older common denominator—is becoming doubtful. As an intellectual style, physical science is coming to be thought by many as somehow

inadequate. The adequacy of scientific styles of thought and feeling, imagination and sensibility, has of course from their beginnings been subject to religious doubt and theological controversy, but our scientific grandfathers and fathers beat down such religious doubts. The current doubts are secular, humanistic—and often quite confused. Recent development in physical science—with its technological climax in the H-bomb and the means of carrying it about the earth—has not been experienced as a solution to any problems widely known and deeply pondered by larger intellectual communities and cultural publics.... With all this, many cultural workmen have come to feel that "science" is a false and pretentious Messiah, or at the very least a highly ambiguous element in modern civilization.[56]

Mills' powerful impetus in the direction of left-wing collectivism was made fully manifest in his passionate propaganda tract in defense of the Cuban revolution and in his apotheosis of its leader in *Listen, Yankee.*

My major aim in this book is to present the voice of the Cuban revolutionary, as clearly and as emphatically as I can, and I have taken up this aim because of its absurd absence from the news of Cuba available in the United States today. You will not find here The Whole Truth about Cuba, nor "an objective appraisal of the Cuban revolution." I do not believe it is possible for anyone to carry out such an appraisal today, nor do I believe that anyone—Cuban or North American—can yet know "the whole truth about Cuba." That truth, whatever it turns out to be, is still being created, and every week it changes. The true story of the Cuban revolution, in all its meaning, will have to wait until some Cuban, who has been part of it all, finds out the universal voice of his revolution.[57]

At no time does the slightest hint of criticism of Fidel Castro ever creep into Mills' account. Castro looms through the pages of *Listen, Yankee,* as an apotheosized superman.

When men seize an opportunity, they make history; this man has. And he is. He is the most directly radical and democratic force in Cuba. He has always appealed, at every juncture, to public opinion, on the TV and also in person. Before any problem is solved, Fidel spends long hours on the TV. In the last eighteen months the power in Cuba has rested upon the people. He explains and he educates, and after he speaks almost every doubt has gone away. Never before has such a force of public opinion prevailed for so long and so intimately with power. So close, for example, that even a weak rumor sends Fidel to the TV to refute it, or to affirm it, to explain what it is all about. So long as Fidel is there, we are going to be all right. His speeches actually create the revolutionary consciousness—and the work gets done. It is fantastic to see how, as it goes along, the revolutionary process transforms one layer after another of the population. And always, there is Fidel's anti-bureaucratic personality and way of going about things, of getting things done, without red tape and without delay and in a thoroughly practical and immediate way.[57]

In his last book, *The Marxists*, Mills divided the most vital of the intellectual currents of modern times into Marxism and liberalism. They are, he argued, animated by common ideals.

Both Marxism and liberalism embody the ideals of Greece and Rome and Jerusalem: the humanism of the Renaissance, the rationalism of the eighteenth century enlightenment.[58]

Of these alternatives, Mills emphatically preferred Marxism.

What is most valuable in classic liberalism is most cogently and most fruitfully incorporated in classic Marxism. Much of the failure to confront Marxism in all its variety is in fact a way of not taking seriously the ideals of liberalism itself, for despite the distortions and vulgarizations of Marx's ideas, and despite his own errors, ambiguities, and inadequacy, Karl Marx remains the thinker who has articulated most clearly—and most perilously—the basic ideals which liberalism shares. Hence, to confront Marx and Marxism is to confront this moral tradition.[59]

A few pages earlier, Mills had formulated the reasons for his preference for Marxism over current social science.

The social scientists study the details of small-scale *milieux*; Marx studied such details, too, but always within the structure of a total society. The social scientists, knowing little history, study at most short-run trends; Marx, using historical materials with superb mastery, takes as his unit of study entire epochs. The values of the social scientists generally lead them to accept their society pretty much as it is; the values of Marx led him to condemn his society—root, stock, and branch.[60]

These passages from Mills, to be sure, contain a fuzzy bundle of half-truths. It is not true, for example, that classic liberalism and Marxism share the same values: classic liberalism is individualistic; Marxism is collectivistic. It is not true that all social scientists study only the details of small-scale *milieux* and have no mastery of historical materials; some do, some do not. Marx's mastery of historical materials—far from being "superb"—has been seriously questioned by some scholars. The ambiguous statement that both Marxism and liberalism embody the ideals of Greece, Rome, and Jerusalem, humanism and rationalism, fails to discriminate the very different aspects of Western thought which are distributed among these positions. Finally, Mills has himself emphatically rejected the linkage between his left-wing collectivism and science—a link which Marxism resoundingly affirmed.

The important point for the present context is this: Mills cast his lot simultaneously with left-wing collectivism and against the linkage between it and science. In his last years, there has been some seething ferment around Mills. If this ferment should condense into a new school of sociology with C. Wright Mills as its charismatic founder, its distinctiveness will be seen to lie in its unique combination of humanism and left-wing collectivism.

Far more important (in terms of numbers of adherents and richness and variety of works) than either right-wing, humanistic collectivism (Neo-Thomistic sociology), or left-wing, humanistic collectivism (the position of C. Wright Mills) are the sociological forms of humanistic individualism represented by social behaviorism and phenomenological sociology.

Social behaviorism, the powerful school of sociological theory which acts as the great counterweight in American sociology to functionalism, represented a reaction both to collectivism (of both right- and left-wing varieties) and to what it conceived to be the excessively rigid positivism which stood in the way of an adaptation of physical methods to the unique properties of social life. All three subbranches of social behaviorism, pluralistic behaviorism stemming from Tarde, Le Bon, Giddings, and Ross, social action theory stemming from Max Weber, Robert MacIver, John R. Commons, and Thorstein Veblen, and symbolic interactionism stemming from William James, Cooley, Goerge Herbert Mead, and W. I. Thomas, represented positions in sociology which combined humanistically modified methods with an individualistic approach to social events. Social behaviorism, thus, is the nearest approach to eighteenth-century rationalism that sociology offers.[61] It should be noted, however, that the social behaviorists actually tried to find a common ground between the methodological perspectives of humanism and science. It thus represented what might be described as either a humanized positivism or scientific humanism. Social action theory, for example, in its methodological perspectives attempted to press to scientific account the typological procedures which Dilthey had offered as an alternative to scientific methods.

Finally, a nonrationalistic form of humanistic individualism took shape as a departure from neo-Kantian formalism.[62] In analogy with a procedure of Kant who had treated science as the empirical study of experience but had drawn a distinction between mind-given forms and empirical content, the neo-Kantian Formalists in sociology drew a distinction between the form and content of social life. The content was studied by other social sciences, but sociology was argued to be similar to geometry. It was said to be a study of pure social forms in separation from their content.

However, if one examined the Kantian view carefully, it quickly became apparent that although both form and content were said to be objects of scientific study, they were assigned very different properties. Since forms are present from the moment experience occurs, and since they are present as possibilities before experience occurs, it is not necessary to employ experimental methods to discover social forms. In fact, experiment is of no help in studying forms, since they are present from the beginning of experience. It should only be necessary to examine experience carefully though introspectively to discover social forms. There was a potential crisis for scientific methodology buried in neo-Kantian sociology, for the most significant of all methods would seem to point toward introspection.

Long before neo-Kantian sociology came face to face with its methodological problems, other developments had been occurring in Western thought which were to offer a possible solution to the sociological formalists. The ferment in the methodology of the humanists of the nineteenth century (in part illustrated by Dilthey above) was forcing them to look to alternatives to science for the analysis of social phenomena. Dilthey, it was noted above, had thought that poetry could be more valuable in the understanding of the operations of the human mind than logic. A primary product of the nineteenth- and early twentieth-century search for a nonscientific and nonlogical (nonrational in this sense) procedure for analyzing the events of human experience was phenomenology. In its most rudimentary sense, phenomenology may be described as a new method of controlled or directed introspection that was believed by its proponents to be more fundamental than either logical analysis or empirical-scientific procedures.

Once it became completely clear that the methodological status being assigned to social forms was potentially quite different from that of social content, phenomenology offered itself as a natural method. Phenomenological sociology pioneered by Alfred Vierkandt was developed with particular brilliance for the analysis of various social and cultural forms by Max Scheler.[63]

Existentialism
and Sociology

With phenomenology sociology had already entered the edifice of existentialism. However, a fully developed existentialist sociology is only now under way. This is no place to consider these problems in detail, but it is useful to sketch some of the major elements of existentialism and indicate the direction of their possible influence on sociology.

It has been argued that the essence of existentialism is found in a profound sense of alienation from their society and their traditions by Western men. However, Marxism, too, has argued that modern workers are alienated by the methods of production and the operation of those forces which separate them from ownership of the instruments of production. It has been argued that the essence of existentialism is found in the formation of an outlook resting on a profound sense of dread. Some existentialists (Kierkegaard, Heidegger) fulfill this definition, but some others (Ortega y Gasset and Jaspers) seem basically to have had Apollonian dispositions. It has been argued that the essence of existentialism is a powerful subjective religious sense (Kierkegaard and Jaspers qualify on this standard), but some persons accepting the label of existentialism have been quite irreligious (Sartre and Ortega y Gasset for certain, Heidegger perhaps). Hence it has finally been argued that existentialism has no coherent position and is, in fact, indefinable (Walter Kaufmann).

However, there are a number of things shared in common by those to whom the label of existentialism has been applied. None of the existentialists is collectivistic. A powerful anticollectivism runs through them all in two respects: they radically reject the collectivistic philosophies of both right and left wing; they are powerfully opposed to collectivisitic trends in contemporary society. Whatever else may be true of it, existentialism is, in the first place, a powerful individualistic reaction in an age of collectivism.

In its individualism existentialism finds a deep echo from ancient traditions of the West, from the civic humanism of the earlier period, and from the tradition in its period of maturity from Descartes to Kant, reaching a kind of culmination in eighteenth-century rationalism. However, existentialism represents an individualistic reaction in an age of collectivism in a world disillusioned with the individualistic rationalism of its classic period. The rationalistic traditions had operated like dissolving acid on the traditional faiths of Western man. When the traditional faiths declined, they left in their place only the unstable compound: faith in reason. But reason rationalized the revolution which ushered in the mass world—a world that powerfully thrust reason aside.

The new individualism that arose in the collectivistic world was disillusioned with the rationalistic formulas of the earlier age. It had no confidence in the products of reason. All "systems" cast up by the thought process in the course of experience were now conceived ultimately as mere "rationalizations" of a more fundamental psychic reality. The new individualism, thus, rejected the rationalism that had served as so powerful a tool for the individualism of the seventeenth and eighteenth centuries. This meant, however, that the new individualism was automatically pressed into the situation, where it had to develop a new analysis of experience. It explored not logic but the nonlogical areas of individual activity for a method of personal orientation. When personal experience is examined, it presents no clear logical distinctions and organized sequences of thought, but an amazing complex of ambiguities, doubts, anxieties, and uncertainties. When thought intervenes in personal experience it often clamps a set of categories as if from the outside, categories which force the ill-fitting densities of experience into a condition of half-fittedness. Hence, the exponents of the new individualism looked to areas thrust into the background by men who had thought that the essence of man was his reason: to poetry, to art, to the experience of the religious mystic, to mythology. And when phenomenology attempted to gather these many impulses into a single procedure for a new analysis of experience, the existentialists were powerfully influenced by them.

Finally, it may be noted, there was good reason why the new individualism might not wish to arm itself with science. For one thing, the rationalistic impulse in Western thought was in considerable measure taken over by science. But more importantly, the great collectivistic movements in modern times had taken over science as a powerful instrument. Science had been utilized with great efficiency by the great business and industrial combinations of modern industry. It has been employed by the great states and powerful armies. Science was the great implement of collectivism!

There was a time when the peculiar ingredients of existentialism would have been quite impossible to assemble in the West. However, a series of powerful individualistic figures responding both to the social trends and to the traditions of the West gradually pulled these ingredients into its eventual synthesis. Perhaps most noteworthy were Schopenhauer, Kierkegaard, Burckhardt, Nietzsche, Dilthey, and Edmund Husserl. Near the turn of the century various of these influences were woven into systematic interpretations of modern man and his times. Among the persons playing a major role in bringing about the existential synthesis are Bergson, Ortega y Gasset, Heidegger, Jaspers, Berdyaev, and Jean-Paul Sartre.

It is not unfair to conceive the social doctrines of the existentialists as constituting an existentialist sociology. An able young writer, Edward A. Tiryakian, accurately summed up the general social doctrines of the existentialists as follows:

> From Kierkegaard's *The Present Age* to Jaspers' *Man in the Modern Age*, the existentialists' evaluation of the individual-and-society relationship remains strikingly the same. What stands out in particular is their rejection and condemnation of modern society as an impersonal environment antithetical and inimical to the development of authentic selfhood.[64]

Tiryakian maintains that there is a need for a reunion of sociology and philosophy and proposes bringing about this union by a fusion of *sociologism* and *existentialism* on the ground that the contemporary predicament of the individual and of society is their common concern. "Basically both are reactions to the disorganization of the modern world."[65] It should be noted that even in the unlikely event one were able to unite existentialism and what is called sociologism, one could still not claim to have united philosophy and sociology. Existentialism is only one, though a vigorous one, of the traditions in contemporary philosophy. What Tiryakian calls *sociologism* is only one of the traditions (again though a vigorous one) of the recent forms of society. By *sociologism* Tiryakian means positivistic organicism and functionalism. Durkheim was his favorite illustration.

Tiryakian accurately sums up the difference between existentialism and this type of sociology in the following passages:

> Durkheim stressed the reality of society as a psychic entity, . . .
> Gabriel Marcel warns against the notion that elements A and B,
> endowed respectively with consciousness C' and C'', may form a
> whole having a synthetic consciousness C'''.[66]

> Durkheim saw no fundamental conflict between the individual
> and society. . . . Heidegger regards the social self as the unauthen-
> tic part of human-being. . . .[67]

> In Durkheim's thought . . . the end of moral action is the collec-
> tivity. . . . In contrast to Durkheim, the existential perspective on
> morality is . . . ambiguous and ambivalent. . . . For Nietzsche, the
> utility of social morality is no proof of its validity. . . . Kierke-
> gaard also took an ambiguous position on morality. The ethical,
> for him, is a higher realm of existence than the aesthetic.[68]

Unlike Kierkegaard, Durkheim did not perceive any opposition
between morality and religion.

> Existentialism is a philosophy of rugged individualism: existential
> thought conceives the individual existent to be without recourse
> to any objective certainty about his position in the world. . . .
> Sociologism is in opposition to the basic rugged individualism
> which underlies all of existential thought, for it takes as basic
> assumptions the solidarity of individuals and the objective reality
> of society.[69]

> Durkheim believed emphatically that society pervades the individ-
> ual. . . . The authentic selfhood of the person is to be found only
> through participation in a collectivity, in social reality. This view
> is antipodal to that of existentialism. . . . Beginning with Kierke-
> gaard all existentialist thinkers have been aware of and disturbed
> by the levelling process of civilization. . . . The levelling process
> affects equality by obliterating individual differences. Kierke-
> gaard, Nietzsche, Marcel, Heidegger, and Jaspers, holding social
> equality to be tantamount to mass mediocrity, make a common
> front in decrying both the process and the advocates of egali-
> tarianism.[70]

After detailing the contrasts between existentialism and the
form of sociology he describes as sociologism, Tiryakian proposed
fusing them in a single perspective. The first step in such synthesis
conceives existentialism and sociology, simply, as alternate responses to the same problem, the moral crisis of the modern
world.[71] By an extraordinarily simple reinterpretation, Tiryakian
sought to reduce sociologism and existentialism to complementary
rather than contrasting perspectives.

Table 6

Sociological Theories in Terms of Their
Humanistic-Scientific and Individualistic-Collectivistic Components

		Main Substantive Issues			
		Individualism		Collectivism	
		Rationalism	Non-rationalism	Left Wing	Right Wing
M P					
E E					
T R					
H S					
O P		Social Behaviorism	Phenomenological Formalism Existential Sociology	The Sociology of C. Wright Mills	Main-stream of Catholic Sociology
D E Humanism					
O C					
L T					
O I					
G V					
I E		Neo-Kantian Branch of Sociological Formalism	Some forms of Conflict Theory	Marxian Sociology and Left-wing collectivism	Positivistic Organicism Functionalism Right-wing conflict theory
C S Science					
A					
L					

> We propose that Durkheim's fundamental concern was really to study objectively a *subjective* reality, not, as is sometimes assumed by existentialists among others, an objective reality.[72]

By one blow Tiryakian claims to have cut the Gordian knot, to have synthesized sociologism and existentialism and reunited sociology and philosophy.

It would surely be a triumph of dialectical reasoning if in this manner and at one blow one were able to synthesize scientific, right-wing collectivism with humanistic, nonrational individualism. However, it is not true that a common moral crisis produced sociologism and existentialism which are merely different evaluations of this crisis. Evaluations come first, and moral crises may or may not ensue. Nor does one wipe away the collectivistic theories of Durkheim or any other positivistic organicist by a gimmick such as discovering that Durkheim was simply trying to treat a subjective reality objectively. One has merely equivocated on the meaning of individuality, i.e., by reducing it to subjectivity.

There is an existentialist sociology or at least an existentialist interpretation of social phenomena, but any such fusion of contradictory positions such as those of the existentialists and the functionalists is out of the question. One is reminded of the old story of the two Russians who found themselves on a train. They found that one was going to Minsk, the other to Pinsk, and broke into a hot argument, since they were going in opposite directions. Peace was restored only when one suggested—"it must be the dialectic."

Summary

The most fundamental of all perspectives in Western thought are those of humanism and science. Humanism arose as a man-oriented secular outlook in the dawn period of the Western cities, when offspring of medievalism were cast as orphans into a new world and forced to exploit the resources of their own natures to solve the unprecedented problems of their existence. Humanism arose in politically-responsible (elitist) circles: the advisers or princes, the tutors in eminent households, diplomatists and secretaries and university professors. In the attempt to solve their problems the humanists searched through the literature of the past, developing philological methods and techniques of historical research. They left a permanent heritage in the humanistic disciplines of the present day. Later, when the city began to crystalize and the rising nation-state took up the curve of development, the humanistic skills and techniques were transferred to the sphere of the nation-state. Perhaps their highest and most full expression was achieved in seventeenth- and eighteenth-century rationalism. However, another phenomena accompanied this transition. In the course of the shift from the city to the nation-state, the old polarity of humanism and theology of the city was lost, and theology was shifted into the sphere of the humanities.

Western science, which fused the rational proof, discovered and worked up by man the classical polis to the systematic experimentalism as a device for developing general knowledge in the world of things, also was born in the Western city. It emerged in quite different circles from humanism and had, originally, a different intent. It proceeded out of the circles of craftsmen and artists. It was intended not to solve problems of man's social experience but to discover new things about the world of physical things. Science powerfully implemented the free technology which formed its medieval birth matrix, and in whatever sphere it was released it worked revolutions.

The primary substantive issues of human social life are formed by the relation between the individual and the collective (society).

236

In every society, including the Western city and later the nation-state, individualistic and collectivistic theories have developed. Individualistic theories see the highest value in the fullest possible development of the individual; collectivistic theories see the highest human values in the most harmonious and smooth-running society possible.

In the period of the Western city, individualistic theories were most frequently advocated by the humanists, while collectivistic theories were most often advocated by the theologians (of both Roman Catholic and Protestant persuasion, though more frequently by the former) as shown in table 7.

In this early period there were only the most sporadic suggestions for lifting science from the world of physical things and applying it to human affairs.

When the curve of development shifted to the nation-state, the early division between humanism and theology was wiped away, and humanism and theology often found themselves making common cause against the forces of a new world. Moreover, a redivision in the forms of individualism and collectivism was carried through and the lines between rationalistic and nonrationalistic individualism and left- and right-wing collectivism were crystalized.

Perhaps the single most dramatic intellectual event of the nineteenth and twentieth centuries has been the rise of the social sciences with their attempt to transplant techniques which proved

Table 7

Humanism and Theology in the Western City

P		Substantive Issues	
E			
R		Individualism	Collectivism
S			
P	Humanism	Main Wing of	Early
E		the Humanists	Nationalism
C			
T	Theology	Some of the	Thomism
I		Protestant	The Inquisition
V		Theologians	
E			

so powerful in dealing with the physical world to the social world. While the social sciences held out the promise of fusing the scientific and humanistic poles of Western thought, they have carried with them the danger (from some points of view) of permanently transforming the ratio between individuality and collectivity and carrying through an unprecedented curtailment of the sphere of individual freedom. Against the forces moving in this direction, existentialism has represented an insurgent protest. Its essence is found in a new antirational and antiscientific individualism.

Some of the major ways in which sociology has evolved under the strains of these diverging forces have been traced. Sociology is a dynamic development opened by the establishment of positivistic organicism dividing into many contrasting and, in part, complementary forms, and continuing in the present with the emergence of an existentialist sociology, on the one hand, and forms of left-wing, humanistic collectivism on the other.

NOTES

1. C. Wright Mills, *The Sociological Imagination* (New York: Oxford University Press, 1959), p. 13.

2. Ibid., pp. 10-11.

3. Don Martindale, *Social Life and Cultural Change* (Princeton: D. Van Nostrand, 1962), pp. 409-15.

4. Ibid., pp. 415-18.

5. Jacob Burckhardt, *The Civilization of the Renaissance* (New York: Oxford University Press, 1945), p. 81.

6. Ibid., p. 128-36.

7. Ernst Cassirer, Paul Oskar Kristeller, and John Herman Randall, Jr., *The Renaissance Philosophy of Man* (Chicago: The University of Chicago Press, 1946), pp. 47-133, 223-24.

8. A. G. Little, "The Mendicant Orders," *The Cambridge Medieval History* (New York: Macmillan, 1929), vol. IV, p. 727.

9. Cassirer, *The Renaissance Philosophy of Man*, pp. 4-6, 185-86.

10. Don Martindale, *The Nature and Types of Sociological Theory* (Boston: Houghton Mifflin, 1960), pp. 6-10.

11. Martindale, *Social Life and Cultural Change*, pp. 353-55.

12. Lynn White, Jr., *Medieval Technology and Social Change* (Oxford: Clarendon Press, 1962), p. 78.

13. Ibid., p. 79.

14. Alexander Goldenweiser, *Anthropology* (New York: F. S. Crofts, 1937), p. 74.

15. Leonardo Da Vinci, *The Notebooks of Leonardo Da Vinci*, ed. Edward MacCurdy (New York: Braziller, 1956), p. 83.

16. Ibid., p. 82.

17. Ibid., p. 67.

18. Ibid., p. 64.

19. Ibid.

20. Martindale, *Social Life and Cultural Change*, pp. 424-63.

21. Ibid., pp. 418-21.

22. Ibid., pp. 440-43.

23. George A. Lundberg, *Can Science Save Us?* (London: Longmans, Green, 1947), p. 2.

24. Ibid., p. 8.

25. Ibid., p. 54.

26. Ibid.

27. Martindale, *Nature and Types*, pp. 110-21.

28. Ibid., pp. 446-50.

29. Edward Shils, "The Calling of Sociology," in *Theories of Society*, ed. Talcott Parsons, Edward Shils, Kasper D. Naegele, and Jesse R. Pitts (New York: The Free Press of Glencoe, 1961), vol. II, pp. 1406-7.

30. Ibid., p. 1410.

31. Ibid., p. 1411.

32. Ibid., p. 1420.

33. Ibid., p. 1430.

34. Ibid., p. 1422.

35. Ibid.

36. Ibid., p. 1440.

37. Martindale, *Nature and Types*, p. 156.

38. Ibid., pp. 127-211.

39. Count Leo Tolstoy, *What to Do?* (New York: Thomas Y. Crowell, 1887), p. 169.

40. Ibid., p. 175.

41. Ibid., p. 176.

42. Ibid., p. 178.

43. Ibid.

44. Ibid., p. 179.

45. Leo Tolstoy, *On Life*, trans. Aylmer Maude (London: Humphrey Milford, 1934), pp. 326-27.

46. Auguste Comte, *Cours de Philosophie Positive* (Paris: Au Siège de la Societé positiviste, 1892), vol. I, p. 9.

47. Ibid., vol. IV, p. 17.

48. John Stuart Mill, *A System of Logic* (New York: Longmans, Green, 1949), pp. 529-32.

49. Johann Gustav Droysen, *Outline of the Principles of History* (Boston: Ginn & Company, 1893), pp. 12 ff.

50. Wilhelm Dilthey, *Weltanschauung und Analyse des Menchen seit Renaissance und Reformation* (Leipzig: G. B. Teubner, 1914), p. 357.

51. Wilhelm Dilthey, *Dilthey's Philosophy of Existence*, trans. William Kluback and Martin Weinbaum (New York: Bookman, 1957), p. 21.

52. William Kluback, *Wilhelm Dilthey's Philosophy of History* (New York: Columbia University Press, 1956), p. 75.

53. Ibid., p. 97.

54. Martindale, *Nature and Types*, pp. 398ff., 430-33.

55. C. Wright Mills, "On Intellectual Craftsmanship," in *Symposium in Sociological Theory*, ed. Llewellyn Gross (Evanston: Row, Peterson, 1959), p. 35.

56. Mills, *The Sociological Imagination*, pp. 15-16.

57. C. Wright Mills, *Listen, Yankee* (New York: Ballantine Books, 1960), p. 8.

58. Ibid., pp. 122-23.

59. C. Wright Mills, *The Marxists* (New York: Dell, 1962), pp. 13-14.

60. Ibid., p. 14.

61. Ibid., pp. 10-11.

62. Martindale, *Nature and Types*, pp. 285-440.

63. Ibid., pp. 267 ff.

64. Ibid., pp. 267-81.

65. Edward A. Tiryakian, *Sociologism and Existentialism* (Englewood Cliffs, N.J.: Prentice-Hall, 1962), p. 144.

66. Ibid., p. 151.

67. Ibid.

68. Ibid., p. 152.

69. Ibid.

70. Ibid., pp. 153-54.

71. Ibid., p. 155.

72. Ibid., pp. 163-64.

73. Ibid., p. 163.

SELECTED BIBLIOGRAPHY

Burckhardt, Jacob. *The Civilization of the Renaissance.* New York: Oxford University Press, 1945.

Cassirer, Ernst; Kristeller, Paul Oskar; and Randall, John Herman, Jr. *The Renaissance Philosophy of Man.* Chicago: The University of Chicago Press, 1946.

Da Vinci, Leonardo. *The Notebooks of Leonardo Da Vinci.* Edited by Edward MacCurdy. New York: Braziller, 1956.

Dilthey, Wilhelm. *Weltenschauung und Analyse des Menchen seit Renaissance und Reformation.* Leipzig: G. B. Teubner, 1914.

―――――. *Dilthey's Philosophy of Existence.* Translated by William Kluback and Martin Weinbaum. New York: Bookman, 1957.

Droysen, Johann Gustav. "Zur Characteristik der europäischen Krisis." In *Politische Schriften.* Edited by Felix Gilbert, pp. 307-42. Munich, 1933.

Goldenweiser, Alexander. *Anthropology.* New York: F. S. Crofts, 1937.

Kluback, William. *Wilhelm Dilthey's Philosophy of History.* New York: Columbia University Press, 1956.

Little, A. G. "The Mendicant Orders," *The Cambridge Medieval History.* New York: Macmillan, 1929, vol. VI.

Martindale, Don. *Social Life and Cultural Change.* Princeton: D. Van Nostrand, 1962.

―――. *The Nature and Types of Sociological Theory.* Boston: Houghton Mifflin, 1960.

Mill, John Stuart. *A System of Logic.* New York: Longmans Green, 1949.

Mills, C. Wright. "On Intellectual Craftsmanship." In *Symposium in Sociological Theory.* Edited by Llewellyn Gross. Evanston: Row, Peterson, 1959.

―――――. *The Sociological Imagination.* New York: Oxford University Press, 1959.

―――――. *Listen, Yankee.* New York: Ballantine Books, 1960.

―――――. *The Marxists.* New York: Dell, 1962.

Shils, Edward. "Epilogue: The Calling of Sociology." In *Theories of Society.* Edited by Talcott Parsons, Edward Shils, Kasper D. Naegle, and Jesse R. Pitts. New York: The Free Press of Glencoe, 1961, vol. II, pp. 1403-49.

Tiryakian, Edward A. *Sociologism and Existentialism.* Englewood Clifts, N.J.: Prentice-Hall, 1962.

White, Lynn, Jr. *Medieval Technology and Social Change.* Oxford: Clarendon Press, 1962.

Index

Social structure
 Comte's views, 130-32
 Durkheim's views, 133-35
 elementaristic theories, 136f, 143-49
 holistic theories, 130f, 143-49
 Parsons' views, 135-36
 Spencer's views, 132-33
 theoretical ambiguities, 130, 149-50, 154
Social theory
 conflict theory, 218-19
 existentialism, 231-36
 functionalism, 214-16, 217
 left-wing collectivism, 226-28
 neo-Kantianism, 230-31
 Neo-Thomism, 226
 positivistic organicism, 211-12, 217
 social behaviorism, 230-31
Society
 as reality *sui generis*, 9
 as source of value, 4-9
Sorokin, Pitirim, 38, 41-43, 189-90, 217
Speier, Hans, 45
Spencer, Herbert, 132f, 149, 178-81, 211-12, 220-22, 224
Spengler, Oswald, 34, 38-39, 44-45
Spinoza, Benedict, 4, 178
Standard operating formula, 61
Stark, Werner, 64-66
Stein, Maurice, 2

Tarde, Gabriel, 184, 229
Taylor, Frederick W., 143-44
Thomas, W.I., 98, 229
Tiryakian, Edward A., 233-34
Tolstoy, Leo, 6f, 220-22, 225
Tönnies, Ferdinand, 217
Totemism, 7-8
Toynbee, Arnold, 32, 38-41, 44-45
Turgot, Jacque, 170-71, 177

Values
 commitment to, 20
 neutrality, 15
 relativity of, 10
 society as source of, 4
Veblen, Thorstein, 229
Vico, G., 169, 172
Vidich, Arthur, 2
Vierkandt, A., 231
Voltaire, 171

Wagner, Richard, 93
Ward, Lester, 211-12
Weber, Alfred, 189
Weber, Max, 16-20, 22, 64, 95-96, 141-42, 147, 188, 229
Weitz, Morris, 53
White, Lynn Jr., 201
Windelband, Wilhelm, 64

Znaniecki, Florian, 98
Zuni Indians, 108-10